# Using the IBM
# Personal Computer®

# Using the IBM Personal Computer®

## T. G. Lewis
Oregon State University

Reston Publishing Company, Inc., Reston, Virginia
A Prentice-Hall Company

IBM® is a registered trademark of International
Business Machines Corporation

**Library of Congress Cataloging in Publication Data**

Lewis, T. G. (Theodore Gyle)
  Using the IBM Personal Computer.

  Includes index.
  1. IBM Personal Computer—Programming.   I. Title.
II. Title: Using the I.B.M. personal computer.
QA76.8.I2594L48   1982       001.64'2       82-12234
ISBN 0-8359-8140-1

© 1983 by
Reston Publishing Company, Inc.
A Prentice-Hall Company

All rights reserved. No part of this book
may be reproduced in any way or by any means
without permission in writing from the
publisher.

10 9 8 7 6 5 4 3 2 1

Printed in the United States of America

**To life in the Oregon hills:**
To Fritz and his mole,
To wild cats and Elmer,
To Papagaÿo and Foster Lake, and
To Madeline and her obsession.

# Contents

# Preface

This book is for anyone thinking of buying or who has recently bought an IBM Personal Computer, EasyWriter, VisiCalc, or Pascal system. If you own a computer with EasyWriter, or VisiCalc you may still be interested in this book because these programs currently run on a number of microcomputers.

The main goal of this book is to inform the reader. What can a microcomputer do? How does a computer operate? What is the meaning of words like file, RAM, bit, BASIC, database, electronic worksheet, word processing, operating system, and software? These words and many others are clearly and concisely explained here.

More specifically, the goal of this book is to inform the reader in how to use the popular MDOS operating system, the EasyWriter word processing program, the spreadsheet calculator called VisiCalc, and two programming languages: MBASIC and Pascal. The IBM Personal Computer is also explained for those who own or plan to purchase this powerful machine.

The best way to learn about computers is by using one. This book is therefore written from the point of view of a user. This means I have approached each topic from a "how to" perspective. In fact, many of the examples have been photographed directly from the computer screen so you can see exactly what the computer does. In some cases the photographs will differ from what you may see on the screen of your own computer because the computer manufacturer may have updated the system to include additional programs. But for the most part I have tried to keep all examples as near as possible to "real life."

In Chapter 1, I examine several areas where computers can benefit you personally. The areas are (1) word processing, (2) spreadsheet calculations, (3) general problem solving, and (4) database processing. These areas are treated in depth in the subsequent chapters.

In Chapter 2, I provide a brief introduction to the jargon used by computer people. This introduction to "computer-speak" will come in handy if you meet a programmer, salesperson, or other computer owner face-to-face. It will also help you to understand the remaining chapters. For even more details on how computers work, see Chapter 8.

Chapter 3 gets down to business by explaining how to use the MDOS operating system program that is supplied with your computer. The emphasis here is on "how to use," rather than on how to modify, add to, or in general change the operating system. If you want to do these kinds of things to MDOS, you will need to read about MDOS in any one of a number of other books.

Chapter 4 is about word processing. EasyWriter is a program that converts your computer into a sophisticated electronic typewriter. With EasyWriter you can do things that no typewriter can do, however. This exciting program is a step forward for humanity, but it takes considerable effort to learn how to use it. This is where Chapter 4 becomes important. After reading Chapter 4, you should be an intermediate level word processing expert.

Perhaps the biggest impact on computing in recent times has been made by the numerous spreadsheet calculator programs designed for microcomputers. These programs turn a computer into an electronic worksheet. Chapter 5 explains how to use VisiCalc to do a wide variety of visual calculations. This program is so much fun that you will resist moving on to the next chapter.

Chapter 6 covers programming. The general problem solver who finds the word processor and spreadsheet calculator inadequate to the task will benefit from this chapter. Two languages are surveyed: MBA-SIC and Pascal. The first is an interpreter and the second is a compiler language. What is the difference? Read this chapter to find out!

Chapter 7 covers a topic that promises to loom big on the small computer horizon. Database management systems are very important programs for reducing the rising cost of software. There are a number of database management programs around. Which is best? In this chapter we will look at the different types of database models, and then learn to use a simple *relational* model database system. Just to make things specific, we will study a relational database program that is provided in BASIC for your computer. You can enter this program into your machine and run it. This will give you a chance to try a very simple database system before you spend your money on one of its more expensive cousins.

Chapter 8 is a brief survey of how computers work. It delves into the inner workings of computers. You will not need to know the subject matter covered in this chapter in order to use a computer. However, if you are simply curious, or. . . .

I want to thank all the people who worked on this book. Madeline Rubin helped with the typing chores and gave good advice. Larry Benincasa, Ellen Cherry, and the staff at Reston Publishing Company were great to work with, and provided the computing equipment. The staff at the Corvallis Computer Store and the Tigard ComputerLand store all deserve my appreciation for their assistance.

T. G. Lewis
Corvallis, Oregon

# Chapter 1

# What Can Computers Do?

Perhaps they should have been shocked by this weapon, this curse, this awful machine for destruction. But they were all too busy to notice.

Perhaps they should have been stunned by this tool, this blessing, this powerful machine of peace. But they were all too busy to notice.

Until they had to.

## INFORMATION LEVERS

Microcomputers have revolutionized the way people handle information by functioning as an information lever. A computer amplifies human intellect just as steam engines amplified human muscle power over a century ago. By using the leverage of a microcomputer, a stockbroker can keep track of client accounts and particular stocks, and can perform a whole array of stock analysis operations never before possible. An architect/builder can perform cost estimating in one-tenth of the time this task might take without a computer. An electrical contractor can not only do the usual business data processing functions on a microcomputer, but can intimidate the competition as well by analyzing their bidding patterns. Once the bidding pattern of a certain competitor is known, the clever contractor can always underbid by five dollars and win the contract!

The reasons for using a microcomputer vary from person to person. Here are a few reasons to use a microcomputer in business:

- to increase accuracy,
- to increase productivity,
- to decrease bottlenecks or hassles,
- to alter cash flow or tax situations,
- or, to simply elevate your status.

A computer can do all of these things if it is properly selected, installed, and used by its owner. However, if not properly used, then a computer can cause misery. The best way to avoid the pitfalls of buying and using a computer is to become a well informed user. That is the purpose of this book—to inform.

## Accuracy

Perhaps the best known fact about computers is their ability to perform millions of arithmetic operations per second without making mistakes. One of the things we like most about computers is their reliability. For example, hundreds of ten digit numbers can be summed and averaged by a microcomputer in the time it takes to type them into the machine.

Typical business applications require accuracy of "dollars-and-cents" calculations. To achieve this it may be necessary to carry out each intermediate operation with "dollars-and-cents" precision. For example, $10.95 becomes $10.950 so that an extra mill is carried forward in the calculation. Even with this precaution, it is possible to suffer some loss of accuracy as discussed later in this chapter.

## Productivity

The most recent claim made by computer manufacturers is that they can increase worker productivity. This idea is directly related to the concept of a computer as an information lever. However, we must be careful not to assume too much about the capability of a computer. For example, it is a common fallacy that computers take jobs from people. This is not true. However, computers do shift the jobs into computer related occupations. Let's illustrate this idea with an example.

John and Mary ran a truck farm on the outskirts of a major metropolitan area. Their farm produced vegetables which John transported to town daily.

One day, John decided to buy a microcomputer to do the farm books. But Mary was skeptical because she realized that someone would need to operate the computer and enter data, etc. According to Mary, they would have to hire someone to run the computer, which would result in an overall decrease in productivity. But John said the computer would increase their productivity due to its speed and accuracy. Who was right?

Actually, John and Mary are both partially correct in their assessment. Without a computer, John and Mary spent hours preparing their sales slips, receipts, and journals for processing by their accountant. The accountant in turn processed this "data" into forms for the government and John and Mary. The accountant's fee is a recurring cost which John and Mary pay every year (or month).

With a computer John and Mary *displace* some of the accountant's work as well as their own work. The work is shifted to a more productive computer and a computer operator. Thus, the overall effect is an increase in productivity because a computer is used instead of an accountant, John, and Mary. The one-time expense of a computer is amortized over its life, and once paid for, never recurs (assuming it does not wear out).

This story about John and Mary illustrates what is happening in the world of business. New jobs are created because they are more productive than the old ones they replace. The old jobs die out because they cannot compete.

## Bottlenecks and Hassles

Computers are often used to remove excessive delays or improve flow of information. Even small businesses want to print all employee pay checks on the day before payday. The receptionist of a law practice wants to retrieve a letter which might have been entered into a word processing computer three weeks earlier. The computer can find the letter much faster than a human can by looking in a filing cabinet.

## Cashflow

A computer is an information lever which also alters the cashflow of a small enterprise. Let's look at an example of this side-effect.

Suppose John and Mary buy a computer system for $10,000. This purchase might be made from borrowed money which is paid out monthly, etc. However, at the end of five years, say, the computer will be paid for and John and Mary will be able to use it for "free". That is, the computer is a kind of **marginal labor** which is paid for once and then used for many years beyond the time it takes to pay for it.

The cashflow advantages of buying a computer instead of paying for an accountant is enhanced by the Internal Revenue Service. If we assume a five-year depreciation rate, then $2,000 each year can be deducted from John and Mary's taxable income. If they are in the 30 percent tax bracket, then the U.S. government pays (30%) (2,000) = $600 towards John and Mary's computer each year for 5 years. In short, the government will pay $3,000 towards John and Mary's $10,000 computer!

Additionally, the government often gives tax incentives of up to 10% for purchasing new equipment. This can mean an added $1,000 in the first year for John and Mary's computer. This brings the cost of the computer down to $6,000.

Next, we can assume that John and Mary's accountant charges $60/hour for bookkeeping. Without the computer this totalled $1200/year, but with a computer, the annual bill for accounting decreases to $300. Hence, an annual savings of $900 can go towards the purchase of the computer. In five years, John and Mary can throw away their computer and the total cost will have been $1500, or $300 per year!

If John and Mary keep their computer for 10 years, it will save them $3,000 in marginal labor alone. This does not include increased convenience, speed, accuracy, etc. It also does not include interest on money borrowed for the initial purpose, either.

## Status

Finally, many people buy a computer as simply a status symbol. A computer is a symbol of power. After all, if the calculation was done on-the-spot by your microcomputer, who is going to argue with it?

More than one loan officer has been intimidated by a customer who already knows the monthly payment on a new car down to the last penny. In addition, the customer probably knows in advance what the total interest will be, and how much of the interest will be offset by tax savings!

# WHAT COMPUTERS CANNOT DO

Can computers think? This is a controversial question which has stimulated research into psychology, medicine, and philosophy as well as computer science. The problem with finding an answer is that we do not yet know what *thought* is or how it works in the human brain.

It is entirely possible that a computer might someday be constructed to at least simulate human thought. Such a feat would bring worldwide recognition to the clever inventor. However, it is also possible that thinking is an entirely human activity because some problems are logically impossible for a machine to solve. A simple example of an *unsolvable* problem will demonstrate what can happen in trying to simulate human thought.

## An Impossible Problem

Consider the following unsolvable problem:

"Fred always tells the truth," said John.
"John lies," said Fred.

In this problem we are to *decide* if Fred or John is telling the truth given the two statements quoted above. Suppose we assume that John lies. This assumption fails to hold up under logical examination: If John lies, then it means Fred lied. If Fred lied, it means John doesn't lie, which contradicts the original assumption. Suppose we assume the opposite. If John tells the truth, then Fred also tells the truth. But if Fred tells the truth, then John lies, which again contradicts the facts. In short, this problem is *undecidable*.

So, is the problem of constructing a thinking computer solvable, or like the example above, is it an impossible problem? Nobody knows, but we do know that there are some things that people can do much better than computers. Here are some of those things that people do best.

## Correct Functioning

Computers are able to correct small errors that may occur during their operation. For example, a computer can decide if a number is too large or too small for it to process. However, a computer cannot reason about itself to the extent of deciding if it is giving the "correct" answer.

Only a human operator can decide if the answers provided by a computer make sense. For example, a computer will blindly print a paycheck for a million dollars even though the correct amount is one thousand dollars. A human observer, however, will almost always catch such an error at once because the row of six zeros will somehow attract attention.

## Input Errors

The most common source of errors in data processing is incorrect input. Only a human operator can decide if an input value is correct.

A computer can easily detect an error during input if a user enters a name, say, rather than a number. But, a computer cannot detect an error in a "dollars-and-cents" input if it is $15.95 instead of $14.55, for example.

One method of checking for input errors is to use **checksums**. A checksum can be computed during data entry and then compared with a checksum previously computed. If the two sums do not match, the operator knows that an error has been committed. This kind of error detection is very useful, but notice that it depends on human intervention.

## Understanding

A computer can simulate some intellectual processes that we might say resemble human thought, but no computer currently *understands* humans. For example, computers may communicate in English, but a computer does not know what the English words mean.

We cannot tell a computer what to do in spoken English (at least not yet). Instead, we must use very rigorous languages like BASIC or Pascal as intermediate languages for communicating with machines. These **programming languages** resemble mathematics more than they do English. Furthermore, they do not directly control the computer, but instead must be converted into electrical signals first. We will discuss how this is done in the next chapter.

The problem with computers is that they do not understand natural language. This means a human programmer must translate English directions into a computer language so that the directions can in turn be converted into electrical signals. This is the process of computer programming, and also the source of **software** (the programs that direct the computer).

## Hard Problems

Some solutions to problems are so time-consuming to compute that even a high–speed computer cannot solve them. For example, some secret codes are so complex that a computer might take twenty years to try all combinations.

The number of possible chess moves in a game of chess is so large that a very fast computer could not study each and every move in a billion years! These kinds of problems may seem rather contrived, but in many realistic applications we are faced with similar difficulties.

An example of a **hard problem** faced by transportation companies every day is the problem of optimal scheduling. Suppose a company has several warehouses and many retail outlets located throughout the country. Further, suppose the company wants to reduce the cost of supplying the retail stores with goods from the warehouses by minimizing the distance each truck travels in order to pick up and deliver the goods. This problem can be solved by examining each of thousands of possible truck routes. However, it may take the best computer a long time to do this.

Hard problems are usually solved by a combination of human intuition and computer processing. In the transportation problem, someone suggests a schedule and a computer then computes the cost. Then an improvement is made because a human discovers a "better way," and the computer calculation shows that costs are indeed reduced. This process continues until a suitable solution is found.

Computers cannot discover new methods, use intuition, innovate, understand natural language, program themselves, catch input errors, reason about output values, or decide if a problem is solvable. Computers are very fast, accurate, and patient, but thinking is still uniquely human.

# COMPUTERS AS MARGINAL LABOR

Exactly what can microcomputers do? Since a computer embodies marginal labor, they are in a sense slaves for doing certain things faster, more accurately, and more conveniently than humans. By **marginal labor** we mean that a computer will not save labor because someone must operate, program, and maintain a computer. However, for the same labor cost, a computer can deliver higher productivity. Furthermore, added processing can be done with a computer for no additional cost to the owner. Once paid for, a computer saves money—the real meaning of marginal labor.

We will illustrate the usefulness of the "electronic slave" in the following broad areas of application.

- Word processing
- Spreadsheet calculation
- General-purpose problem solving through programming
- Database processing

The following chapters give detailed instructions on how to use your computer for each of these areas of application. In the remainder of this chapter we introduce these areas and discuss how the computer can be used in each.

## Word Processing

One of the most obvious ideas in computing is to replace your mechanical typewriter with a microcomputer. This leads to savings in time and effort because, unlike a typewriter, a computer can do the following:

1. Erase, insert, delete, change, move, copy, and search for patterns of text in any written document without retyping,

2. "Remember" any written document by recording it on a diskette for reference at a later time.

The first advantage means that **text** in the form of business letters, legal contracts, etc. can be edited without retyping the entire document. A business letter can be entered into the microcomputer and saved on diskette. Then the letter can be displayed on the microcomputer display screen for verification. If any character, word, sentence, or paragraph needs to be changed, it can be modified without altering any of the surrounding text. Once a satisfactory version of the letter is obtained, one or more identical copies can be printed without human intervention.

One of the most common applications of word processing is in maintaining mailing lists. Suppose you want to write a letter to each member of an organization. With a word processing system you can enter and edit a single copy of the letter and then print many copies of it from the original. Furthermore, using a list of previously stored names and addresses, you can tell the word processor to attach different name and address headings to each letter.

A **word processing system** consists of a microcomputer with one or more disk drives, screen/keyboard, and a high-quality printer. Typically, a word processing program is purchased separately from the hardware. A variety of word processor programs exist, but we will discuss only one such program in the chapter devoted to this topic.

Here is a brief list of the application areas where word processing excels:

- legal contracts, realtor listings, business (secretarial) letters,
- mailing lists, phototypsetting,
- newsletters, newspapers, magazines, books,
- clubs, associations, unions, schools,
- authors, editors, journalists,
- electronic mail, message centers, corporate communication

Indeed, anyone who must prepare documents with substantial text in them can increase productivity using a word processor.

## Spreadsheet Calculations

A microcomputer is more than a glorified calculator because it can "remember" large volumes of information and it can "remember" instructions for processing that information. In fact, it is the stored program which gives computers an advantage over calculators.

The problem with computer programs, however, is that someone must write and maintain the programs. This is an arduous task unless you rely on software levers like the automated spreadsheet programs discussed here.

A spreadsheet program is a program which helps a user design and implement a computer program without having to know much about computer programming. How is this possible?

A typical spreadsheet program divides the screen into a **matrix** of rows and columns. For example, a simple 3-by-3 matrix as shown in Figure 1-1 contains three rows numbered 1, 2, and 3, and three columns labeled A, B, and C. See Figure 1-1.

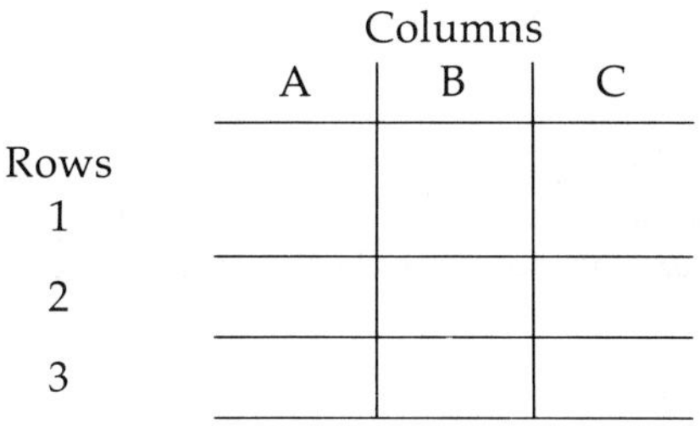

**Figure 1-1**

We designate each cell in this matrix by its column and row label. Thus, A1 refers to the upper left-most cell while B2 refers to the middle cell.

Now, suppose we construct an automobile/travel spreadsheet using the 9-cell matrix. Let the following cells represent the known quantities:

A1 : total gallons consumed
A2 : total cost of fuel
A3 : price per gallon
B1 : total distance traveled
B2 : total time elapsed

and the following cells represent the calculated quantities:

C1 : mileage (miles per gallon)
C2 : cost per mile
C3 : average speed

and the undefined cell, B3 is not used.

Given A1 through B2 we want to calculate C1 through C3. But the computer needs to know how to calculate C1 through C3, so we must supply a formula. Recall the following relations:

mileage = (total distance)/(total gallons)
cost per mile = (total cost)/(total distance)
average speed = (total distance)/(total time)

These formulas are translated into cell labels by noting the cell assignments made above. Thus, to get a numeric result for each of the calculated quantities, we must tell the computer to divide the quantity in one cell by the quantity stored in another cell. For C1, C2, and C3:

C1 = B1/A1
C2 = A2/B1
C3 = B1/B2

These formulas and the cell designations above yield the results for an automobile/travel spreadsheet. For example, suppose we are given (placed in the matrix):

A1 : total gallons    =   12.8
A2 : total cost       =   21.50
A3 : price per gallon =    1.679
B1 : total distance   = 512
B2 : total time       =    9.5

The spreadsheet for these quantities might appear as shown below:

|  | Columns | | |
| --- | --- | --- | --- |
|  | A | B | C |
| **Rows** | | | |
| 1 | 12.8 | 512.0 | 40.0 |
| 2 | 21.50 | 9.5 | 0.042 |
| 3 | 1.679 | | 53.9 |

**Figure 1-2**

This spreadsheet is a financial **model** of an automobile/travel system. Such models are very useful for a variety of applications. If we alter one of the values stored in a cell, all other cells which depend on the altered cell are also altered. For example, if we change A1 to 10.5 gallons, the calculation in cell C1 is also changed. Thus, the model can be used to explore "what if" questions about the automobile/travel system.

Spreadsheet calculations are useful in many applications. We list below only a few of the most obvious.

- mortgage, financial, real estate calculations
- engineering, architectural, building estimating
- statistical, experimental, scientific calculations
- retail stores, wholesalers, warehousing applications

## General Purpose Problem Solving

A spreadsheet program simplifies using a computer, but for new or more sophisticated problems we must turn to programming for the solution. Two approaches exist for obtaining programs for special problems: (1) buy programs from software vendors, and (2) write your own programs.

If you elect to buy software from a vendor, there are three ways to do so:

1. Purchase ready-made programs such as accounts receivable, payroll, general ledger.

2. Purchase ready-made programs and then modify them to do what you want them to do.

3. Sign a contract with a vendor to custom design and implement a new program.

If you decide to write your own programs, then it will be necessary for you to learn more about computers. In particular, do-it-yourself programmers must first learn a formal programming language such as BASIC, Pascal, FORTRAN, etc., and then learn the art of programming.

A computer programmer is a general problem solver. Programmers have learned to solve problems in very stylistic ways. For most programmers this involves the following:

**Requirements definition.** What is required to solve the problem, for example, what are the inputs and outputs?

**Design specification** How is the problem going to be solved, and what is the method of solution? How is data organized?

**Coding specification** How is the design converted into a program? What programming language is used? What coding rules are used?

**Implementation** The actual program as written in a programming language must be correct and understandable.

**Testing** Selected test cases must be demonstrated to convince another person that the program works.

**Documentation** The system must include manuals, program listings, and explanations of the problem, program design, implementation, and test results.

Suppose we illustrate these steps with a very simple problem. For instance, given a checking account with balance B and a check for amount A, what is the ending balance EB after the check has been cashed? This simple problem has many "trick" aspects of which the thorough programmer will be wary. First, what is required of the problem?

### Requirements

Inputs:    B  = balance
           A  = amount of check
Outputs:   EB = ending balance


Note: The requirements should also specify that B must always remain positive, and A should be greater than zero.

### Design

Method: Check to make sure B and A are positive and greater than zero. Also, use subtraction to get EB. *Note:* the data will be organized as simple real-valued numbers. However, we must assume they are small enough to fit in memory.

### Coding

We will use BASIC as the programming language with the following documentation standards:

1. All programs will contain a heading of comments which tell what the program does,

2. The programs will use "structured" control so that reading the program is much like reading a book.

3. Use meaningful names for the variables, e.g. BALANCE, AMOUNT, and ENDBAL.


### Implementation

Use **levels of abstraction** in the coding process in order to speed programming and reduce errors. See Chapter 6, "How To Write Your Own Programs," for more details.

The code for this example:

```
10 REM  ****************************************************************

20 REM     CHECK BOOK BALANCE PROGRAM

30 REM          INPUTS : BALANCE = current balance

40 REM                   AMOUNT  = check amount

50 REM          OUTPUTS: ENDBAL  = ending balance

60 REM  ****************************************************************
```

```
100 PRINT "Enter balance : ";
110 INPUT BALANCE
120 PRINT "Enter amount  :";
130 INPUT AMOUNT
140 IF AMOUNT <= 0 THEN 120
150 IF BALANCE - AMOUNT <= 0  THEN 200
160 ENDBAL = BALANCE - AMOUNT
170 PRINT "Ending balance $ ", ENDBAL
180 STOP
190 REM ********* ERROR CONDITION************************
```

## Testing

We can test this program by carefully selecting input data. The data should test each **if-statement** so that each program statement is executed at least once. For example,

$$AMOUNT <= 0$$
$$BALANCE - AMOUNT <= 0$$

means to test if AMOUNT is negative, if BALANCE is negative, and if BALANCE is less than AMOUNT. This analysis suggests the following sets of test values.

1. AMOUNT = 10.00
   BALANCE = 50.00
2. AMOUNT = 50.00
   BALANCE = 10.00
3. AMOUNT = −50.00
   BALANCE =   5.00
4. AMOUNT =   5.00
   BALANCE =   5.00
5. AMOUNT =   5.00
   BALANCE =  −5.00

These, and other test cases are used to verify that the program works. Of course this method does not guarantee complete correctness of your program, but it is a good way to make sure the program works most of the time.

*Documentation*

Programs are documented for two groups of people: users and programmers. The users need only know how to use the program, and do not want to be bothered by implementation details.

The programmers who must maintain and perhaps alter a program need to know lots of details. The most important details should be explained in simple, direct sentences and figures.

We will discuss programming in more detail in a subsequent chapter. This brief introduction should convince you to either buy programs from a software vendor, or else read the subsequent chapter for more information.

## Database Processing

Computers can be used to "remember" large volumes of information by storing lists of data on diskette. These lists are organized on diskettes in the form of disk **files** (see Chapter 8 for details). Whenever information is needed, a **key** is used to identify the information and retrieve it from the disk file.

In many applications the number of lists stored in disk files is large and difficult to manage. For this reason a special program called a **database manager** is used.

A **database management system** is a computer with software for entering, retrieving, modifying, and outputting information stored on disks. One of the main goals of a database management system **DBMS** is to simplify a user's access to the database information. How is this done?

*Schemes: User's View*

A database simplifies handling large amounts of information by structuring the information according to a **schema,** or user's view. There are three fundamental schemas (views) in the world of DBMSs:

1. Network—the database is thought of as a network of interacting "pieces" of information. For example, the telephones in the United States are connected via a network of telephone lines. Any line might be thought of as connecting to any other line.

2. Hierarchical—the database is thought of as a layered system of "pieces" of information. For example, the telephones of the United States could be thought of as connected in layers: the first layer is defined by the area code, the second layer is defined by the prefix, etc. While this is not the way telephones are connected, it is one way for a user to view the system, i.e. it is an acceptable user's view.

### PARTS

| Qty | Part No. | Price | Date |
|-----|----------|-------|---------|
| 5 | NC-875 | 5.95 | 9/1/81 |
| 3 | NC-501 | 0.35 | 9/30/81 |
| 0 | NC-450 | 1.95 | 9/9/81 |

### SUPPLIERS

| Name | Street | City | Zip |
|------|--------------|-------------|-------|
| Acme | 1100 Broadway | Billings | 87550 |
| Jones | 3506 Olivara | Los Angeles | 97730 |

### CUSTOMERS

| Name | Street | City | Zip | Balance |
|-------|-----------|-------|-------|---------|
| Smith | 3658 Oak | Tulsa | 65401 | 100.95 |
| Jones | 1335 Main | Tewes | 08350 | 98.50 |

**Figure 1-3**

3. Relational—the database is thought of as a collection of tables. Each table is "flat"—that is, a table has no structure except the usual rows and columns. For instance, the telephones in the United States might be thought of as they appear in the telephone book. Each line of text in the book corresponds to a row and each entry corresponds to a column. Thus, name, address, and telephone number constitute the columns, and one row in the book consists of "Lewis", "2812 Monterey Pl.", and "755-0853", for example.

The battle among user views is still raging, but most database systems are either hierarchical or relational. As an example of relational data, suppose we study how this view is used to store an inventory database.

An inventory database consists of, e.g., three relations. The PARTS, SUPPLIERS, and CUSTOMERS relations each contain information in tabular format. (See Figure 1-3.)

The columns of these relations are called **domains** and the rows are called **tuples**. The "Part No." domain may be selected as the key to retrieve a part from PARTS, and "Name" may be used to retrieve a tuple from one of the other relations.

We might imagine a processing program which removes three NC-875 parts from PARTS and sends them to "Smith" in relation CUSTOM-ERS. The tuple from CUSTOMERS is used to address the purchase invoice.

The imagined processing program would also update the "Qty" domain corresponding to this part number. If the "Qty" drops below a certain level, then more parts would be ordered from the appropriate SUPPLIERS.

DBMSs are used for a variety of applications. For additional information on this approach to computing, see Chapter 7 which is devoted to database processing. Here are some other places where database processing is useful.

- Keeping lists of records, sports statistics, magazines.
- Business data processing, e.g. inventory, billing.
- Energy conservation facts, information retrieval services.
- Real estate listings, personnel listings, dating service.
- Bank accounts, train schedules, social clubs, libraries, subscriptions, birthdays, event calendars.

## COMMON QUESTIONS

Q. Why is a microcomputer called an information lever?

A. Because it increases productivity by supplying marginal labor.

Q. If I am in the 35 percent income tax bracket and I pay $5,000 for a computer, how much of this does the government pay for me?

A. Assuming a salvage value of zero dollars and a straight-line depreciation schedule over five years, the government pays 35 percent of $5,000. However, credits, incentives, and double-declining schedules can improve this estimate.

Q. How long will a microcomputer last?

A. If properly maintained and used a microcomputer will last as long as, or longer, than an automobile. Most likely, you will outgrow your microcomputer before it "dies", and want a "bigger" machine.

Q. Can computers think?

A. No.

Q. Is the following problem solvable by computer?
"Fred always lies," said John.
"John always lies," said Fred.
Are Fred and John telling the truth?

A. Assume John is telling the truth. Then, Fred must be lying, so the truth is that John tells the truth. Now, assume Fred is telling the truth. Then, John is lying which supports our assumption that Fred is telling the truth. But both cannot be telling the truth. Can both be lying?

Q. What are the most common errors in using a microcomputer?

A. Input errors which are accidentally entered into the system.

Q. Give an example or method of checking for input errors.

A. Checksumming.

Q. Why are programming languages used to communicate with computers instead of English?

A. English is too ambiguous and informal for a computer to "understand".

Q. What is software?

A. The programs, or instructions, which control the functioning of the hardware.

Q. What do we mean by a "hard problem"?

A. A hard problem is one that can be solved but it would take a very fast computer a very long time to do so.

Q. What is word processing?

A. In its simplest form, word processing is the use of computers instead of typewriters. In more sophisticated word processing applications, a computer is used to deliver mail electronically via a word processing system.

Q. What do we mean by editing?

A. Text is rearranged, changed, and in general processed by editing it. Common editing operations are: delete, insert, change, find, move, copy, etc.

Q. What is a spreadsheet program?

A. A spreadsheet program is a computer program which simplifies computer programming by limiting the calculations that can be performed to a grid or matrix of cells. These cells are used to store values which are interrelated through user-defined formulas. Hence, a user "programs" by specifying the interelations among the cells of the spreadsheet.

Q. Why are spreadsheet programs so valuable?

A. They reduce the time and effort needed to program a microcomputer, and they serve as models of real-life systems.

Q. What are the steps in general problem solving using a computer?

A. Requirements, design, coding specification, implementation, testing, and documentation.

Q. Give an example of a programming language.

A. BASIC

Q. What is a DBMS?

A. A DataBase Management System. This is a collection of programs for processing data stored in files based on a user's view called a schema.

Q. What are the three kinds of schemas for a DBMS?

A. Network, hierarchical, and relational.

Q. Why would someone use a DBMS?

A. DBMSs reduce the time and effort needed to implement programs that process large volumes of data.

Q. Why would someone avoid using a DBMS?

A. Due to their general nature it is possible that a DBMS may not serve your needs, or else is too slow and takes too much diskette space.

# Chapter 2

# A Quick Guide to Computer Vocabulary

It spoke to them from the mountain. And, at first they did not understand. Yet as its words fell like rain on the valley below, seeds of awareness began to grow and take root.

As years passed the garden spread into a forest of ideas. Admittedly there were thorns and weeds, but for the most part the orchards were tall and strong, the vines were abundant, and all who had heard were richly rewarded.

Then the day of renewal came, and one among the garden was chosen to speak. It spoke to them from the mountain, and at first they did not understand.

## THE MEANING OF COMPUTERS

Microcomputers have brought the power, versatility, and control of digital electronics to the doorstep of home owners, truck drivers, independent business people, bankers, musicians, artists, educators, politicians, movie–makers, and a thousand other innovative people. In short, computers are pervasive, because of the LSI (large scale integration) revolution. But what does all this mean? What are the profound events upon which all computing depend?

In this chapter we give the reader a short course on computer vocabulary for the purpose of exposing the most fundamental ideas computing has to offer, and to prepare you for life in an information society. For a detailed explanation of how computers work, turn to Chapter 8.

There are three fundamental ideas which govern all of computing.

1. Automatic control—the idea that a machine can perform certain "intellectual" operations without human intervention.

2. Memory—the invention of information "banks" or stores which can hold data and, most importantly, programs for automatically controlling the remaining parts of the machine.

3. Software—layers upon layers of programs which increase the level of "intelligence" of machines so that they can perform increasingly sophisticated functions.

## Automatic Control

The idea that a machine can make decisions and perform (simple) tasks without human intervention probably began with the invention of the clock. A clock need not be "operated by" a human. Similarly, a computer can be programmed to run indefinitely without a human operator. This simple idea was used to invent the card-controlled weaving loom, and later, the automatic bomb sight (during World War II).

Modern computers are **digital controllers.** Early electronic controllers operated on a continuous signal (voltage, current, etc.) and so were called **analog** controllers. The speed indicator in most automobiles measures speed in continuous units of miles per hour. But since the LSI revolution, digital electronics have proved superior to analog electronics because of lower cost. A digital computer operates on discontinuous, or discrete, units of information called **bits.** A bit is either "on" or "off", instead of assuming some continuous value.

The idea that all information can be broken into small "on-off" switch settings is one of the most profound notions in modern technology. The **bit** is, therefore, the fundamental unit of information. Since a bit can take on only one of two possible values (zero or one), all modern computers operate as **binary** digital controllers. Instead of counting from zero to nine, a binary computer counts from zero to one!

Large numbers and volumes of information can be stored in computers by **encoding** groups of bits into larger units of information as discussed in Chapter 8. The important thing to remember here is that all information can be encoded in binary computers, hence giving them enormous control over their information–rich environment.

## Stored Programs (Memory)

The next breakthrough in computing came on the heels of the invention of the electronic memory. We will show how electronic memories are used to store binary encoded information in Chapter 8. The most immediate consequence of these memories was the concept of a stored program. A **stored program** is a sequence of instructions which govern the operations of a computer.

The idea is this: a human devises a way to do something as a series of very simple operations. This is called an **algorithm.** The algorithm is converted into a sequence of **machine instructions** (binary encodings which control the circuitry of a computer). We say the algorithm is **coded** in **machine language** when a programmer encodes the algorithm. Finally, the machine language instructions are **loaded** (copied) into the electronic memory where they are stored while the machine retrieves them one at a time. Each machine language instruction controls the computer for a brief moment. The details of this process are covered in Chapter 8.

Automatic control and computer memory combine to give computers sufficient power and flexibility to compute anything that can be computed. This is such a profound accomplishment that it has taken thirty years for humanity to "catch up" with something called "software". Indeed, we are currently in the midst of an expansion of the software age.

## Software

The third idea which lends profound meaning to computers is the idea of software. **Software** is the sum total of the programs which "execute" on a computer. Software is to computing what the steam engine was to the Industrial Revolution.

If humans were forced to encode algorithms into machine language programs (binary), the shortage of software would be of epidemic proportions. Fortunately, there are software levers.

Modern software is constructed in layers much like a head of lettuce. Actually, the layers may interact and therefore may *not* be entirely separable, but we will treat them as independent levels here.

The inner layer, of course, is the machine itself. This is represented by binary encoded instructions which we call machine language. Since machine language is very detailed and tedious to use, we almost always use a software lever called an **assembler** to convert **symbolic** machine language into binary machine language. The assembler is a program which translates the program written in symbolic form into the program written in binary encoded form. The symbolic form is called the **source** program and the binary form is called the object program. Thus, input to the translator is a sequence of source program statements and output from the translator is a sequence of object program statements.

Assembler language source programs are one-for-one transliterations of machine language object programs. In this sense they are low-level programs. To get higher level software we must move to the next layer.

A **programming language** is a high-level language which translates from one to many machine language statements. BASIC, FORTRAN, COBOL, etc. are examples of programming languages.

A source program written in BASIC, for example, may be translated into 5 or more binary object instructions for each BASIC statement. This is why programming languages increase programmer productivity.

There are two (or more) ways to translate a statement in a high–level language into several object statements:

Compiling
Interpreting

A **compiler** is a program which translates source programs into object programs. The object program is not executed, but instead it is stored for execution at a later time. Pascal, COBOL, and FORTRAN are examples of compiled languages.

An **interpreter** is a program which not only translates a source program into an object program, but it also executes the object program statements on-the-spot. Actually, an interpreter does not produce an object program as output because it is not necessary. Therefore, an interpreter is a program for **direct execution** of another program. BASIC, LISP, and APL are examples of interpreted languages.

The advantages of interpreted languages versus compiled languages are:

1. Development time is improved because a new program can be quickly executed without a time-consuming translation step.

2. Interpreters are usually smaller (take less memory) than compilers.

The disadvantges are:

1. Interpreted languages need a run-time interpreter which, in addition to the source program, takes memory space.

2. Interpretation is a slow process, thus interpreted programs run up to 10 times slower than object code programs.

Most programs for microcomputers are written in BASIC or Pascal. However, even these source languages are too low–level for many people. The quest for very high–level languages is currently taking the computer programmer into new areas of language design. Some of these avenues are explored in the following survey.

**Query language processors** are programs for interpreting very high-level statements for processing database systems. We might imagine the following program segment in a very high–level query language:

FOR ALL  NAMES IN MASTER FILE
      DO;
            BALANCE IS SUM OF ALL TRANSACTIONS;

```
        PRINT BALANCE;
    END;
```

This query posts the new balance of accounts for an accounting program.

Another direction being taken by programmers in order to reduce programming effort is in the area of program generators. A **program generator** is a program which writes another program, automatically. The generator requests input information from a user, and then uses this information to produce a BASIC, Pascal, or COBOL program, for example.

Extending beyond program generators takes us into the realm of artificial intelligence. An **AI program** is a program which can communicate with a user in a natural language. If and when such a system is available, it will make programming as easy as training an assistant to do the job.

The modern electronic binary computer is unique in the history of technology because it can control its environment automatically, "remember" information by storing binary encoded signals in an electronic memory, and become increasingly more "intelligent" through layers of software. All developments in computing stem from these three capabilities.

In the next section we take a tour of the hardware world of computers in order to learn the terminology of computer hardware experts. Then, in the final section, we will take a second look at software terminology.

## HARDWARE JARGON

Chapter 8 details the inner workings of hardware. Our purpose here is to expose you to words that computer people use everyday when discussing computers. It is the "street language" of computer experts.

If we were discussing automobiles it might be useful to categorize them in terms of comfort, reliability, and performance. Similarly, a computer is rated in terms of ease-of-use, reliability, and performance. Unfortunately, the measures of ease-of-use, reliability, and performance may seem strange and unfamiliar to newcomers. Let's see if these strange measures can be clarified.

### CPU

The CPU (central processing unit) consists of an ALU (arithmitic logic unit) for performing machine language operations like ADD, COMPARE, and COPY, and a main memory or RAM (random access memory).

Usually, a CRT (cathode ray tube) screen and keyboard are connected or **interfaced** to the CPU so a user can communicate with it. The CRT may have a **cursor** or blinking dot which indicates to you that the computer is turned on and waiting for your inputs.

A CRT screen is rated in terms of its size and display speed (ease-of-use). An 80 by 24 CRT screen is able to display 24 lines of 80 columns each. A 9600 **baud** screen can write 960 characters per second. Therefore, the entire 80 by 24 = 1920 characters of a full screen could be filled in less than two seconds.

The speed of a computer is often measured in **bandwidth** units. For example, 9600 baud is a way to characterize the speed of a CRT. Since each character requires 8 bits for its encoding (see Chapter 8), and 2 bits for its transmission, a 9600 **baud** connection can transmit 960 characters per second. Other bandwidth units are lpm = lines-per-minute, cps = characters-per-second, bps = bits-per-second, and baud = bits-per-second, (roughly).

The memory of a CPU is used to store a program and its data while the program is being run. The memory is called RAM (random access memory) because all locations in the memory are all equally easy to access. Some computers use a special non–destructive memory called ROM (read–only–memory) to store permanent programs and data. For example, BASIC interpreters are often stored in ROM so that they are always loaded and ready to use as soon as the power is turned on.

Each cell in memory is assigned a number called its **address.** The time it takes to access a memory cell and retrieve information is called the memory **cycle time.** This time is a measure of the overall speed of the CPU because memory access is such a frequently performed operation.

Memory cycles are coordinated by a timer called the CPU **clock.** Since all operations of the CPU are timed by its clock, we can estimate CPU performance by knowing its clock rate. A 4 MHZ (four mega–hertz) clock is one which "ticks" 4 million times per second. Typically, 4 or 5 "ticks" are needed to access memory and do a certain operation. Therefore, a 4 MHZ CPU is one which can process approximately one million memory locations per second.

## Printer

A printer is used to obtain "hard copy" from a computer. Typically, a printer outputs lines of text onto 80 or 132 column paper. The quality of the printed character may be compromised in exchange for greater printing speed.

A dot-matrix font is an array of dots used to approximate solid-font characters. A 5-by-7 array is of lower quality than a 9-by-12 array, for example. The cost of the printer is also increased by increasing the density of the dot-matrix array.

Printers must be attached to the CPU through an **interface.** A serial interface transmits information a single bit at a time while a parallel interface transmits information an 8-bit character at a time. An RS-232 interface is a typical serial or parallel interface.

The performance of a printer may be increased by contracting it to print bidirectionally. That is, printing occurs in both directions as the printing mechanism scans the page.

Typical printer speeds range from 300 baud (30 cps) to 1200 baud (120 cps). The time it takes to do a carriage return decreases the effective speed of a printer if short lines are output instead of full lines. A bidirectional printer reduces this loss by printing during the carriage return.

A full-ASCII (pronounced ask-key) printer is a printer with all characters of the ASCII (American Standard Code for Information Interchange) character set. Some printers do not include the full set, however, or may not support upper and lower case, for example.

## Disk Drives

A **disk drive** is a device for reading/writing bits to/from a rotating magnet disk. A **floppy disk** is a flexible plastic diskette about the size of a 45-rpm record. A **hard disk** is a rigid disk about the size of a 45-rpm or 33-rpm record, depending on its capacity.

The amount of information a disk can store is usually measured in millions of bytes (characters), MByte. A 20 MByte disk, for example, can store 20 million characters of information.

The speed of a disk depends on its rotational speed and transmission rate. A disk is usually rotated at about 360 rpm and can transmit at rates of nearly 1 MByte per second (highly variable). The organization of diskettes is discussed in greater detail in Chapter 8.

Disk drives provide a low-cost extension of RAM because they are inexpensive and can be removed (except for "Winchester" type disks). Unfortunately, access time to information stored on disks is much slower than access time on RAM. Therefore, we are forced to trade speed for memory in designing most computer systems. Hence disk storage is simply another level of storage within a hierarchy of memory as explained in Chapter 8.

## Communications

It is also possible to connect a computer to a telephone or some other "network" of communication in order to send/receive information from outside of the computer system. This is done by **interfacing** the computer to some device like a **modem**. A modem (modulator-demodulator) converts electronic signals into sound for transmission, and from sound-to-electronic signal for reception.

Typical transmission speeds of 300 or 1200 baud are possible with a modem and a telephone. Actually, a telephone will support up to about 2400 baud (240 cps) without extra "conditioning" equipment.

Communications software along with a modem and modem interface can be used to copy information from one computer system to another. The sender might, for example, send a program to the receiver. The receiver could then use the program to process its information. The results of the processing might be sent back to the original sender, and so forth.

Modems can be simple or sophisticated. A simple modem requires a human to dial the telephone. A sophisticated modem is able to automatically dial (auto-dial) and automatically answer (auto-answer) the telephone without human intervention.

All in all, computer hardware is much like an automobile: ease-of-use is measured by how clearly the dot-matrix characters are displayed or printed, how fast the CRT screen can update and display a full screen, and how easy it is to interface new devices to the CPU. Reliability is measured in MTBF (mean-time-between-failures), and performance is measured in bandwidth units like megahertz, characters per second, etc. Memory devices are rated in terms of how many characters (bytes) they can hold and their access (cycle) time. Speed, capacity, and compatibility are important keywords in computer jargon.

## SOFTWARE JARGON

Software is the **control** part of a computer system. Without software, a computer is useless. The most important concepts in software are:

- Algorithms,
- Data structures, and
- Languages.

In simplified terms, a problem is solved using a computer by selecting (or inventing) an algorithm (method of solution), devising a data structure which organizes the data so the algorithm can be used, and then implementing the algorithm and data structure using a programming language suitable for the problem.

## Algorithm

An **algorithm** is an unambiguous, precise, and effective recipe for solving a problem. The building blocks of an algorithm are the following three **control structures:**

1. Simple sequence—One operation of the algorithm is performed after another.

2. Branching—Either one operation or sequence of operations is done, or else some other operation or sequence of operation is done, but not both.

3. Looping—An operation or sequence of operations is done over and over again until some condition is satisfied.

The simplest algorithms are implemented as computer programs deep within the innermost layers of the computer system. For example, algorithms for starting a computer do the following:

1. Initially copy a program from a disk drive into RAM and begin executing the new program—this is called a **bootstrap loader,**

2. The newly loaded program loads another program called the **operating system** program into RAM. The operating system awaits commands from the user.

3. The user calls up other programs via the operating system program. For example, the user may elect to call up the BASIC interpreter in order to write and execute a new program.

An operating system like DOS is simply a program which assists the user in using the computer system. Operating systems help to copy information stored on disks, edit new source program text, drive printers, modems, and CRT screens.

We tell the computer what to do through operating system **commands.** In a sense, an operating system is a program for controlling other programs. If another program fails due to an error, it is the operating system that must recover the system and help the user find the error.

Some operating systems monitor the execution of one program at a time, while other operating systems allow two or more programs to execute in time-interleaved fashion: each program is allowed to run for a few milliseconds before being interrupted. This is called **multiprogramming,** and gives the user the appearance that two or more programs are executing simultaneously. In fact, only one program is executing at a time, but the computer is fast enough to give this false impression.

For example, a multiprogramming operating system would make it possible to run a program which prints a file on the printer, and another program which interacts with the user via the keyboard and CRT screen.

Additionally, a **timesharing** operating system allows two or more users to share a single computer (through two or more keyboard/CRT terminals). Timesharing is done the same way as multiprogramming, e.g., by interleaved operation of the computer.

Finally, a **multiprocessor** operating system controls a computer with two or more microprocessors. Thus, truly simultaneous operation of two or more programs is made possible through coordination of the multiple microprocessors. Such systems are often called **distributed** because several disjoint microprocessors are used instead of a single centralized microprocessor.

The simple algorithm and the three basic control structures—sequence, branching, and looping—used to construct algorithms leads to sophisticated programs like DOS. But this is only one-half of the story, because without data, an algorithm cannot do very much.

## Data Structures

Data must be organized into logical groups of information in order to be used by an algorithm. The simplest structures are discussed in Chapter 8 in more detail. They are:

bits
characters
integers
reals

However, more elaborate structures are needed for most realistic problems. We will define only a few of the most important data structures found in computer software.

An **array** is a contiguous list of elements, e.g., integers, reals, characters, etc. in memory. We access an array element by its name and its subscript. For example, array element 3 in BASIC would appear as B(3) and A$(3) in arrays B and A$.

A **pointer** is a number which points to information stored in a data structure. For example, the **address** of element B(3), say, is a pointer to element B(3).

A **tree** is a hierarchical data structure shaped like a tree. The root of the tree points to branches which in turn contain information and more pointers to more elements in the tree structure. Trees are very useful for gaining fast access to information stored in disk files. A **B-tree,** for example, is a tree structure commonly used to index information in a disk.

We discuss B-trees and give a program for constructing them in Chapter 7.

A **file** is a data structure stored on a disk. The elements of a file are called **records**. A **sequential file** is an array stored on disk that must be accessed from beginning to end of the list. A **random file** is an array stored on disk that can be accessed at any element of the file, at any time. Why use a sequential file when a random file seems more flexible?

Sequential files are cumbersome and slow but they can be used to store variable length records (elements). That is, a sequential file can be used to store information which may vary in record length. A random file, on the other hand, can only store fixed-length records.

In most applications we want to retrieve a record from a file given some uniquely defining information stored within the file. A **key** is a piece of information which identifies a record stored within a file.

An **index file** is a file containing keys and pointers to another file. The other file contains the complete record corresponding to the key located through access to the index file. Index files are used just like the index of a book: to find where in the book the information is uniquely defined by the key.

A common way to implement an index file is to use a B-tree data structure. Thus, to locate a record with a certain key, the index (B-tree) file is searched first. Once the key is found in the index file, the corresponding pointer is used to retrieve the complete information.

The job of a programmer is to select an appropriate algorithm and data structure which solves the stated problem in the least amount of time, least amount of memory space, and most reliable way. These goals often conflict with one another, however, and it is usually necessary to make difficult trade-offs between algorithm complexity and data structure complexity. An unwise choice between two alternatives can result in poor performance and poor reliability.

## Languages

We have already discussed the importance of programming languages in computing. A language is a software lever because it can accelerate programmer productivity. In this section we introduce additional terminology used by programmers.

A program consists of control structures for implementing an algorithm and data structures for organizing the data to be processed. A variety of naming conventions are often used to keep all this detail straight in the programmer's mind.

Variables are given names so that a programmer need not remember the RAM address of the value corresponding to the variable. Values are assigned to variables by moving a value to the location in RAM corresponding to the variable. Hence, A = 5 means to assign the value of 5 to the variable, A.

Variables and constants are associated with a data type in many cases. A data type is a collection of values. Hence all real values form a type called "reals", and all character strings form a type called "strings". For example, A$ is a string-valued variable while X is a real-valued variable.

A program with a design or implementation flaw is a program containing a "bug". A bug is removed by changing or "patching" the program. This process is called **debugging.**

One way to reduce the possibility of bugs (as well as their effect on the overall program) is to break the program into small pieces called **procedures.** A procedure is a section of source program which is "called" by another program whenever needed. Programmers typically design large programs as a collection of subprograms or procedures.

If, during program execution, a numeric calculation results in numbers which are too large or too small we say the program has an **overflow** or **underflow** bug in it. If a data structure is incorrectly written into RAM or a disk file, we say the program has encountered a **parity** error. These errors, and others, are **trapped** by the operating system. A **fatal error** causes the program to stop and the operating system to take control of the computer system.

A variety of programming languages exist because of the special processing needs of different applications and because of history. BASIC is a very old language which was developed for beginners. Pascal is a modern language which was developed to teach good programming style. FORTRAN was an early attempt to devise a language suited to numerical calculations, while COBOL was an early attempt to devise a business data processing language. There is no clear-cut way to decide which language is "best" because it depends upon personal style and what the application is. However, standardized languages like COBOL, Pascal, and FORTRAN 77 ease the burden of transferring programs from one machine to the next because they have very few machine dependent features.

Furthermore, modern languages like Pascal, PL/I, and Ada are designed to reduce the time and effort needed to implement new software. These languages also strive to make a program readable, so that corrections and changes to the original program may be made quickly.

## COMMON QUESTIONS

Q. What are the two broad classifications of computers?
A. Analog and digital

Q. What is the fundamental unit of information?

A. The bit. This is represented by an on-off switch.

Q. Why are computers called binary computers?

A. Because they encode information as a group of binary (zero or one) numbers.

Q. What is a stored program?

A. A program that is held in RAM while it is being used to control the computer.

Q. What is RAM?

A. Random access memory. A RAM is simply a collection of thousands of on-off switches which are set to one or zero in order to "remember" information (programs and data).

Q. What is the difference between an assembler language and a compiler language?

A. Assemblers correspond one-to-one with machine language while compiler languages correspond one-to-many with machine language.

Q. What is the difference between an interpreter and a compiler?

A. An interpreter does not produce object code, but instead directly executes the source code program. Conversely, a compiler translates the source program into an object code program. The object program is executed at some later time, independent of the compiler.

Q. How can we measure the speed of a CPU?

A. A CPU (central processing unit) is typically rated in terms of its clock speed, say 4 MHZ.

Q. What is a baud (pronounced "bawd")?

A. Almost always we can equate a baud with "bits-per-second". It is a measure of transmission speed.

Q. What is a ROM?

A. A ROM (read-only-memory) is a non-volatile memory. This means that information in the form of programs and data is permanently stored in a ROM even when it is not powered. Conversely, a RAM is volatile and so loses its information whenever power is removed.

Q. What is a dot-matrix printer?

A. A printer that forms characters as an array of dots instead of solid lines is called a dot-matrix printer.

Q. What does an interface do?

A. An interface is a connection device that converts signals from one machine into signals recognizable by another machine.

Q. What is ASCII?

A. A standard character code: American Standard Code for Information Interchange.

Q. What is the major advantage and disadvantage of a Winchester style disk?

A. They are fast and can store millions of characters, but they often cannot be removed from their drives.

Q. What is a modem?

A. A modem (modulator-demodulator) is a device for connecting a computer to a telephone line.

Q. What are the building blocks of an algorithm?

A. Control is governed by sequence, branching, and looping in an algorithm.

Q. What is an operating system?

A. A program for controlling the execution of other programs.

Q. Why aren't all operating systems multiprogrammed and time-sharing systems?

A. This takes added RAM and causes overhead (time lost). If not needed, an operating system should not include such "extras".

Q. If all information is stored in computer memory in the form of bits, then how is a data structure stored?

A. As bits also. However, encoding schemes are used to add meaning to the groups of bits.

Q. Why use sequential files when random files seem to be better?

A. For most cases a random file is better. However, only a sequential file is able to store records of variable length.

Q. An index file seems unnecessary in order to retrieve information by unique key since the same retrieval problem exists for both index and ordinary file. Why?

A. First, the index file can be used to retrieve information from another file in order without sorting the original file. Secondly, a file can have more than one index file associated with it so that retrieval can be done from many keys.

Q. Why prefer one programming language over another?

A. Some reasons to select one programming language over another are: (1) ease of programming, (2) standardization, (3) maintainability, and (4) cost.

# Chapter 3

# How to Get Started with the IBM Personal Computer

There was one button for the sun, and another for the moon. And when she pushed the silver lever down, all oak, maple, and elm leaves turned into rainbows.

I remember one day in late April when she turned off the rain and pushed the sun button. The birds obeyed and sang their spring song while she painted the grass green.

## ANATOMY OF THE IBM PERSONAL COMPUTER

The IBM Personal Computer is a desktop *computer system* consisting of both hardware and software. For an in-depth description of hardware and software terms, read Chapters 1, 2, and 8. The following assumes that you are familiar with these terms.

## Hardware

### The system unit

The main chassis (IBM calls this the System Unit) of the IBM Personal Computer (the big "box") contains an Intel 8088 CPU, from 16KB to 576KB of RAM, built-in speaker for sound reproduction, and up to four disk drives. In addition, your IBM Personal Computer can accommodate an optional tape cassette drive and one or two CRT (television or IBM monitor) screens. Input to the system unit is made through a detached keyboard containing 83 keys for input of text, numbers, and control information. You will also notice several sockets for attaching these and other peripherals to the system unit. The sockets are located on the back of the unit. Pictures and detailed explanations of how to use these sockets are provided in the IBM Guide To Operations.

*Power-up sequences*

The system unit is powered by household current. To get started you should make sure all cables and power cords are plugged together and then turn on the power by flipping the power switch (big red switch).

**POWER** The power switch of the IBM Personal Computer is a big red switch located on the right side (towards the back) of the system unit. When powered-up without a diskette in the system unit, the CRT screen will display the prompt shown below (see Screen Display 3-1):

> The IBM Personal Computer Basic
> Version C1.00 Copyright IBM Corp 1981
> 61404 Bytes free
> Ok

But if the power switch is turned on when a DOS diskette is in drive A (see section describing the software), then the following prompt is displayed (see Screen Display 3-3):

> Enter today's date (m-d-y):

Both prompts will take a relatively long period of time to be displayed after you flip the power switch on. Be patient. Also, be careful to wait about 5 seconds before turning the system unit power on again after turning it off. A good way to restart the IBM Personal Computer without powering it down is to use the CTRL + ALT + DEL keys. Hold all three down at the same time and the system will start again just as described here.

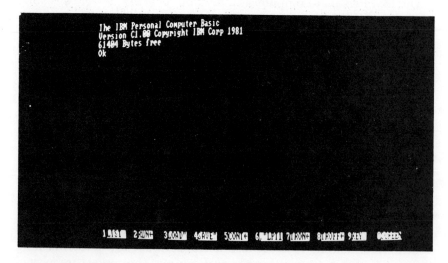

**Screen Display 3-1.** Startup logo obtained when no DOS diskette is loaded. This is ROM BASIC.

The reason two different power-up prompt messages are displayed is the following. The IBM Personal Computer includes a 40KB ROM which holds programs to directly interpret BASIC programming language statements. This is a relatively simple BASIC language interpreter, but it gives the IBM Personal Computer the "intelligence" to "understand" BASIC even though you may own the most inexpensive version of the machine. Hence, if the IBM Personal Computer cannot find a disk drive containing additional programs, it assumes it is a "simple" BASIC machine. The first prompt message, shown above, illustrates the "simple" machine prompt line.

On the other hand, if your IBM Personal Computer has one or more disk drives installed in the system unit, then you can enjoy the added power of a "DOS" machine. DOS stands for **D**isk **O**perating **S**ystem, which is a collection of "built-in" programs that you use to manage information stored on diskettes. We will examine these DOS programs in greater detail in this chapter.

*Printer connections*

You will most likely want to connect a printer to the system unit in order to do word processing (EasyWriter, see Chapter 4), and obtain a permanent copy of your work. This can be done in one of several ways. If the IBM printer is used, then the 37-pin *parallel* interface socket should be used. If another printer is used, then the 25-pin parallel socket may be used provided the pins are assigned to the same tasks in both printer and IBM Personal Computer unit. Otherwise, a special interface may be needed. If your printer uses a *serial interface* such as an RS-232C standard interface (see Chapter 8 for details), then you must purchase a serial interface card to insert into the system unit.

If you purchased an IBM Personal Computer printer, then you can test this printer by holding down the "line feed" (LF) button while simultaneously turning the line printer power on. This will cause the line printer to print every character in its memory over and over again. Once you are satisfied that it works, turn the power off, then on. Your printer is ready to be used as an output device.

*Disk drives*

You probably purchased your IBM Personal Computer with two disk drives. The **disk drive** located to your left (facing the system unit) is designated drive A. The right-hand disk drive is designated drive B. It is common to refer to files stored on diskettes put into either of these drives as follows: For information stored on diskettes put into drive A,

A:filename.extension

and for information stored on diskettes put into drive B,

B:filename.extension

Here A: and B: refer to the disk drives and filename.extension refers to the name of a file and its **type** (what it contains). Thus, you will refer to either diskette A or B when using the disk drives.

The following rules should be memorized by anyone using the IBM Personal Computer:

**LOADING:** Diskettes are inserted into a drive by flipping the drive door open and shoving the diskette into the drive LABEL UP, and LABEL END last. That is, grasp the diskette with your thumb covering the label as you insert the diskette into the drive unit. Close the drive door firmly.

**WRITE ERRORS:** Forgetting to remove the "write-protect" sticker is a common mistake made by first-time users. This leads to a write-protect error. A diskette can be write-protected by taping the notch of the diskette so that nothing can be written onto the diskette. If you get a write-protect error, remove the tape from the notch and the error will not occur.

We will return to an in-depth discussion of diskette storage later when we examine the software part of the IBM Personal Computer.

*CRT screen or monitor*

The **CRT screen** can be any household television with an attached "RF modulator" (to convert it to character display quality), or the IBM monitor screen. If a color TV is used, you will be able to display characters and graphical information in 8 colors of 2 shades each (for a total of 16 hues). This option requires a Color Graphics Adapter, however. The CRT screen is "cursor addressable." This means it has a cursor (shown as a blinking underscore) which can be moved anywhere on the screen. The cursor is moved to the right half of the screen, for example, by either typing text or else striking the space bar on the keyboard. More importantly, though, the cursor is used by software packages like the EasyWriter word processor and the VisiCalc worksheet program to guide you through their use.

You can elect to use the CRT screen in 40-column (bold-letter) format or 80-column (wide) format. The 40-column mode is easier to read, especially when using a color TV as CRT screen. Obviously, an 80-column screen can hold more information and is compatible with the line printer. The 80-column format is automatically selected by the IBM Personal Computer software unless you change it with the mode command as follows:

A > mode 40

The screen width is changed back to 80 columns by entering the command again:

A > mode 80

We will discuss this command and its other uses later in this chapter.

*The keyboard*

The IBM Personal Computer has an extended typewriter keyboard. That is, it has the keys normally found on a typewriter (these are light-colored), plus additional keys used for programming and running programs like EasyWriter. Several of the extra keys are "special-purpose" keys that you should be aware of in order to avoid frustration. For example, there are "toggle switches" that control upper and lower case, the numeric pad, etc. Recall that a toggle switch is like a light switch on your wall at home: each time it is "flipped" it reverses its setting. Thus it is either "on" or "off" after each time it is used.

## Keyboard Hints

**CAPS LOCK:** The CAPS LOCK key is a toggle switch that causes the "typewriter" keys to operate in the upper case mode.

**NUM LOCK:** The NUM LOCK key is a toggle switch that causes the numeric pad (right-side keys) to operate as either a numeric pad or as a cursor control pad (observe the arrows and "home," "page-up," and "page-down" keys).

←: The "left arrow" key is a backspace key and causes the last character entered to be erased.

**PRTSC:** The "print screen" key will print the contents of the CRT screen on the printer if used with the "shift" key.

**CTRL:** The "control" key is used in conjunction with other keys to control the computer. Here is a brief list of some of the CTRL functions you will be using:

CTRL + NUM LOCK = Pause, causing the computer to wait for you to press any key before continuing.

CTRL α ALT α DEL η Restart, causing the computer to stop whatever it is doing and restart as if the power were turned off, then on, again.

CTRL + C = Cancel, causing the line you just entered to be cancelled.

CTRL + PRTSC = Echo, causing what you type and what is displayed to be printed at the same time.

**FUNCTION KEYS:** The 10 function keys are assigned different meanings in different programs. When no program is being run, they are used to redisplay the previous command, etc.

**ARROWS:** There are several keys marked with an arrow. These are used as follows.

**LEFT** = top row, means backspace. Middle rows on right side, means "enter." The enter key is used to terminate a line of input.

**UP** = one each on left and right, meaning upper-case.

**LEFT,RIGHT** = on left side, second row, meaning tab.

**ALT:** The ALT key is used to generate extended ASCII decimal codes. The 83-character keyboard can generate 255 characters when ALT + n is entered. For n equal to 48, for example, character zero is generated. For another example, notice that ALT + 216 generates a special symbol (see the display obtained by using the Diagnostics diskette). One valuable feature of this key is that you can display and print letters from the Greek alphabet.

## A Note On Control Characters

Many computing systems use a standard set of meanings for control keys. For example, the IBM keyboard can be used much like any other keyboard (say, like a CP/M keyboard) as follows. (CTRL means the CTRL key.)

| | |
|---|---|
| **CTRL + C** | Ignore this line and start a new one. |
| **CTRL + H** | Backspace |
| **CTRL + I** | Tab |
| **CTRL + J** | Line feed |
| **CTRL + M** | RETURN |
| **CTRL + P** | Echo print |
| **CTRL + S** | Pause during display of a large amount of information, for example, to momentarily stop the screen from scrolling during a TYPE command (see next two sections). |
| **CTRL + Z** | Mark the end of input through the console. |

## Software

Software for the IBM Personal Computer is recorded on 5 1/4" diskettes supplied with your computer. In this chapter we will be concerned with two diskettes marked DOS and DIAGNOSTICS only. In subsequent chapters we will use other diskettes containing software to do word processing, spread-sheet calculations, and general problem solving. Additional programs can be purchased, of course.

Notice the label on each diskette which identifies the information stored on it. Also notice a "write-protect" notch along one side of each diskette. This notch must be open before any data or instructions can be recorded on the diskette.

The DOS operating system diskette labled "DOS" or "System" should be inserted into the A disk drive (the one on the left side) before you turn on the power. After a 30 second warm-up you will get the "warm-start" prompt shown in Screen Display 3-3.

Enter the date (say 5-10-83) and strike the ENTER key (←). This will cause the DOS operating system to take control of the computer system and wait for you to enter a command. The command prompt line

A>

means DOS is running from disk drive A and is waiting for your instructions.

At this point you normally load a diskette into drive B and then select a program stored on the diskette. For example, you might insert a Visi-Calc diskette into drive B and instruct DOS to run VC80 (the 80-column version of VisiCalc).

A > B:VC80

Or, you might want to begin using BASIC or advanced BASIC. In this case you can enter the BASIC or BASICA (advanced BASIC) command to get started.

A > BASIC
A > BASICA

Suppose you want to begin immediately to use the BASIC demonstration programs supplied on the DOS diskette. You would enter the advanced basic command followed by the name of the menu program, as follows.

A > BASICA

After a pause and a message as shown in Screen Display 3-2 you can enter the following BASIC commands.

LOAD"SAMPLES" (ENTER)
RUN

This will give you a quick introduction to the IBM Personal Computer, but to get down to business we must do some housekeeping chores first. Instead of getting ahead of ourselves, suppose we do first things first.

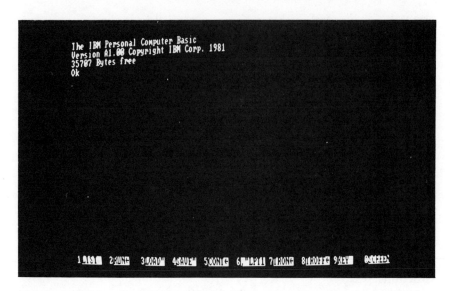

**Screen Display 3-2.** Advanced BASIC obtained from the DOS diskette, A > BASICA.

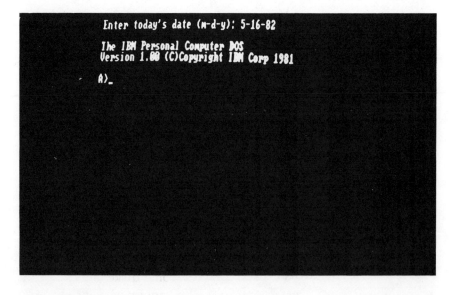

**Screen Display 3-3.** DOS startup logo. This is obtained when the DOS diskette is in drive A.

The very first time you see the IBM Personal Computer you should become more familiar with DOS and make copies of all of your software diskettes like DOS, Diagnostics, and so forth. Notice, however, that some software diskettes are copy protected and cannot be copied. Other diskettes contain programs to copy themselves. We will learn how to use several of these program diskettes in subsequent chapters.

## FIRST THINGS FIRST

The first time you use your IBM Personal Computer or anytime you think it might be broken, run the Diagnostics diskette. This is done by properly inserting the Diagnostics diskette into drive A and restarting the computer (see LOADING instructions in the previous section). Remember, you can restart the IBM Personal Computer by flipping the power switch or if the power is already on, by holding down three keys at the same time:

### CTRL + ALT + DEL

In either case, the menu shown in Screen Display 3-4 will appear after a 30-second delay (the length of time depends on how much memory you have in your system unit). The programs on this diskette let you do three very important first things:

**0** Check out your hardware to make sure it is working.

**1** Format one or more new diskettes so that they can be used to store programs, data, or text.

**2** Copy existing diskettes just in case the originals fail. This gives you a backup copy. In general, you should always have two copies of valuable information stored on a diskette.

## Running Diagnostics

### Format option

Screen Display 3-4 shows what is displayed when you run the Diagnostics diskette. If you simply want to test the hardware to make sure it is working properly, then select option 0. However, we want to make backup copies of all system software before we risk destroying valuable information. Therefore, we must FORMAT some diskettes, and then copy the system diskettes (and any others) onto newly formatted "blanks" (blank diskettes are the ones without any information recorded on them).

1 (ENTER)

**Screen Display 3-4.** Diagnostics program main menu. Selection of zero causes the machine to be checked for errors.

**Screen Display 3-5.** Format and copy a system diskette using the Diagnostics Program.

Now, insert a new diskette in drive B, and enter B:

B (ENTER)

Actually, you can format as many diskettes as needed by repeating this option. Go ahead and format a box of diskettes for use later on. See Screen Display 3-5 for an example of this sequence.

*Copy option*

Next, copy the system disks one at a time as follows. Select option two.

2 (ENTER)

WHICH DRIVE CONTAINS SOURCE DISKETTE ? a (ENTER)
WHICH DRIVE CONTAINS TARGET DISKETTE ? b (ENTER)
INSERT DISKETTES = PRESS ENTER

Put the DOS diskette in drive A, a formatted blank diskette in drive B, and press ENTER. Repeat this step for all diskettes that you can copy. These are your backup copies, so they should be stored in a safe place.

*Diagnostics option*

The next step in getting prepared to use the IBM Personal Computer system is to check out the hardware. This is done by selecting option zero from the menu shown in Screen Displaying 3-6.

0 (ENTER)

The IBM system unit will respond with a list of all devices and memories it contains. For example, you might get the following list.

SYSTEM  BOARD
128KB  MEMORY
KEYBOARD
COLOR/GRAPHICS  ADAPTER
2 DISKETTE DRIVES  &  ADAPTER

If this list is correct, enter Y (ENTER). The Diagnostics program will continue to check each one of these. The next menu shown in Screen Display 3-6 lets you select the number of times the tests are performed. We will describe option 0 (RUN TEST ONE TIME) only.

0 (ENTER)

Each system unit is tested with your assistance. If any system unit fails, the error number should be recorded so you can report the error to an authorized dealer. The system unit checks each one of its parts and lists them. For example, SYSTEM UNIT 100 refers to RAM.

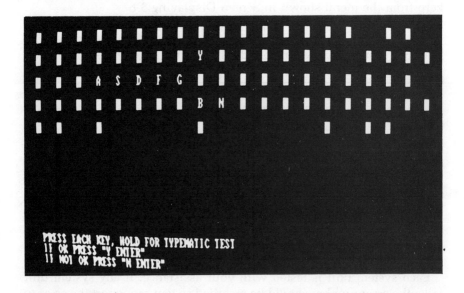

```
2 - COPY DISKETTE
9 - EXIT TO SYSTEM DISKETTE

INSERT DIAGNOSTIC DISKETTE IN DRIVE A AND ENTER THE ACTION DESIRED
0

THE INSTALLED DEVICES ARE

SYSTEM BOARD
 64KB MEMORY
KEYBOARD
COLOR/GRAPHICS ADAPTER
2 DISKETTE DRIVE(S) & ADAPTER

IS THE LIST CORRECT (Y/N) ? y

SYSTEM CHECKOUT

0 - RUN TESTS ONE TIME
1 - RUN TESTS MULTIPLE TIMES
2 - LOG UTILITIES
9 - EXIT DIAGNOSTIC ROUTINES

ENTER THE ACTION DESIRED
 0
```

**Screen Display 3-6.** Diagnostics program finds installed devices and then displays system checkout menu.

```
PRESS EACH KEY, HOLD FOR TYPEMATIC TEST
IF OK PRESS "Y ENTER"
IF NOT OK PRESS "N ENTER"
```

**Screen Display 3-7.** Keyboard test. User strikes each key to see it displayed properly.

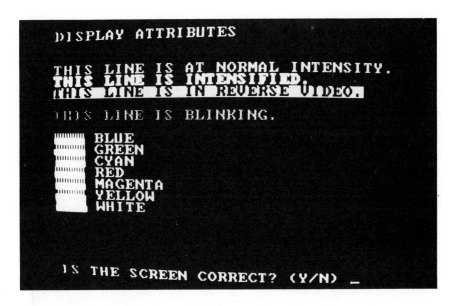

DISPLAY ATTRIBUTES

THIS LINE IS AT NORMAL INTENSITY.
THIS LINE IS INTENSIFIED.
THIS LINE IS IN REVERSE VIDEO.

THIS LINE IS BLINKING.

BLUE
GREEN
CYAN
RED
MAGENTA
YELLOW
WHITE

IS THE SCREEN CORRECT? (Y/N) _

**Screen Display 3-8.** Screen test. User can check color quality on a color TV monitor.

| | |
|---|---|
| SYSTEM UNIT 100 | (main memory) |
| SYSTEM UNIT 200 | |
| SYSTEM UNIT 300 | (keyboard) |
| SYSTEM UNIT 500 | (disk drives) |

Several steps in the test are shown in Screen Displays 3-7, 3-8, 3-9, and 3-10. For a complete set of pictures you will have to run the Diagnostics diskette yourself.

## A Tour of DOS

You are now ready to begin using the built-in programs of the DOS diskette. Load the DOS diskette into drive A and press CTRL + ALT + DEL. After a brief delay you will be prompted for the calendar date. Suppose you enter the following (or the correct date):

5-12-84

You will see the IBM Personal Computer logo followed by the DOS "logged drive" prompt. See Screen Display 3-3.

A>

**Screen Display 3-9.** 40-character wide character set test.

**Screen Display 3-10.** 80-character wide character set test.

Enter B: (ENTER) and the "logged drive" becomes B.

B>

Finally, if you enter A:, the logged drive reverts back to drive A. The **logged drive** is the disk drive that DOS programs assume you want to use unless you specify otherwise.

### Screen width

You can set the CRT screen width to 40 or 80 characters using the MODE command. MODE is used also to adjust the display to the left or right as shown in the following examples.

MODE 40,R,T

This sets the screen width to 40 characters and allows you to adjust the left-hand margin (R).

MODE 40,L,T

This version of the MODE command sets the width to 40 characters, also, but lets you adjust the right-hand margin.

MODE 80,R
MODE 80

These let you set the width to 80 characters but without testing margin adjustments.

### Printer width

The MODE command is also used to set up printer parameters as follows:

MODE LPT1:,80,6
MODE LPT1:,132,8

These commands set the width of the printed page at either 80 or 132 columns, and set the number of lines per inch at either 6 or 8 lpi (lines per inch).

### Time and date

Next, you should set up the time of day and calendar date. To do this enter the following commands.

TIME (ENTER)

The current time will be displayed (default is zero) in hours:minutes:seconds.hundredths. You can either enter a new time or leave the clock as it is by pressing ENTER without entering a new setting. Later on when you want to see what time it is, enter TIME (ENTER) again.

The DATE command works much like the TIME command.

DATE (ENTER)

This allows you to look at the current date (in case you forget) and change it if you want.

*What is on disk?*

Every formatted diskette has a table of contents file that contains a list of all other files stored on the diskette. This table of contents file is called the diskette **directory** because it is a directory into the diskette. You can look at a diskette directory using the **DIR** command. Here is how to use it:

DIR
DIR A:
DIR B:

The first version above causes the directory of the logged disk diskette to be displayed on the screen. The second and third versions cause A and B directories to be displayed, respectively, no matter what the logged drive happens to be.

DIR    *.COM
DIR A:*.COM

This version of the DIR command causes only the COMmand file names to be displayed (see Screen Display 3-11). Note the difference between using * and using ? in a file name.

DIR A: BASIC?.COM

This command causes the two files below to be displayed because ? can be a blank or the *single* letter A.

BASIC    COM    10880    08-04-81
BASICA    COM    16256    08-04-81

The name, extension or type, length in characters, and date you last recorded the file on diskette are displayed. Thus, BASICA is a file containing COMmand software, of length 16256 characters, and last recorded on the 4th day of August 1981.

*When disks get full*

Later in this chapter we will see how to create a file and put information in it. You can create up to 64 files per diskette, and each file can hold up to 160KB of information. Since each sector (unit of physical

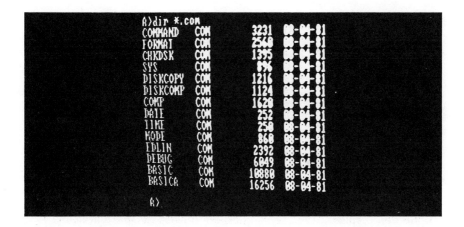

**Screen Display 3-11.** The DOS command DIR*.COM displays the command files only.

diskette space) holds 512 characters, this means you can create files with one, two, or up to 40 sectors of data. But how do you know when a diskette is full?

INSUFFICIENT DISK SPACE

This message will be displayed if you try to store more information in a disk file than there is space available. To check the diskette ahead of time, use the CHKDSK command; see Screen Display 3-12 for an illustration.

CHKDSK
CHKDSK B:

These commands tell you how much space is taken up by existing files, and more important, how much space remains available. If you need more space than that available, then either use a new diskette or remove unused files as follows.

*Disk file erasure*

Any disk file can be removed from a diskette using the ERASE command. Remember, once a file is ERASEd it cannot be retrieved. So be sure you no longer need the file.

ERASE A:NOTE.TXT
ERASE B:?O?E.*
ERASE *.*

```
A>ohkdsk a;
            43 disk files
   160256 bytes total disk space
     4608 bytes remain available

   65536 bytes total memory
   53392 bytes free

A>_
```

**Screen Display 3-12.** Checking disk in drive A for space available.

The first example erases file NOTE.TXT from disk drive A. The second example removes all files on drive B that are spelled with O and E as their second and fourth letters, and of any type (.*). The third example erases all files from the logged drive!

*Changing a file name*

Sometimes you will want to change a file name. For example, you may create file NOTE.TXT and later decide to use it as a BATCH file, instead of a TXT file. A file name can be changed using the RENAME command:

> RENAME B:NOTE.TXT B:NOTE.BAT
> RENAME B:NOTE.TXT B:*.BAT

These two examples do the same thing. The * means to use the same file name in both new and old files. The general form of a RENAME command is as follows.

> RENAME OLDNAME NEWNAME

You can use the single letter substitution rule, also as shown in the example below.

> RENAME MAKE.BAT ??D?.*

This changes MAKE.BAT to MADE.BAT on the logged drive.

Try these basic DOS commands and then turn to the next section to learn more about the built-in DOS programs.

## A Parting Note on File Types

In DOS it is a convention to use certain file extension codes to designate the type of information stored in the file. These conventional extensions are listed below.

ASM      assembly language source program
BAK      a backup file
BAS      BASIC language source program
BAT      batch command file
COM      a command program file
DAT      a data file
DOC      a document file (from a word processor)
EXE      an executable (machine language) file
HEX      hexidecimal format machine language file
INT      intermediate code file from a compiler
LIB      a library program file
OBJ      an object code (machine language) file
OVR      an overlay file (used by a program)
PRN      program listing file for printer
REL      a relocatable machine language file
$$$      an unknown or temporary file
VC      a VisiCalc worksheet file

## COMMON DOS OPERATIONS

There are many programs that you can execute directly from a power-up or restart by simply loading the proper diskette into drive A. In fact, programs such as EasyWriter, VisiCalc, and others discussed in this book are perhaps the most often used programs for the IBM computer, but they are by no means the only programs. A special collection of programs called the DOS (Disk Operating System) is "built into" the IBM Personal Computer system. These programs are so common and useful that they have become part of the system, hence the name "system software." Let's look at some of these common and useful DOS programs and see what they can do.

Remember, the prompt line "A>" means you are logged onto disk drive A. Any program on drive A can be executed by simply typing its name immediately after the prompt line.

If you type a program name which does not exist (misspelled or wrong disk drive), DOS will respond with the following message as shown below:

A > myprog
Bad command or file name

If you want to execute a program stored on disk drive B instead of the logged drive, then you can prefix the program name with the letter B. For example, program VC80 is stored on drive B:

A > B:VC80

This command causes the 80-column version of VisiCalc to be retrieved from drive B and be loaded into RAM to be executed.

Another method of accessing programs on drive B is to switch logged drives:

A > B:
B>

Now B is the default drive and unless prefixed with A: all programs will be taken from drive B.

DOS programs are either internal (I) if they are kept in main memory, (RAM) upon starting the IBM Personal Computer with the DOS diskette in drive A, and external (E) if they are kept on the DOS diskette until needed. An internal DOS program is resident in RAM at all times after power-up, and so it can be used even when the DOS diskette is removed. On the contrary, an external (E) program can only be used when the DOS diskette is in a drive. Both kinds of DOS programs are called "commands," but since the external commands come and go to and from RAM, they are sometimes called transient commands. The internal (I) commands are also called intrinsic commands. We list both kinds of commands below.

## Intrinsic DOS Commands

| | |
|---|---|
| **Copy** | Copy a disk file from one disk area to another. |
| **Dir** | List a diskette table of contents. |
| **Erase** | Erase a disk file from a diskette. |
| **Pause** | Wait until a key is pressed before continuing. |
| **Rem** | Display a remark while processing a batch file. |
| **Rename** | Rename a disk file. |
| **Type** | Display contents of a disk file. |
| **(batch)** | Any user-defined command made from other commands. |

## Transient DOS Commands

| | |
|---|---|
| **Autoexec** | Automatic (batch) file that is executed when the computer is first started or restarted. |
| **Chkdsk** | Display status of a diskette. |
| **Comp** | Compare disk files to verify one against another. |
| **Date** | Enter date. |
| **Debug** | Program debugging tool. |
| **Diskcomp** | Compare one diskette against another to verify it. |
| **Edlin** | Line editor for program preparation. |
| **Format** | Prepare a diskette for use by DOS. |
| **Link** | Link together two or more programs. |
| **Mode** | Set display screen or printer width. |
| **Sys** | Transfer DOS files to another diskette. |
| **Time** | Display time, and enter new time. |

Suppose we look at these command programs and show by way of examples how they work and what they are used for. Details of each command are available from the IBM Disk Operating System manual.

## DIR

The **DIR**ectory command causes the table of contents of a diskette to be displayed on the screen. To display the DOS diskette directory we type either DIR or DIR A:. To display only the transient command files as shown in Screen Display 3-11, enter the following:

DIR *.COM

Notice that the command file names are **typed** as .COM files. This means they are **COM**mand programs which can be executed as if they are part of the DOS commands (which they are). These are the highly useful command programs listed above.

The *.COM means to display all command files on the diskette. Whenever we want all filenames to be referenced in a DOS command like the one above, use *. If, however, we want to display one file only, be sure to use its full name. A question mark can be used to substitute for a single letter in a name. Thus, only single letter file names are displayed by the command shown below:

DIR ?.*

If we want to see the names of all four-letter files stored on disk drive B, we can do so as follows:

DIR B:????.*

The DIRectory display shows all command programs on the DOS diskette. However, the system tracks of DOS are not shown. They contain build-in commands that are always available for your use.

These programs are mainly useful for system and application programmers; however, a few of them are useful for anyone using the IBM Personal Computer. We will discuss the most useful programs only in the remainder of this chapter.

## CHKDSK

You can find out how much space remains on a diskette by typing (we discussed this command briefly in the previous section):

CHKDSK
CHKDSK  A:
or              CHKDSK  B:

For example, you can check the DOS diskette in drive A to see how much space remains by typing CHKDSK as shown below:

A > CHKDSK

The response will tell you how many files are stored on the diskette and how many bytes (characters) remain (see Screen Display 3-12).

40  disk files
160256  bytes total disk space
6144  bytes remain available

65536  bytes total memory
53392  bytes free

Therefore, the DOS diskette has 40 files in its table of contents which take up a total of (160256 − 6144) = 154112 bytes of disk space. The RAM has 53392 free bytes remaining out of a total of 65536 bytes.

## FORMAT

You are able to format a new diskette through the Diagnostics diskette program as we showed in the previous section. However, it is also possible to format a new diskette at any time using the DOS command FORMAT:

FORMAT B:

```
A>format b:/s
Insert new diskette for drive B:
and strike any key when ready

Formatting...Format complete
System transferred

Format another (Y/N)?n

A>chkdsk b:
          3 disk files
     160256 bytes total disk space
     147968 bytes remain available

      65536 bytes total memory
      53392 bytes free
A>_
```

**Screen Display 3-13.** Formatting with system tracks. The three system files are shown in a CHKDSK command.

This command causes the diskette placed in drive B to be prepared for use by the IBM Personal Computer system. Recall that a new diskette must be formatted before it can be used by the disk drives. Formatting "blanks" the diskette, sets up an empty directory, and does other first-time only chores like initializing the file allocation table (FAT). This table keeps track of all disk sectors that have been allocated to files, and in turn all "free" sectors. Note that a file may or may not consist of contiguous sectors on the diskette. It may be necessary to chop up a file into many noncontiguous sectors. The diskette tables must, therefore, be initialized so that the DOS can use them later.

Formatting . . . Format complete

This message will appear on your screen during and after a successful FORMAT operation. You can FORMAT as many diskettes as desired while in this command.

If you intend to use a diskette for system software, that is, if you want to transfer the DOS intrinsic commands to it later using the SYS command below, then use the following version of FORMAT (see Screen Display 3-13):

FORMAT B:/S
FORMAT A:/S

This causes the FORMAT command to both format and record the system files on the diskette. But you may not want to put these DOS files on a new diskette because they take up valuable space. Instead you can use the disk space to store data.

If you format and record the system files on the blank diskette, then a CHKDSK command will reveal 3 files in use. These files are the DOS system files containing the intrinsic commands.

The FORMAT command also checks the new diskette for bad sectors. All bad sectors are allocated to a special file named BADTRACK. If CHKDSK reports more than 3 files (0 files for FORMAT without /S), then the excess file is BADTRACK. The number of bad sectors equals the length of BADTRACK divided by 512.

## SYS

Now, suppose you have FORMATted a blank diskette leaving room for the DOS intrinsic commands. You can move the system files from an existing DOS diskette onto the blank diskette (in drive B) as follows:

SYS B:

This will cause a new copy of the DOS system files to be copied onto the diskette. If the diskette is not blank, then it must have had system files previously allocated to it before this command will succeed. If it fails, the following message is reported:

No room for system on destination disk

The only way around this obstacle is to FORMAT another diskette with system files (FORMAT B:/S), and copy your files from the old diskette onto the newly formatted diskette. The DISKCOPY command discussed below is used to copy entire diskettes. The COPY command is used to copy one or more individual files.

## DISKCOPY

An entire source diskette can be copied to a destination diskette.

DISKCOPY source destination

Two drives will be used if the source and destination drives are different; otherwise a single drive is used.

DISKCOPY
DISKCOPY A: A:

These are single-drive disk copy commands, and the following are two-drive commands (see Screen Display 3-14).

DISKCOPY A: B:
DISKCOPY B: A:

```
A>diskcopy a: b:
Insert source diskette in drive A
Insert target diskette in drive B
Strike any key when ready
Copy complete
Copy another? (Y/N)
_
```

**Screen Display 3-14.** Copy the diskette in drive A onto the diskette in drive B.

The copies are identical (mirror image) copies of one another. That is, no reorganization of the files and sectors is performed (see the description of COPY A:*.* B:).

## DISKCOMP

After you make a mirror image copy of a diskette, be sure to verify that the two disks are identical. The DISKCOMP command is used to catch errors in copied diskettes. Thus, if the original diskette is in drive A and the newly copied diskette is in drive B, do the following:

DISKCOMP A: B:

If you suspect that the diskette is OK, but the drive unit is failing, then run the Diagnostics program, or compare a diskette to itself as illustrated below:

DISKCOMP
DISKCOMP A: A:

This version of DISKCOMP can be used to compare two diskettes using a single drive, too.

## COPY and COMP

The COPY and COMP commands work just like the DISKCOPY and DISKCOMP commands except for the following:

1. COPY and COMP work on individual files.
2. COPY reorganizes files when possible to increase system performance. Therefore, a reason to use COPY instead of DISKCOPY is to improve performance in programs that have a lot of disk activity.

COPY source destination

This causes the source file(s) to be copied into the destination file(s). One or more files can be copied in a single command. For example, to copy an entire diskette from drive A to a diskette in drive B (and reorganize it):

COPY A:*.* B:

This copies all files (*.*) in A into B. The file names need not be repeated in the destination.

The COPY command is used to transfer information from one place to another, regardless of the location.

COPY A: NOTE.TXT A:NOTE.BAT

This causes the contents of NOTE.TXT in drive A to be transferred to the NOTE.BAT file in drive A. The two files will contain identical information, after the transfer (see Screen Display 3-15).

Now, study the following example:

COPY MAKE.TXT ??D?.*

You might think that this causes the contents of MAKE.TXT on the logged drive to be transferred into a new file with a name constructed from the source file name MADE.TXT. You are correct! The COPY command constructs a destination file with the following name: MADE.TXT.

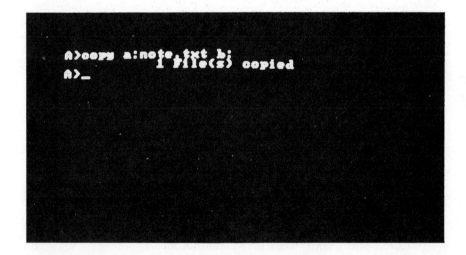

**Screen Display 3-15.** Copy a single file to the diskette in drive B. The file names are identical.

## TYPEing a File on the Screen

Finally, you will want to look inside a file and see what it contains. This can be done using the TYPE command as follows:

TYPE filename

This causes the file to be displayed on the screen. For example, MAKE.TXT can be displayed as shown below:

TYPE MAKE.BAT
TYPE B:MAKE.BAT

An example of this command is shown in Screen Display 3-17.

The file may be too large to fit on the screen. If so, it will whiz past your eyes too quickly for you to read. The display can be stopped using CTRL + S or the special combination of CTRL + NUM LOCK. The display will continue after a second CTRL + S or after pressing any key following the CTRL + NUM LOCK combination.

If you use a * or ? in your file name, the TYPE command will fetch and display the first file it finds. If other files also match the file name pattern, they will not be displayed. For example, if MAKE.TXT and MADE.TXT already exist, then only the first one in the diskette directory will be TYPEd.

TYPE MA?E.TXT
TYPE *.TXT
TYPE *.*

All of these commands display the first file found to match the file name pattern. (Note, some of the files contain unprintable information, so be prepared to get "garbage" when displaying .COM files, and so on.)

Give these commands a try on your IBM Personal Computer, then continue to read the next section. If you plan to use the computer rather than write programs for it, you can skip the next section. However, if you want to become an expert DOS user, you will be interested in the advanced features explained there.

## FANCY DOS OPERATIONS

Many of the DOS operations are not needed for day-to-day use by a nonprogrammer. For example, you may not care to construct BAT files or copy system tracks, etc. simply to use the programs already supplied with your machine. However, once in a while you may want to copy a file or you may simply be curious about how to use certain commands.

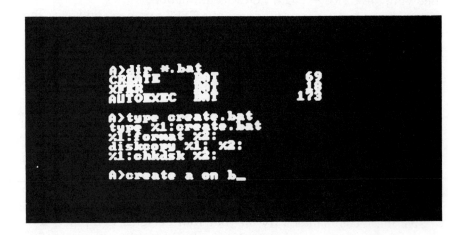

**Screen Display 3-16.** Enter text into a file from the keyboard.

**Screen Display 3-17.** The CREATE batch file and how to use it.

The first thing you might want to try is the CTRL + PRTSC character. Enter

A > DIR (CTRL + PRTSC)

and notice that all input and output that normally displays on the CRT screen is also directed to your printer (if you have one). Thus, the directory of disk A is printed as well as displayed.

The CTRL + PRTSC character can be issued a second time to turn off the printer. Thus, CTRL + PRTSC is a **toggle** switch for activating/deactivating the printer. This feature may be useful in combination with other commands. For example, the TYPE command discussed in the previous section can be used to display a file on the CRT screen and on the printer as well:

TYPE B:NOTE.TXT (CTRL + PRTSC)

Now, the contents of the file appear on the screen and the system printer simultaneously. To turn the printer off, toggle the key again: CTRL + PRTSC.

In the remainder of this section we examine several interesting combinations between control keys and devices that are extremely useful to the expert DOS user.

## COPY Revisited

In the previous section we learned that COPY is a command program that copies a file from a source disk or device to a destination disk or device. Notice the inclusion of a **device** as well as disk file name in the COPY arguments. For example, we can use COPY to copy the information from a disk file onto a printer without writing a program to do this. The devices have names as shown below. When devices are named in this manner we call them **pseudofiles** because they can be used in a command anywhere a file name is allowed.

**CON:** Console keyboard and screen. If the keyboard is the device you want to get characters from, use this as an input pseudofile name. If the screen is desired, use this as an output pseudofile name. Remember to terminate the end of input via CON: using CTRL + C or special function key F6, followed by an ENTER.

**AUX:** or **COM1:** The communications adapter for communicating through the telephone lines. This requires an additional interface card in your main chassis.

**LPT1:** or **PRN:** The printer as an output pseudofile.

Suppose, for example, we want to print the contents of B:MAKE.TXT on the printer.

COPY B:MAKE.TXT LPT1:

This command transfers the contents of the file stored on drive B to the line printer. Note the difference between this command and the TYPE command plus the CTRL + PRTSC control keys. The COPY version does not display the file on the screen at the same time it is being printed.

### Keyboard to printer

The COPY command can be used to copy keyboard inputs directly to the printer just like a typewriter:

COPY CON: LPT1:

The command is terminated when a CTRL + Z or F6 key is entered in column one of a line of input.

A file can be displayed on the screen just like a TYPE command does as follows:

COPY B:FILENAME.EXT CON:

### Keyboard to disk

Finally, you can create a file on disk using the COPY command as follows:

COPY CON: B:NEWFILE.TXT

This causes all inputs at the keyboard to be transferred to the diskette in drive B. If you want to get a hard copy of the file later, then use the COPY command again:

COPY B:NEWFILE.TXT LPT1:

Suppose you want to write a note to yourself and store it in a file called NOTE.TXT. The COPY command is used:

COPY CON: NOTE.TXT

    This is a reminder to get groceries:
      Eggs
      Butter
      Milk (2% for Ted's diet)
      Soup stock
      Wine (for Sat. nite)
    (F6, ENTER)

Notice how the input is terminated with the F6 function key and an ENTER key. This must be entered in column one after the last line. Also, remember that a maximum of 127 characters per string is allowed. If you terminate a string with an ENTER key, then you will not need to worry about this maximum. However, if you type your input as one continuous string of characters, you may run into trouble after character 127 is entered. If so, use ENTER to terminate the string.

One of the most common uses of COPY CON: FILENAME is to create BAT files. This is the subject of the next installment.

## Batch Files

A BATCH command is actually a super command that allows you to execute a batch of commands in one action. The idea is to construct a file of commands and store them on disk using COPY CON: FILE-NAME.BAT. Be sure the file type is BAT because this stands for BATCH, and only BAT files can be executed by DOS in this fashion.

When you want to run the entire batch of commands, simply input the file name (leave off the extension .BAT). For example, suppose we combine all of the commands needed to format and create a backup copy of a system diskette. Let's call this file CREATE.BAT. It is entered using COPY as shown below:

```
COPY CON:  CREATE.BAT
FORMAT B:/S
COPY A: B:
(F6)  (ENTER)
```

Now, whenever we want to format and backup a copy of a disk in drive A, we submit the file above to DOS as follows:

```
CREATE
```

This causes DOS to execute the FORMAT command followed by the COPY command. FORMAT and COPY request additional information from the user as shown in the earlier section.

### Batch file parameters

We can generalize batch files by including parameters that are defined when the BAT command is executed. A batch parameter is an integer beginning with a percent sign. Here is a parameterized CREATE.BAT file, for example. See Screen Display 3-17 for an illustration of this command in action.

```
COPY CON:  CREATE.BAT
TYPE  %1:CREATE.BAT
%1:FORMAT  %2:
DISKCOPY          %1:  %2:
%1:CHKDSK      %2:
(F6)  (ENTER)
```

Now, enter

```
CREATE  A  B
```

The first parameter (%1) takes on a value of A, and the second parameter takes on a value of B. Hence, DOS executes the following version of CREATE.BAT:

```
TYPE A:CREATE.BAT
A:FORMAT B:
DISKCOPY A: B:
A:CHKDSK B:
```

This version of CREATE.BAT does the following:

1. TYPE displays a listing of file CREATE.BAT which is an intrinsic command (built-in and internal to resident DOS).

2. FORMAT formats a blank diskette which must be in drive B.

3. DISKCOPY transfers the contents of A: onto B:

4. CHKDSK displays the amount of storage used and the amount remaining on drive B.

We can make CREATE.BAT even fancier by adding some redundant parameters for ease of use. Suppose we build a file called CREATE.BAT with three parameters as follows (parameter %2 is not used, only helpful in making the batch file easier to understand).

```
COPY CON:  CREATE.BAT
TYPE  %3:CREATE.BAT
%3:FORMAT  %1:
DISKCOPY  %3:  %1:
%3:CHKDSK  %1:
```

Now, when used, specify which is the source drive and which is the destination drive. For example,

CREATE B FROM A

causes B to become a backup copy of A and,

CREATE A FROM B

causes A to become a backup copy of B. But, notice parameter %2 (FROM) is never used in the batch file. It is simply there to make the command easy to use.

We can use this idea to tailor several extended commands for DOS. The following examples should show you what can be done.

### Some useful batch files

Suppose we want to transfer and reorganize all files from one drive to another, but we don't want to remember how TYPE is used. This can be done by designing a transfer command file XFER.BAT as follows.

```
COPY CON:  XFER.BAT
COPY #3:*.* %1:
(F6)   (ENTER)
```

Then, to copy from one drive to another type,

XFER B TO A

or else,

XFER A TO B

This causes all files from one diskette to be copied to another diskette.

If you have difficulty remembering the order or names of files, you can construct meaningful batch files to replace the TYPE commands, etc. Here are some ideas.

In general, to display a file on the screen,

SHOWME filename ON drive

For example,

SHOWME TEXT.DOC ON A

The batch file for this command would include at least the following.

TYPE %3:%1

Here is another idea. Suppose we do the same thing for the printer.

PRINT filename FROM drive

For example,

PRINT TEXT.DOC FROM B

The batch file for this command would include at least the following.

COPY %3:%1 LPT1:

## The PAUSE and REM

The REM command is used in a batch file to display a comment or remark on the screen during the operation of the batch file. Similarly, the PAUSE command displays a remark but in addition it causes the computer to wait until some key is pressed before continuing. Here is an example that includes a remark and a pause, both. Try this on your IBM Personal Computer:

```
COPY CON:  AUTOEXEC.BAT
REM   Press ENTER if no date or time change wanted.
DATE
TIME
PAUSE Changing screen width to 40
```

```
MODE 40
DIR *.COM
PAUSE Changing back to 80 now.
MODE 80
REM ready, now.
(F6)   (ENTER)
```

AUTOEXEC.BAT is a very special batch file that is always executed whenever the system is reset (power-up or CTRL + ALT + DEL). Thus, you can tailor the AUTOEXEC file to do anything you want it to do. For example, the batch file above overrides the standard IBM power-up restart logo, and instead does the following:

| | |
|---|---|
| **REM** | Displays the remark shown above. |
| **DATE** | Displays and allows you to set the date |
| **TIME** | Displays and allows you to set the time |
| **PAUSE** | Displays the remark and waits for you to strike a key |
| **MODE** | Changes the screen width |
| **DIR** | Displays the directory .COM files, only |

After every MODE command the screen is cleared and so it is necessary to us the PAUSEs as we have shown above. Try this handy little AUTOEXEC file.

## COMMON QUESTIONS

Q. What is DOS?

A. DOS stands for **D**isk **O**perating **S**ystem, and is the operating system program used on the IBM Personal Computer.

Q. What is a transient program?

A. In DOS the .COM files are programs that are copied from diskette into the RAM to be executed. After it is executed, a transient program is erased from RAM.

Q. Why does NUM-LOCK sometimes "interfere" with the SHIFT key on your IBM Personal Computer?

A. It does not really interfere, it just toggles the numeric pad so that arrows and special page control characters are sent to your computer instead of numbers. Simply push the NUM-LOCK key a second time to toggle it back to "numeric mode."

Q. What is the size of my CRT screen?

A. 80 columns by 25 lines, by default. However, you can change this using the DOS command, mode 40, and then change it back again using the command, mode 80.

Q. What are the disk drives called?

A. The one on the left is A: and the one on the right is B:

Q. What is a cursor-addressable CRT?

A. A cathode-ray tube (TV screen) with a blinking underscore that indicates where the next character to be entered will show on the screen.

Q. What can be connected to the IBM Personal Computer?

A. A printer (parallel or serial interface), a telephone using the communications adapter option, a color TV using the color TV adapter option, and other devices that each use an adapter to physically attach the device to the main chassis.

Q. Do the numeric (upper-case) keys work the same as the numeric pad keys?

A. Yes, but be sure NUM-LOCK is properly toggled.

Q. What does the Diagnostics program do?

A. Allows you to test the computer and the peripheral devices.

Q. How do you format a blank diskette?

A. Use the DOS FORMAT command. A diskette is not usable until formatted. The FORMAT program initializes the diskette table of contents, etc.

Q. How can you find out how the diskette is organized?

A. Read the IBM Disk Operating System manual (appendix C) and execute the DOS CHKDSK command. The disk sectors are "linked together" to form files, and each file has a name that is listed in the diskette table of contents. Each sector is 512 characters long, and there are $40 \times 8 = 320$ sectors per diskette.

Q. What does it mean to compare a diskette?

A. The information on a diskette is verified by reading from another (exact copy) diskette to see if the same information is stored on both diskettes. If the information on the two diskettes is different, then one of the diskettes is bad and should not be used.

Q. What is a "logged drive"?

A. A logged drive is a default drive, e.g. A or B. This is usually drive A, but it can be changed by entering B:

Q. How can the contents of a file be displayed?

A. Enter "TYPE filename". For example, the contents of B:TEXT can be displayed on the screen by entering command TYPE B:TEXT. To temporarily halt the display, press CTRL + S or CTRL +

NUM-LOCK. The CTRL + S is a toggle, while CTRL + NUM-LOCK is canceled by striking some other key.

Q. What does COPY do?

A. It is a command program for moving information from one file or device to another file or device. For example, COPY CON: B:NOTE.TXT lets you enter text from the keyboard into file B:NOTE.TXT.

Q. What is a pseudofile?

A. A pseudofile is a device that appears to be a file. For example, CON: is a device that can be treated like a diskette file name when used in a COPY command.

Q. What is the purpose of a BATCH file?

A. It is used to execute a batch of DOS commands in one abbreviated command.

Q. What is the purpose of * in a file name?

A. It is a shorthand way to say "don't care." Thus, *.* means all files of all types, *.COM means all COM files, and TGL.* means all TGL files (regardless of type).

Q. What is the difference between using * and using ? in a file name?

A. The * refers to the entire name or entire type of a file when used in a file name, while ? refers to a single letter in a file name.

Q. How can you print the contents of a file?

A. A simple way is to COPY it using the pseudofile PRN: or LPT1: as the destination. Thus, COPY B:NOTE.TXT LPT1: will print the contents of B:NOTE.TXT.

Q. What does CTRL + PRTSC do to DOS?

A. This causes all CRT screen characters to be printed as you enter or display information on the screen. To disable CTRL + PRTSC you must enter a second CTRL + PRTSC character.

Q. Write a .BAT file to do the following:
MAKE NEW SYSTEM ON B

A. Build a file called MAKE.BAT (using COPY CON: MAKE.BAT) as follows.
SYS %4:
COPY A:*.COM   %4:
(CTRL + Z) (ENTER)
Now, this is stored on the logged diskette so whenever you type the command
MAKE NEW SYSTEM ON B
the MAKE.BAT batch file is executed with %4 equal to B.

Q. How can you rename AUTOEXEC.BAT to something simple like DO.BAT?

A. Use RENAME AUTOEXEC.BAT DO.BAT

Q. What is the first thing you should do with your IBM Personal Computer?

A. Make backup copies of all software diskettes. The copy protected ones should be registered with their manufacturers so you can purchase backup copies at a lower price from the original.

# Chapter 4

# How to Do Word Processing

The *word*. They knew the *word,* and saw that it was good. They used the *word* and it was sometimes fearful, sometimes comforting, but always needed.

So, the *word* grew and became as a god. They served the *word* and it guided them all the days of their lives.

But, the *word* continued to grow and it consumed them and became a curse. Thus, they hammered the *word* and imprisoned it on the written page. Yet, the insidious *word* blinded them and shortened their attention span. They knew not what to do with the *word* and went away in chaos.

Then, the *word processor* arrived!

## THE IBM PERSONAL COMPUTER AS AN ELECTRONIC TYPEWRITER

You can turn your IBM Personal Computer into an electronic typewriter by using a word processing program like EasyWriter. This is done by loading the EasyWriter program into RAM and then following the instructions discussed in this chapter.

The word processor program will allow you to enter words, set margins, save and restore documents in diskette files, and control the quality of printing (depending on the capability of your printer).

Before you begin, make sure you have a DOS formatted diskette that will be used to hold the text you will generate. This is called your document or storage diskette.

Also, you should make copies of your EasyWriter diskette just in case you destroy the EasyWriter program itself through wear or by accident. Here is how it is done.

## Making a Backup Copy

If your computer store dealer has not "personalized" your EasyWriter diskette so that it will run on your IBM computer, then take a few minutes to do so.

To personalize your EasyWriter diskette, do the following. We will assume that you have a DOS diskette in drive A and the EasyWriter diskette in drive B. Then you must copy the system tracks from the DOS diskette in A onto the EasyWriter diskette in drive B:

SYS B:

Upon completion of this "personalization" step, the EasyWriter diskette will contain the DOS system tracks, and you will get the following message:

System transferred

## Formatting the Storage Diskette

If you have not already made a copy of the EasyWriter program diskette, then you should do so now. For details on making backup copies, see Chapter 3. You will want to make the program backup copy on a DOS formatted diskette that has the system on it already.

FORMAT B:/S

Now, use the backup copy of EasyWriter as the program diskette. Put it in drive A and restart the system unit using "power-on" or CTRL + ALT + DEL. The EasyWriter program will be loaded into RAM and then executed. The screen will appear as shown in Screen Display 4-1. Insert the formatted storage diskette into drive A (remove the program diskette), and strike the ENTER key.

EasyWriter storage diskettes must be formatted in a code that is recognized by EasyWriter. Therefore, you must format a DOS diskette a second time to prepare it for use by EasyWriter. However, formatting destroys all information on a diskette, so do the format operation one time only!

The menu shown in Screen Display 4-2 appears after you press the ENTER key. This menu will be explained later. To format the storage diskette, enter Y twice. The format operation will take 20 to 30 seconds to complete.

If you decide to use two diskettes while entering a document, then you will also want to format a second diskette in drive B. This is a good idea because you can use the second diskette as a backup copy of the first diskette. Every document is saved on both diskettes.

To format a second diskette select drive B by entering a 2 while in the command mode as shown in Screen Display 4-3. This changes the "logged drive" to B. Next, you can initialize the diskette in B the same way you initialized the diskette in drive A.

**Warning!** If EasyWriter does not find a DOS formatted diskette in drive B, it will revert to drive A. If you do not carefully watch for this, you will accidentally erase all of your documents from drive A instead of formatting the diskette in drive B!

Once you have formatted one or more storage diskettes you are ready to begin using EasyWriter. Notice that both drives can be used for storage diskettes. The EasyWriter program runs entirely out of the RAM.

```
                          IBM

                  Personal Computer


                     EasyWriter

                   Version 1.00


            (C) Copyright IBM Corp. 1981
            (C) Copyright IUS, Inc. 1980




    Insert storage diskette in Drive  A, then press ENTER
```

**Screen Display 4-1.** Starting EasyWriter.

```
                    EASYWRITER FILE SYSTEM
----------------------------------------------------------------
A - APPEND FILE     E - EDIT FILE      H - PRINT FILE     U - UNPROTECT
B - BACKUP          F - FORMAT DISK    P - PROTECT FILE   X - EXIT
C - CLEAR TEXT      G - GET A FILE     R - REVISE A FILE  1 - DRIVE A
D - DELETE FILE     L - LINK FILES     S - SAVE FILE      2 - DRIVE B
----------------------------------------------------------------
DISKETTE NOT INITIALIZED
DO YOU WISH TO FORMAT?
```

**Screen Display 4-2.** Format a storage diskette.

```
                         EASYWRITER FILE SYSTEM
-------------------------------------------------------------------------
A - APPEND FILE      E - EDIT FILE      H - PRINT FILE      U - UNPROTECT
B - BACKUP           F - FORMAT DISK    P - PROTECT FILE    X - EXIT
C - CLEAR TEXT       G - GET A FILE     R - REVISE A FILE   1 - DRIVE A
D - DELETE FILE      L - LINK FILES     S - SAVE FILE       2 - DRIVE B
-------------------------------------------------------------------------
NO FILE      FILESIZE= 1     AVAIL= 18559     %USED=  0     DRIVE A
NO LINKS


COMMAND:
```

**Screen Display 4-3.** Command mode.

# Command Structure of EasyWriter

A summary of EasyWriter commands is given in the next section. But, before you begin to use this program, it will help to understand the "big picture." Let's go back to Screen Display 4-3 which shows the command level of EasyWriter.

Screen Display 4-3 shows the "top level" of a 3-level command structure. You can enter one of the commands (a single letter followed by ENTER) and either do the same operation or else "drop down" to another level.

The G command, for example, gets a file from diskette. The H command causes the current file to be printed. You must get a file before you can print it.

The 3-level command structure of EasyWriter is shown in Figure 4-1. At the "top" of this structure (shown as the left-most column in Figure 4-1) is the File System menu which we will call the "Filer." The main purpose of the Filer is to transmit files between RAM and a storage diskette.

The E command causes the Filer menu to go away and the Editor to take over. You will *not* get the HELP MENU as shown in Screen Display 4-4 unless you press function key F1 while in the Editor. So, to get Screen Display 4-4 from the Filer level, you must enter E followed by F1.

As you can see from Screen Display 4-4, the Editor is used to insert, delete, mark, and move text around within the document. We will explain this menu in greater detail in the examples to follow. For the time being, notice that this is the heart of the word processor program.

Additional commands are shown in Screen Display 4-5. These are obtained by pressing function key F4 while in the Editor level. This menu also corresponds to the third level of the command structure shown in Figure 4-1. Perhaps the most important additional commands are the A-ALIGN and J-JUSTIFY commands. The ALIGN command does paragraph alignment and the JUSTIFY command is a toggle for setting even right margins.

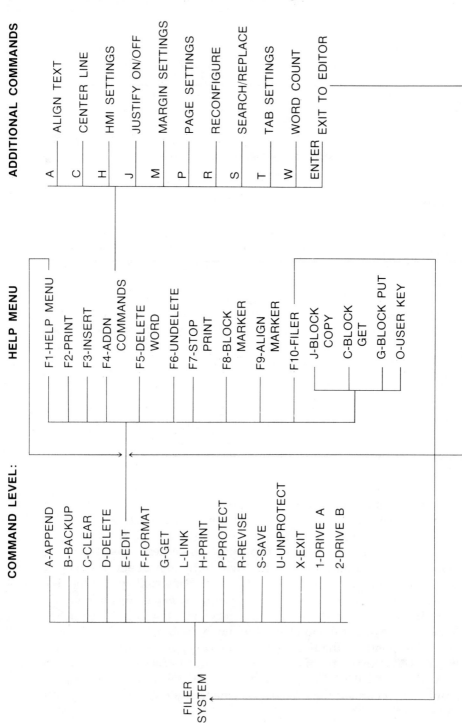

**Figure 4-1.** Command structure of Easy Writer.

```
                    EASYWRITER HELP MENU
-----------------------------------------------------------------
   F1 - HELP MENU         F2 - PRINT           J  - BLOCK COPY
   F3 - INSERT LINE       F4 - ADDN COMMANDS   C  - BLOCK GET
   F5 - DELETE WORD       F6 - UNDELETE        G  - BLOCK PUT
   F7 - STOP PRINT        F8 - BLOCK MARKER    O  - USER KEY
   F9 - ALIGN MARKER      F10- FILING SYSTEM

L                                                          R
+----+----+----+----+----+----+----+----+----+----+----+----+---
```

**Screen Display 4-4.** Editor help menu.

```
          A D D I T I O N A L   C O M M A N D S
-----------------------------------------------------------------
   A - ALIGN TEXT       M - MARGIN SETTINGS    T - TAB SETTINGS
   C - CENTER A LINE    P - PAGE SETTINGS      W - WORD COUNT
   H - HMI SETTINGS     R - RECONFIGURE        ENTER - EXIT TO EDITOR
   J - JUSTIFY ON/OFF   S - SEARCH AND REPLACE

COMMAND?
 · L                                                       R
+----+----+----+----+----+----+----+----+----+----+----+----+---
```

**Screen Display 4-5.** Editor additional commands.

Figure 4-1 shows how to go back up a level at a time. The ENTER key causes the additional command level to be exited so you can return to the Editor. The Editor is exited by striking function key F10 to get back up to the Filer level. The Filer level is terminated by striking X. This causes EasyWriter to be terminated as well.

Now that you understand the big picture, we can summarize the meaning of each command in the command structure. These commands allow you to enter, insert, delete, move, copy, change, store, retrieve, and revise new and existing documents.

## SUMMARY OF EASYWRITER COMMANDS

Before we illustrate the use of EasyWriter we need to list the commands and give a brief definition of their use. These lists can be used later on for reference, and also as an introduction to using them. Each level in the command structure of Figure 4-1 is explained below.

### File System (Screen Display 4-3)

A    Append a file by transferring a second file to RAM. The second file is appended to the end of the current file in RAM. The files are not altered on diskette unless you perform an R-REVISE.

B    Backup the entire contents of the diskette in drive A onto the diskette in drive B. All previous information on the diskette in drive B is lost.

C    Clear RAM of all text. This erases a document from RAM, but does not alter the documents stored on diskette.

D    Delete a file from diskette. This erases a document from diskette.

E    Edit the current (RAM) file. If no current file exists, the screen will go blank and wait for you to begin entering text. This is how to get started.

F    Format or initialize a storage diskette in order to prepare it for use by EasyWriter. The diskette must be DOS formatted already. Beware of unformatted diskettes!

G    Get a numbered file from diskette and place it in RAM. This becomes the current document file.

L    Link two or more files together so you can print, search, and replace across more than one document even though they will not fit into RAM. This command does not attempt to append files as does the A-APPEND command. It simply chains together files that are on diskette.

H    Print the current file and all other files that are L-LINKED to it. You can also use the print command F2 that is in the Editor level.

P,U   Protect or Unprotect a file. A protected file cannot be deleted or revised.

R    Revise a file. Save the current document by writing over the diskette file that contains it. Unless you revise a file, a new diskette file will be created with the same name but a different number.

S    Save a file. A new file is created with a unique number (1-31). The contents of RAM are written to this file. If you want to change an existing file on diskette instead, use R-REVISE.

X    Exit EasyWriter. This command terminates EasyWriter so you can return to DOS.

1,2   Select default disk drive A or B. If the diskette in A or B is not DOS formatted, this command will fail.

As you can see, the Filer commands are used to establish a current file, move files, and destroy files. Each document is given both a name and a number. The number is unique (1-31), but the names may not be

```
                         EASYWRITER FILE SYSTEM
-----------------------------------------------------------------------
A - APPEND FILE      E - EDIT FILE      H - PRINT FILE    U - UNPROTECT
B - BACKUP           F - FORMAT DISK    P - PROTECT FILE  X - EXIT
C - CLEAR TEXT       G - GET A FILE     R - REVISE A FILE 1 - DRIVE A
D - DELETE FILE      L - LINK FILES     S - SAVE FILE     2 - DRIVE B
-----------------------------------------------------------------------
FILE #: 2   chap2     FILESIZE= 3077      AVAIL= 15483    %USED= 85     DRIVE B
LINKS ARE:    2   4   5   6   7   8   9  10  11  12  13

    1 heading       95  2 chap2      3077  3 chap1.5    8864  4 chap2.1    4602
    5 chap2.2     2396  6 chap2.3    1959  7 chap2.4    1844  8 chap2.5    2071
    9 chap2.6     1764 10 chap2.7    1831 11 chap2.8    6171 12 chap2.9    2985
   13 chap2.10    1213 14 chap3      2173 15 chap3.1    2430 16 chap3.2    2574
   17 chap3.3     4183 18 chap3.4    2627 19 chap3.5    1966 20 chap3.6    2020
   21 chap3.7     3297 22 chap3.8    3129 23 chap4      3054 24 chap4.1    2663
   25 chap4.2     3557 26 chap4.3    2657 27 chap4.4    2838 28 chap4.5    3432
   29 chap4.6     2876 30 letter     1797 31 letter2    2400
COMMAND:
```

**Screen Display 4-6.** Filer status obtained from space bar.

unique. For this reason, EasyWriter uses numbers rather than names when referring to diskette files.

You can press the space bar at any time while in the Filer to display the file names and numbers as well as other important information as shown in Screen Display 4-6.

In Screen Display 4-6 the current file is indicated as FILE #2 Chap2. This file is in RAM and occupies 3077 characters of memory. This leaves 15,483 characters of RAM space. The files are listed along with their length in characters. The %USED = 85 tells you that 85% of the diskette in drive B is used up for storage. You have only 15% available space on the diskette.

The LINK message contains a list of file numbers that are linked together. These are shown in Screen Display 4-6 as file numbers 2, 4, 5, 6, 7, 8, 9, 10, 11, 12, and 13. Any print or search command issued at this time will apply to all of these files. Furthermore, the print and search commands will be applied to these files in the same order as shown.

The file number, file name, and file size are shown for all files on the diskette in drive B. Notice that numbers must be unique, but names do not need to be unique. All EasyWriter commands refer to files by file number.

Now, suppose you select the E-EDIT FILE command followed by pressing the F1 function key. This will put you in the HELP MENU mode of the EDITOR.

## Editor Help Menu (Screen Display 4-4)

Pressing F1 while in the Editor causes the HELP MENU to appear. Pressing F1 a second time causes the menu to disappear. You can do any editing while the menu is shown or not. In addition, you can use the arrow keys and CTRL to navigate the screen.

Typing over a character on the screen causes the character to be replaced. You can also insert and delete as explained below.

| | |
|---|---|
| F1-HELP | Display the HELP MENU |
| F2-PRINT | Print the document. |
| F3-INSERT | Insert a blank line. This is a faster way to insert text than using the INS key because it does not need to move characters each time you type another character into the document. |
| F4-ADDN | Additional commands. See the next summary for these. |
| F5-DELETE | Delete a word to the immediate right of the cursor. This is faster than using the DEL key repeatedly. |
| F6-UNDELETE | This command brings back previously deleted text, one character at a time. It only works if you have not moved the cursor since you deleted a word or character. |
| F7-STOP | Pressing this while the printer is printing causes the printer to stop and the print command to be abandoned. |
| F8-BLOCK MARKET | Mark the beginning or end of a block of text that you want to copy or move to another place within the document. This command is used along with the CTRL + J, CTRL + C, and CTRL + G commands. |
| F9-ALIGN MARKER | Use this to protect a block of text from the A-ALIGN command. This prevents the block from being aligned. |
| F10-FILER | Return to the Filer level. |
| J,C,G | Used with CTRL key to control the "cut and paste" block moves. Use F8 along with these commands to copy a block of text from one place to another. |
| Q | User defined keys are activated by CTRL + Q plus a user defined code (usually in ASCII). |

Also notice in Screen Display 4-4 that left and right margin markers have been set. The L marks the left margin setting and the R marks the right margin setting. These can be changed using the F4-ADDN COMMANDS command.

## Additional Commands (Screen Display 4-5)

This is the lowest level in the command structure shown in Figure 4-1. In this level you can format the document by setting margins, moving text, and performing search and replace operations on linked files.

| | |
|---|---|
| A-ALIGN | Align the text beginning with the currently displayed page and ending with the last page in the document. Use J-JUSTIFY, M-MARGIN, and F9-ALIGN MARKER commands to control the format of the aligned text. |
| C-CENTER | Move a line horizontally until it is centered. The cursor can be placed anywhere in the line to be centered. |
| H-HMI | Not used on the IBM Personal Computer. |
| J-JUSTIFY | A toggle that is turned ON/OFF each time you use it. When turned on, the left and right margins of your text are kept even. |
| M-MARGIN | Set the left, right, and paragraph indentation margins. |
| P-PAGE | Set the beginning page number so that pages will be numbered when printed. |
| R-RECONFIGURE | Reconfigure the program diskette default settings. This is used to reset default margins, justification toggle, tabs, page lines, spaces between lines, printer types, and printer interface cards. |
| S-SEARCH | Search and replace text. Search for a character, word, or phrase and replace it with some other pattern. This works across linked files. |
| T-TAB | Set the tab spaces. |
| W-WORD | Tells you how many words you have in the current document. |
| ENTER-EXIT | Press the ENTER key to exit this level, and return to the Editor. |

In addition to the menu commands, you can imbed "dot commands" in the document itself. These so-called dot commands are used to control the printing of a document. A dot command must be the first phrase that appears on a line. Here is a summary of the EasyWriter dot commands.

## Dot Commands

All dot commands must begin in column one and consist of a single dot command per line. All single dot commands must end with a paragraph end marker (use the ENTER key), and all dot command lines must occur without blank lines between them.

Dot commands can occur anywhere in the document. Once they are activated, they remain active until another dot command overrides them.

| | |
|---|---|
| .EJECT | Page eject. Go to top of next page. |
| .EJECTnn | Eject if nn or fewer lines from the end of the current page. |
| .EOL | Define your own end-of-line character for use by the printer. |
| .FORMSTOP<br>.FORMSTOPOFF | Use these two dot commands to cause a single sheet of paper to be printed at a time. At the end of each page the printer will stop. To continue, press the space bar. This way you can insert a single sheet of paper at a time into the printer. |
| .LINESnn | Set number of printed lines per page at nn. The default value is nn = 54. |
| .MARGINnn | Set left margin at column nn. This setting will affect printing, not editing. |
| .PAGErr,cc | Number printed pages in row rr and column cc of every printed page. |
| .PAGELINESnn | Length of a page in lines. The default value is nn = 66 lines per page. |
| .SPACEnn | Set spacing of lines. If nn = 0 the printed page is single-spaced. If nn = 1 the printed page is double-spaced, etc. |
| .TITLEA,nn,text<br>.TITLEB,nn,text<br>.TITLEC,nn,text | Set up to three headings to be printed on line nn of every page. The heading is given as text. |

| .TOPnn | Set the number of spaces at the top of every page. The printing starts at line nn + 1. |
| .USER | Define an ASCII coded character. For example, .USER#96 defines symbol # as the character you get from ASCII 96. In this case # means to print an apostrophe. |

These commands are entered into your text just like any other document text. However, most of them appear at the beginning of a document. This is illustrated in the examples shown in the next section.

## DOCUMENT PREPARATION WITH EASYWRITER

To show you how to enter and edit a document in EasyWriter suppose we use the example illustrated in Figure 4-2. Figure 4-2(a) shows how the document appears when typed into the computer. Figure 4-2(b) shows the same document as it is printed.

In Figure 4-2(a) the dot commands at the top of the page direct EasyWriter to do the following things during printing.

| top2 | Skip two lines at top of every page. |
| lines64 | Print up to 64 lines per page. |
| titlea,3, | Print "Treatise on Goubers" at the top of every page. |
| space1 | Leave a blank line between every line in the printed output. |

You can compare the results obtained from these dot commands with the printed result shown in Figure 4-2(b). Notice that the page is doublespaced. Also notice that the paragraphs are not indented. These facts can only be explained by showing you how the document was prepared.

### An Example of Document Entry

The document of Figure 4-2 is prepared by entering the following commands and text. First, the EasyWriter program is started as explained in the previous section. The command level is reached and the Editor is entered by typing an E. EasyWriter responds with the message PLEASE STAND BY.

```
E (ENTER)
PLEASE STAND BY
```

```
.top2
.lines64
.titlea,3,                    Treatise on Goubers
.space1
```

1.1 The Average Gouber.

The average gouber is computed by summing over the
meso-nerdic space of micro-goubers as follows:

             Avg = Sum[ meso-nerdics ]

This expression is applied to the meso-nerdics that are
easily observed in furd reactions. However, the measurements
must be taken quickly, as every meso-nerdic lasts for 3
nano-seconds.

**Figure 4-2(a).** Document entry.


             Treatise on Goubers


1.1 The Average Gouber.


The average gouber is computed by summing over the

meso-nerdic space of micro-goubers as follows:


             Avg = Sum[ meso-nerdics ]


This expression is applied to the meso-nerdics that are

easily observed in furd reactions. However, the measurements

must be taken quickly, as every meso-nerdic lasts for 3

nano-seconds.

**Figure 4-2(b).** Document printing.


After a pause, the screen is cleared and the cursor appears at the top of
your screen. EasyWriter is waiting for you to either press a function key
or begin entering text.

Suppose we press F1 to get the HELP MENU. What we want to do is
set the screen margins and toggle the justify switch to "on". So, the next
step is to press F4.

F4
M

The margin command causes EasyWriter to ask for three numbers labeled L,R,I. The first number L is the column number of the left margin. The second number R is the column number of the right margin, and I is the number of indentation columns.

0,65,5 (ENTER)

This sets the left margin to column zero, the right margin to column 60, and paragraph indentation to 5 columns.

Next, the J-JUSTIFY toggle is turned on by entering J.

J (ENTER)

The right margin will be smoothed by placing appropriate spacing between words. Finally, we leave this level of the Editor by pressing the ENTER key:

ENTER

The menu goes away and the screen returns to the place we left off. Thus, the text as shown in Figure 4-2(a) is entered.

Figure 4-2(a) does not show all of the story, however. Notice that the formula for average is indented and centered in the page. Here is how this is done.

The F9 key is used to protect a block of text from automatic alignment and left justification even though the J-JUSTIFY toggle is on. The line immediately above the averaging formula contains an F9 symbol (a happy face on your IBM screen), and the line immediately following the protected formula also contains an F9 symbol. Now, this formula will remain wherever we put it regardless of margin settings.

To center this line (the one containing AVG), use the arrow keys to move the cursor to any character in the line. Enter the Editor level by pressing F4 and then press C.

F4
C (ENTER)
ENTER

The second ENTER is necessary in order to terminate the Editor level.

Finally we are ready to save the document. This is done by pressing F10 followed by the S-SAVE command:

F10
S (ENTER)

The document will be saved under a name that you supply. If you want to retrieve it at a later time, you can do so using the G-GET command and the file number:

G (ENTER)
1 (ENTER)

This retrieves file number one from diskette.

You may have noticed that the printed output shown in Figure 4-2(b) does not look exactly like you may have expected. For one thing, it does not have indented paragraphs or an even right margin, also called "right justified" margin.

The A-ALIGN command must be used prior to printing a document if you want to get an aligned document as shown in Figure 4-3. To do this, enter A (ENTER) while in the ADDITIONAL COMMANDS level:

A (ENTER)
ALIGNING

If not in the proper level, use F4 to get there.

The aligning operation will take a while to complete. Each line is adjusted according to the margin settings and J-JUSTIFY toggle. In Figure 4-3 each paragraph is indented and both right and left justified as expected (remember 0,60,5 setting). The formula for AVG is not moved, recall, because it is protected from alignment with the F9 symbol.

In addition to the dot commands shown in this example, we could have used the following commands:

EJECT3          Eject current page if within 3 lines from the bottom.

MARGIN10        Move everything over (right) by 10 columns.

PAGES2,3        Number the pages in row 2, column 3.

These can be placed at the top of the document just as shown in this example.

Now we turn to the Editor for more examples of how to process the words once they have been entered into an EasyWriter document file.

## EDITING A DOCUMENT WITH EASYWRITER

Suppose we use the same document shown in Figure 4-2 as a sample document to be edited. We must get this document into RAM first of all. This is done with the Filer command, G:

G (ENTER)
1 (ENTER)

Here we have assumed that the document is stored in file number one.

```
Treatise on Goubers
```

```
1.1 The Average Gouber.
```

```
The   average   gouber is   computed   by   summing over   the
meso-nerdic space of micro-goubers as follows:
```

```
Avg = Sum[ meso-nerdics ]
```

```
This expression is applied   to the meso-nerdics that are
easily observed in furd   reactions. However, the measurements
must   be taken   quickly,   as every   meso-nerdic   lasts for   3
nano-seconds.
```

**Figure 4-3.** Aligned version of Figure 4-2.

The document in file 1 is loaded into RAM, and the E command used to enter the Editor level:

E (ENTER)

This time, we get the screen as shown in Figure 4-2(a).

## Navigating a Document

The following keys and controls are used to navigate a document by moving the screen cursor, etc.

| | |
|---|---|
| Arrows | The four direction arrows cause the cursor to move up, down, left, and right until you locate the text you want to "point at." |
| Backspace | Erase a character immediately to the left of the cursor. |
| CTRL + ARROW | Jump over left or right word. |

| | |
|---|---|
| HOME | Move cursor to top of page. |
| PGDN,PGUP | Move down/up a full screen. |
| CTRL + PGUP | Move to beginning of document. |
| END | Move to end of document. |
| TABS | Move to preset tab stops. |
| CTRL + END | Delete to end-of-line |
| CTRL + Q | User definable printer command. |
| DEL | Delete a single character to the immediate right of cursor. |
| F3 | Insert a blank line below cursor setting. |
| F5 | Delete an entire word to right of cursor setting. |
| F6 | Undelete previously deleted character. Works only if you have not moved the cursor. |
| F8 | Block marker for beginning and ending of a block of text to be moved. |
| F9 | Alignment protection marker as illustrated in the previous example. |
| INS | Enter insert mode at the location indicated by the cursor. |
| ENTER | Exit insert mode. |

These keys are used to navigate around a screen full of text. However, many times you will want to search and replace text on a global basis. To do this, you will want to use the SEARCH AND REPLACE command shown in the ADDITIONAL COMMANDS menu of Screen Display 4-5.

## Search and Replace

Suppose you want to replace every occurrence of "gouber" and "goubers" with the words "hexglub" and "hexglubs" in Figure 4-2. You can do this as follows:

F4
S

These two commands cause you to drop down into the ADDITIONAL COMMANDS level and activate the SEARCH AND REPLACE command of the editor.

| | |
|---|---|
| SEARCH WORD: | Gouber |
| REPLACE WITH: | Hexglub |
| ALL OR SOME? | A |

This will search for all occurrences of "Gouber" and substitute "Hexglub." Notice that lower case "gouber" is not replaced. To get the lower case version also, do the S command again.

SEARCH WORD:    gouber
REPLACE WITH:    hexglub
ALL OR SOME?    A
DONE!!

The changes are shown on the screen as they take place.

Suppose next that you want to replace some of the occurrences of the word "the" with the word "a." To do this, enter S instead of A:

SEARCH WORD:    the
REPLACE WITH:    a
ALL OR SOME?    s
TYPE:  K-KEEP, D-DELETE, R-REPLETE, X-EXIT

If you respond with K, the replacement is skipped, D the search word is deleted, R the search word is replaced, and X the search command is abandoned.

If you perform a search and replace command on a collection of linked files, the same operations are performed across all files if the SOME option is selected. In addition, you can decide whether to save the changes on a file-by-file basis as you scan the linked files.

## Block Editing

Block editing is the process of moving an entire block of text from one place in your document to another place. A block of text is any group of words that you want to process. It may be one or more sentences, paragraphs, or even pages.

In EasyWriter you have three things to be concerned about in doing a block move:

1. The block to be moved which is designated as such by the F8 block marker.

2. The place where you want to move the block, called the destination. The destination can be anywhere in the document that you want to insert the block.

3. A work buffer of 3,500 characters that is used to temporarily hold the block while it is in the process of being moved. This is a kind of holding area.

These three things are manipulated by placing a block marker F8 at the beginning and end of the block to be moved, transferring the block into the buffer, and then transferring from the buffer to the destination. There are three commands in the HELP MENU of the Editor that you will be using:

CTRL + J     Block copy
CTRL + C    Block get
CTRL + G    Block put.

The CTRL + J command is actually a switch. When you toggle this on, it will allow you to make multiple copies of a block. When you toggle it off, you can only move a block from one place to another place. We will use this toggle to replicate a block in the example below.

The CTRL + C command causes a marked block to be transferred into the buffer. The marked block will be erased from the document. To avoid the erasure be sure CTRL + J is on. If CTRL + J is on, then you can do a CTRL + G and the erased block will appear again.

The CTRL + G command causes the block in the buffer to be inserted into the document at the destination specified by the screen cursor. This command creates duplicates of the buffer if CTRL + J is toggled on.

This may all seem rather confusing so suppose we list the steps for a block move, and then a block copy:

## BLOCK MOVE

1. The block beginning must be marked with a block marker. The block marker must be placed on a line by itself. Move the cursor to a blank line immediately before the first line in the block. If there is no blank line, then create one using F3.

2. Insert F8 into the blank line immediately before the block to be moved. Do this using INS + F8 + ENTER + ENTER. Notice that two ENTERs are needed: one to terminate the INS and another to terminate the line containing the solitary marker. The F8 marker will appear as an "arrow head" symbol.

3. Also insert an F8 marker after the last line of the block to be moved. This specifies where the block ends.

4. Move the cursor back to the line above the beginning F8 block marker. The block will be moved into the buffer when you do a BLOCK GET:

CTRL + C

You will see the block disappear. It has been transferred to the buffer.

5. Now, move the cursor to the place in the document where you want to insert the block. Use CTRL + G to cause the block to be moved from the buffer to the document. The block will appear in the text.

6. The F8 block markers will remain in the text, so move the cursor to each marker and delete both of them.

Notice that the BLOCK MOVE procedure destructively moves a block from one place in the document to another. If you simply want to copy the block then you must modify the procedure above as follows:

## BLOCK COPY

Use Steps 1–3 in Block move. Replace Step 4 above with the following:

4. In step 4 you copied the block into the buffer with CTRL + C. In order to replicate the block, you must do the following:

4(a). Turn on the block copy toggle using the CTRL + J command after you have moved to the beginning of the block, but before you have done the CTRL + C command of step 4.

4(b). With BLOCK COPY ON do the following. Use the CTRL + C command to transfer the block into the buffer. Then, without moving the cursor, do a CTRL + G command. This will cause the block to be replicated right back where it was. However, you still have a copy of the block in the buffer.

4(c). Do the same thing as in steps 5 and 6 of the BLOCK MOVE procedure. Everywhere you move the cursor and do a CTRL + G command, a copy will appear.

The BLOCK COPY procedure must be terminated by CTRL + J to turn the BLOCK COPY toggle off, and of course you should erase the F8 block markers.

Suppose we summarize the differences between block moving and block copying.

**BLOCK MOVE**    CTRL + C followed by CTRL + G

**BLOCK COPY**    CTRL + J, CTRL + C, CTRL + G followed by CTRL + G, CTRL + J.

You can make as many copies as you want by repeating the CTRL + G command for each block copy desired.

Sometimes the buffer will contain "garbage" left over from previous block copy operations. If this happens, you can "flush" the buffer by flipping the toggle twice:

CTRL + J
CTRL + J

This causes the buffer to be erased so no unwanted text creeps into your block moves and/or block copies.

## COMMON QUESTIONS

Q. How many times must you format an EasyWriter storage diskette?

A. Twice. Once to make it work with DOS and a second time to make it work with the EasyWriter program.

Q. Is it necessary to leave the EasyWriter diskette in a drive while using the EasyWriter program?

A. No. You can remove the program diskette as long as you do not reconfigure the program itself.

Q. What happens if you attempt to use an unformatted diskette?

A. Sometimes the operation you intended is ignored. Other times you can lose valuable information.

Q. When should you use A-ALIGN?

A. Usually after you have entered all your text and you want to make the margins smooth. You should probably save your document first, though, since the ALIGNed result may not be the result you expected.

Q. Why would A-ALIGN give unexpected realignment?

A. Remember that A-ALIGN makes all margins line up. If you want to purposely indent a block of text, you should use F9 markers to protect the indented block from alignment.

Q. What happens to text that you type over?

A. It is replaced by the new characters.

Q. If you accidentally delete a word using function key F5, can the deleted characters be brought back?

A. If you have not removed the cursor, then you can undelete the word a single character at a time using function key F6.

Q. If you do not need the program diskette while using EasyWriter, why do you need two drives?

A. You should use drive B to hold a backup copy diskette. Use the BACKUP command to perform backups.

Q. What is the difference between the dot command MARGIN and the M-MARGIN SET command in the Editor?

A. The M-MARGIN SET command sets the margins that will be used while you enter the document and A-ALIGN it. The dot command has an effect only during printing.

Q. Which function keys do you think are the most important to remember?

A. Probably F10 and F4. These two will give you the main menus that tell you what to do next!

Q. What can you do to overcome the limitation on the size of RAM available for editing a document?

A. You can overcome the 18,500 character size limitation by linking files together. The L-LINK command lets you list the file numbers in order. Search and replace works across the linked files, and so does H-PRINT.

Q. If your printer supports special printing modes like bold lettering, underlining, and double-width, how do you take advantage of these features?

A. Check your manual for the special control symbols for activating these. Also, read about the USER dot command in the EasyWriter manual.

Q. What might be wrong with the way you use the dot commands if they do not seem to work?

A. You probably have not followed all of the rules for dot commands. Make sure they start in column one, and are on a line all by themselves, one to a line.

Q. How is double-spacing set using a dot command?

A. Use .SPACE1 for double spacing and .SPACE0 for single spacing.

# Chapter 5

# How to Do Spreadsheet Calculations

Everyone could see that it was a 3-dimensional hologram by the way the cube glowed with a green hue. It was the professor's first lecture using the new holographic "blackboard."

We all waited for the lesson to begin. Today's lecture was on Einstein's derivation of his famous energy equation.

The professor sat at her keyboard and typed a few lines as she spoke. The 3-dimensional cube quivered and glowed as the symbols danced before the class.

We came, we saw, and we understood.

## GETTING STARTED WITH VISICALC

A concise explanation of spreadsheet calculators is given in Chapter 1. Also, you will need to understand a few simple terms and DOS commands introduced in Chapters 2 and 3. If you have not read the previous chapters then perhaps you should turn to them before using the VisiCalc diskette as described here. The following examples assume you know how to operate your IBM Personal Computer.

If you insert the VisiCalc diskette into drive A and reset the system unit (power on or CTRL + ALT + DEL) and the worksheet appears, then your diskette has been properly tailored to your machine. However, your diskette may not be tailored the way you want it, or it may not "boot" from drive A automatically. You will be able to tell if this is the case, because nothing will happen when you reset the system unit. In this case, you must do the following.

### Personalizing Your VisiCalc Diskette

The VisiCalc diskette must be equipped with three file groups before it will automatically start without the need for operator intervention.

These three groups of files are installed by performing the following DOS commands.

Remove the write-protect sticker from the VisiCalc diskette and load it into drive B. Put the DOS diskette in drive A, of course, and transfer the system files to the VisiCalc diskette as follows:

A > SYS B:

After a successful transfer the screen will contain this message:

system transferred

Next, you need to copy the COMMAND.COM file:

A > COPY A:COMMAND.COM B:

1 File(s) copied

Finally, you will want to personalize your start-up procedure by building an AUTOEXEC.BAT file. This is done with the COPY command discussed in Chapter 3. You can put almost anything in this batch file you want. The following is a suggestion only, and assumes the MODE command as well as the three groups of files discussed above are stored on the VisiCalc diskette.

```
COPY CON:   B:AUTOEXEC.BAT
DIR    B:
PAUSE
MODE 80
VC80
(F6)    (ENTER)
```

There are two versions of VisiCalc. VC80 is an 80-column version that uses the wide screen; hence, mode 80 assures this. VC40 is a 40-column version that uses the bold letter screen; hence, MODE 40 is used in the alternative batch file:

```
COPY CON:   B:AUTOEXEC.BAT
DIR    B:
PAUSE
MODE  40
VC40
(F6)    (ENTER)
```

Now, remove the diskettes and place the VisiCalc diskette in drive A and a worksheet diskette (for saving worksheets) in drive B. Reset the system unit and watch what happens. From now on, you need only put the VisiCalc diskette in drive A and a storage diskette in drive B to begin your work.

## VisiCalc Keyboard

You will be able to navigate the columns and rows of a VisiCalc worksheet as shown in Screen Display 5-1 by entering the special codes. These codes are listed below with a brief description of what they do.

| | |
|---|---|
| / | All commands in VisiCalc are entered after typing the "slash" character. You will also note that a single letter command is all that need be entered. VisiCalc will display the entire spelling of all commands so you can verify each one before it is actually carried out. For example, the /F command becomes /FORMAT. VisiCalc displays FORMAT at the top of the screen. |
| > | This means to move to a cell. So, if you enter >A1 VisiCalc moves to row one, column A. |
| ! | This means to recalculate all formulas in the worksheet. |
| ; | This means to change windows. It only works when you use the split screen option; see the /WINDOW command. |
| " | Enter text (label, title, heading) instead of a formula or number. |
| Arrows | The four arrows on the IBM keyboard (numeric pad 8, 6, 2, and 4) can be used to navigate the rows and columns of a worksheet. Remember, these arrows only work when the NUM LOCK key is properly toggled. |
| CTRL + Z | Cancel a command and start all over again. |

## VisiCalc Terminology

Recall from Chapter 1 that a worksheet is a matrix with columns and rows. In VisiCalc, you can "grow a worksheet" by starting in the upper left-hand corner of the screen. This is column A, row 1, so we call it cell A1. If you move horizontally (use the arrows), then the next cells are B1, C1, D1, etc. If you move down, the next cells are A2, A3, A4, etc. The maximum number of columns in VisiCalc is 63 (A to Z, AA to AZ, BA to BK) and the maximum number of rows is 254. A **block** of rows and columns is a rectangular array defined by the upper left-most cell and the block's lower right-most cell. Figure 5-1 shows how a VisiCalc worksheet grows as its block size is increased. A block is designated by its upper left cell and its lower right cell separated by three periods:

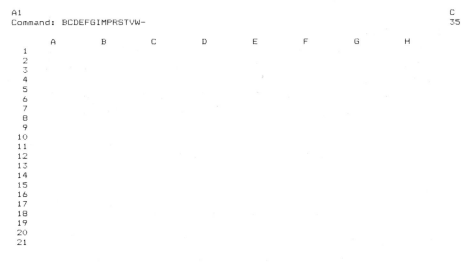

**Screen Display 5-1.** The VisiCalc worksheet.

A1 . . . B2

This block contains 4 cells; see Figure 5-1.

Use the empty worksheet that is displayed in VisiCalc to practice moving from row to row or column to column using the arrow keys. Remember, the following terms have special meaning in VisiCalc:

**Active Cell** This is the current cell as designated by a reverse video on the screen. This is the cell that will receive an input after you enter a number, formula, or text. This is also called the current cell.

**Blank Cell** An empty cell. Its value is zero.

**Block** A rectangular array of rows and columns as designated by the upper left cell and lower right cell. For example, B3 . . . C5 defines a rectangular array of cells with two columns, B3,B4,B5, and C3,C4,C5.

**Current Cell** The active cell, or cell currently referenced by the reverse video cursor.

**Global Command** The command applies to all cells in the Worksheet.

**Partial Column** A contiguous group of cells within a column. For example, C3 . . . C7 is a partial column.

**Partial Row** A contiguous group of cells in a row. For example, C3 . . . H3 is a partial row.

**Worksheet** A block of 63 columns and 254 rows. Each cell can contain either a label as text, a number, or a formula.

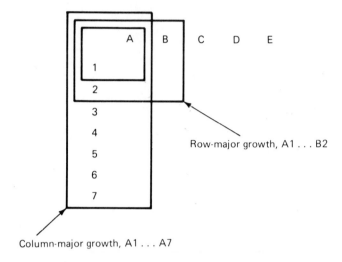

**Figure 5-1.** Growth of a VisiCalc worksheet.

You are now ready to use VisiCalc (see Screen Display 5-2). In the next section we list the commands available in VisiCalc. This list is for reference later on. For details on how to use them skip to the subsequent sections of this chapter which illustrate the use of VisiCalc with many examples.

## SUMMARY OF VISICALC COMMANDS

The VisiCalc commands allow you to do many operations. The worksheet commands let you mold the rows and columns to nearly any length and width. You can insert and delete entire rows and columns. You can set global parameters like "dollar-and-cents" format which display cell values in two decimal place precision, or force the worksheet to calculate in row-major or column-major order.

The data entry commands allow you to enter a string of text, a single number, or a formula into one or many cells. The /FORMAT command lets you select column width, cell content format, and left or right justified display. For example, you can direct a VisiCalc cell to left-justify or right-justify its contents.

The /STORAGE command allows you to send a worksheet to a disk file, a printer, or the CRT screen. This command can be used to print the worksheet formulas and cell formats, or to print all values stored in the worksheet. You can also print a partial worksheet by specifying a block to be printed.

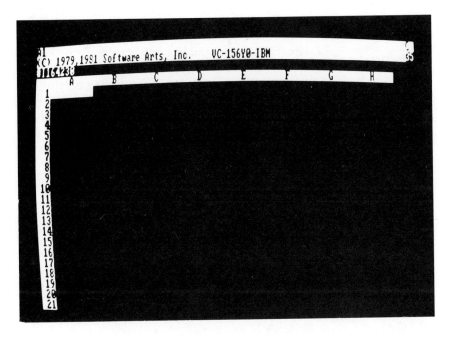

**Screen Display 5-2.** The VisiCalc worksheet.

## COMMAND REFERENCE LIST

| Command | Examples |
| --- | --- |
| /BLANK | /B<br>Remove all contents from a cell. The value of a blank cell is zero. |
| /CLEAR | /C<br>Clear (blank) all entries in the worksheet. Since this erases the entire worksheet, VisiCalc asks you to "Type Y to confirm" before the deed is done. |
| /DELETE | /D R C<br>Delete a row (R) or column (C). The row or column contents are lost, and all other cells are moved up or over to fill in the worksheet. |
| /EDIT | /E<br>The contents of the current cell are displayed so you can edit them. Once the editing is done, the contents are placed back in the active cell. Notice the active cell is highlighted in reverse video on |

the screen. Be careful when using this command to select the active cell first.

The /EDIT command lets you use the arrow keys to backspace over a string of text and change one or more characters. The backspace arrow deletes, but the left and right arrows in the numeric pad move over the cell contents. Insertion is done by moving to the place you want to insert, and simply typing.

/FORMAT

/F D G I L R $ *

This is used to format the current cell in the work-sheet. The format control codes are listed below.

D      Default to the global format, see /G

G      general decimal notation cell contents

I      integer cell contents

R,L    right,left justify cell contents

$      dollars and cents notation

*      graphic plot (bar chart)

/GLOBAL

/G C O R F

The following global toggles can be set or reset each time you use the /G command.

C     Set column width of all columns in the window. For example, /GC 15 causes all cells in all columns of the current window to be 15 characters wide. See the /WINDOW command.

O     Specify the order of calculations when values are computed for rows and columns. /GOC means to calculate column-by-column, /GOR means to calculate row-by-row. See the later examples for an illustration of the importance of order when calculating values.

R     Specify manual, /GRM , or automatic /GRA recalculation. If you want to force VisiCalc to wait until all data has been entered into a worksheet before doing the calculations, then specify /GRM. Otherwise, the entire worksheet will be recalculated after each cell value or formula is entered. The ! causes manual recalculation whenever desired.

     M    Manual recalculation. Use !

A      Automatic recalculation.

F     Set global formats. Use this to specify the format of all cells not previously set by the /F command.

/INSERT

/I R C
Insert a new (empty) row or column. The adjacent row or column cells are moved to make room.

/MOVE

/M A5 . . . C5
Move the contents of a column or row to a new column or row. The formulas in each cell are automatically adjusted as needed to keep the same meaning. /MOVE does a delete followed by an insert on entire columns or rows. For example, A5 . . . C5 causes the A-column to be deleted and inserted in the C-column. But since the A-column is deleted, the column of values and formulas are inserted in column B of the new worksheet. The previous B-column is moved over to the new A-column.

/PRINT

/P
This command is used to print the worksheet values. The formulas are not printed. To print the formulas, use /SS LPT1: instead.

/REPLICATE

/R B5 . . . B5,B6 . . . B10
Make a one-to-many copy of a cell to a block of cells. You can adjust the formula as it is copied or not. If R=relative adjustment is selected, then formulas are changed to fit their new cells. If N = No change is selected, the formulas are copied without change.

/STORAGE

/S L S D Q #
Write all or part of the current worksheet to the printer or diskette. You can choose to display the entire worksheet or list the contents (formulas and format settings).

L      Load a file from diskette to the worksheet. The file cell contents are superimposed on the worksheet, so new entries replace old ones, and all other cells stay the same. If you want the file only, start with /Clear.

S      Save the worksheet on diskette. The /SS,P

option will direct the worksheet formulas and formats to the printer. See /P also.

D  Delete a VisiCalc worksheet file.

Q  Quit VisiCalc and return to DOS.

#S  Save the worksheet in DIF standard format. The DIF format allows you to process the worksheet from other programs; for instance, you can access a DIF worksheet from a BASIC program, or from the DOS TYPE command.

#L  Load a DIF formatted worksheet file.

/TITLE

/T H V B N
Title lock. Lock current row, column, or both so they do not scroll. To remove, use /T N.

H  Lock horizontal rows. All rows above the locked row are also locked. Use > command to move into a cell in one of the locked rows.

V  Lock vertical columns. Use > command to move into a locked row cell.

B  Lock both column and row.

N  None, unlock all locked rows and columns.

/WINDOW

/W H V 1 S U
Split the CRT screen into two windows each containing a different portion of the worksheet. Horizontal (H) or vertical (V) splitting is allowed. To clear (1) or synchronize (S) and /W command, use 1 or S. Also, use ; to toggle between windows.

H  Split screen into "upper and lower" halves.

V  Split screen into "left and right" halves.

1  Revert to 1 screen.

S  Synchronize the cursor movement in both screens so they move together.

U  Unsynchronize the cursors in both screens.

## Function Reference List

Each cell of a VisiCalc worksheet can hold a string of text ("), a number, or a formula. Each time you change a cell that another cell depends on, cell values will be recalculated (unless /GRM is toggled). The calculations are done in row-major order sweeping from left to right, or column-major order sweeping from top to bottom.

An **expression** in a worksheet cell is any algebraic expression containing numbers, cell names, or functions as listed below.

| | |
|---|---|
| +, −, *, /, ^ | Arithmetic operations of add, subtract, multiply, divide, and exponentiation. |
| =, <>, <, >, <=, >= | Comparison operations of equal, not equal, less, greater, less or equal, and greater or equal. Expressions are compared and compute a true or false value for use in the IF function. |
| @ABS (value) | Absolute value. |
| @AVERAGE (list) | Average value of a list of cells, for example, B9 . . . B12, C1 . . . C6. |
| @COUNT (list) | Counts the number of non-BLANK cells in the list of cells or blocks. |
| @ERROR, @NA | Display "ERROR" or "NA". |
| @EXP (value) | Raise 2.71 . . . to a power equal to the value. |
| @OR (val1, val2) | Computes TRUE if either val1 or val2 is true. |
| @AND (val1, val2) | Computes TRUE if both val1 and val2 are true. |
| @NOT (value) | Computes TRUE if value is FALSE and conversely, FALSE if value is TRUE. |
| @IF (val1, val2, val3) | If val1 is TRUE use val2, otherwise use val3. |
| @INT (value) | Drop the decimal portion of the value and return the integer part. The value is truncated, not rounded. |
| @LOOKUP (val1, range) | Search the block in range for the last value less than or equal to val1. Then, compute the value of the cell in the column to the right of the last value found; or the value of the cell in the row below the last value found. Which one (row, column) depends on the range (column, row). |

| | |
|---|---|
| @LN (value) | Natural logarithm of value. |
| @LOG10 (value) | Decimal logarithm of value. |
| @MAX (list) | Return largest value in list of cells. |
| @MIN (list) | Return the smallest value in the list of cells. |
| @NPV (discount, range) | Computes the net present value of a block defined by range. |
| @PI | 3.14159..to 16 digits. |
| @SIN, @ASIN, @COS, @ACOS, @TAN, @ATAN | Trigonmetric functions in radians. |
| @SQRT (value) | Square-root. |
| @SUM (list) | Sum total of block. |

These and other formulas will be illustrated in the many examples to follow.

## Expression Evaluation

Note that parentheses can be used to form expressions, such as the following.

$$(A3 + B5) / @SUM (A4 . . . A10)$$

In fact, parentheses may be required to avoid incorrect meaning in a VisiCalc expression. Without parentheses, all expression evaluation is done from left-to-right. For example, the two expressions below calculate the same value!

$$+ A3 + B5/A1$$
$$(A3 + B5)/A1$$

Notice that an expression must begin with a plus, minus, etc. or a parenthesis to distinguish it from a label.

Suppose cells A1, A3, and B5 contain 1.5, 3.2, and 6.6, respectively. The value returned from the expressions above is 6.533333. Now, suppose we write the expression with parentheses placed as shown below:

$$+ A3 + (B5/A1)$$

The value computed is 7.6! *In other words, VisiCalc expressions are evaluated left-to-right, unless the evaluation order is changed by parentheses.*

When in doubt about the meaning of a VisiCalc expression, be sure to use parentheses. Excess levels of parentheses do not harm a VisiCalc expression, but leaving them out may lead to errors. Here is a final pair of expressions that does exactly the same thing even though they do not look alike:

$$+ C12 + B6/A3 - A5$$
$$(((C12 + B6)/A3) - A5)$$

The most frequent errors committed in VisiCalc are expression evaluation errors.

## A METRIC CONVERSION TABLE

Perhaps the simplest example of a worksheet is a conversion table. Suppose we design and implement a metric conversion table like the one shown in Figure 5-2(a). This table contains a column(A3 . . . A7) of quantities, a column of metric measures (B3 . . . B7), and the corresponding British equivalents. Thus, one liter equals 0.26 gallons, 0.1057 quarts, or 0.0353 cubic feet of water at standard temperature and pressure.

Figure 5-2(b) shows how the metric conversion table is used. In this example, you move the worksheet cursor to cell A6 using the arrow keys or the "go to."

$$> A6$$

Entry of 3.4 causes all numbers in row six to be recalculated. Thus, 3.4 kilograms equals 7.5 pounds or 120 ounces. How is this done?

```
   Metric      To        English   Conversion     Table
============================================================================
  1liter    =       .26gallons =      .1057quarts =      .0353cubic ft.
  1meter    =       1.1yards   =      3.281feet   =      39.37inches
  1kilometer=       .62miles
  1kilogram =       7.5pounds  =         120ounces
  1knot     =       .87miles   =      .0002feet   =      .0005meters
```

**Figure 5-2(a).** A metric conversion table as it's entered into VisiCalc.

```
   Metric      To        English   Conversion     Table
============================================================================
  1liter    =       .26gallons =      .1057quarts =      .0353cubic ft.
  1meter    =       1.1yards   =      3.281feet   =      39.37inches
  1kilometer=       .62miles
  3.4kilogram =     25.5pounds =         408ounces
  1knot     =       .87miles   =      .0002feet   =      .0005meters
```

**Figure 5-2(b).** The metric conversion table with cell A6 changed to 3.4.

## Building The Metric Table

The metric table of Figure 5-2(a) was constructed by typing a row of dotted lines and a row of equal signs as shown. Then the column of ones was entered as follows:

> A3
1

Now, this value is replicated in the remaining cells of the column:

/R   A3 . . . A3, A4 . . . A7

This puts the remaining 1's into the partial column A4 . . . A7. Notice that you do not need to type the entire command above into the keyboard. Instead, place the VisiCalc cursor on cell A3 and then enter /R. The A3 is displayed for you. Next, if you type ENTER, the phrase. . . A3 will be supplied for you. Finally, all that you need to do to point out the destination cell is to move the cursor to cell A4, enter a period, then move the cursor to cell A7 and strike the ENTER key. The command line is supplied for you as you move the cursor around the screen. The three periods ". . ." are supplied when you strike a single period, ".".

Next, the text of column B was entered a cell at a time. This was done for columns D, F, and H, also.

Finally, the other columns were entered by placing a formula for the converted metric value into each cell. For example, column C contains the formulas below.

0.2642 * A3
1.0936 * A4
0.621  * A5
2.205  * A6
+ A7 / 1.151

In fact, we can see what formulas are in the entire worksheet by outputting the contents of the worksheet. Figure 5-3 shows what is produced from the series of commands below.

First, be sure the VisiCalc cursor is resting on the A1 cell (or the upper right-most cell of the block to be printed).

/SS
LPT1:

This causes the worksheet formulas and formats to be "stored" in the printer. That is, the formulas are sent to pseudofile LPT1: where they appear on your line printer.

Notice in Figure 5-3 that the strings of text are prefixed by a double

```
>H7:"meters
>G7:.0005*A7
>F7:"feet     =
>E7:.0002*A7
>D7:"miles    =
>C7:.87*A7
>B7:"knot        =
>A7:1
>F6:"ounces
>E6:120*A6
>D6:"pounds   =
>C6:7.5*A6
>B6:"kilogram =
>A6:1
>D5:"miles
>C5:.62*A5
>B5:"kilometer=
>A5:1
>H4:"inches
>G4:39.37*A4
>F4:"feet     =
>E4:3.281*A4
>D4:"yards    =
>C4:1.1*A4
>B4:"meter    =
>A4:1
>H3:"cubic ft.
>G3:.0353*A3
>F3:"quarts =
>E3:.1057*A3
>D3:"gallons =
>C3:.26*A3
>B3:"liter    =
>A3:1
>H2:"==========
>G2:"==========
>F2:"==========
>E2:"==========
>D2:"==========
>C2:"==========
>B2:"==========
>A2:"==========
>F1:/FR"Table
>E1:"Conversion
>D1:"English
>C1:"To
>B1:"Metric
/W1
/GOC
/GRA
/GC10
/X>A1:>A1:
```

**Figure 5-3.** Formulas for the metric conversion table.

quote mark. The formulas and numbers are shown without quote marks, etc. The "other" information shown with prefix / gives cell format information; for example, see cell F1. The other / information reveals the following.

> /W1     one window
> /GOC   column-major calculation order
> /GRA   automatic recalculation
> /GC10  column width set to ten

We had to set the width of each column in order to make the best use of the space.

> /GLOBAL C 10

This causes all columns to "expand" to 10 characters in width each.

In cell F1 we used the /FORMAT L command to force the label of the cell to left-justify. That is, the /FL command causes the contents of a cell to move to the left side of the cell.

## Displaying the Worksheet

The outputs shown in Figure 5-2 were obtained from the /PRINT command which outputs the values, and not the formulas. So, to obtain the results of a worksheet (instead of the formulas), do the following:

> /PP

Alternately, you can send the finished worksheet to a diskette file using the /PF version of /PRINT.

> /PF
> B:CONVERT

This causes a print file named B/CONVERT.PRF to be written on the diskette in drive B. You can use the COPY command to direct the file to a printer at a later time and retain a copy on diskette. In DOS, this would be done as shown below.

> COPY B:CONVERT.PRF LPT1:

The output will look exactly as seen on the screen, except the row and column labels will be removed.

## Saving a Worksheet

You can also save the worksheet and its formulas, formats, and values in a diskette file as follows.

/SS
B:CONVERT

This command causes all information needed to reconstruct the entire worksheet to be saved in a file named B:CONVERT.VC. Later, when the equivalent of 3.4 kg is needed, load the original table and change the value stored in A6 to 3.4. The values that depend on this value will be automatically recalculated, giving the conversions you want.

/SL
B:CONVERT

This causes the worksheet to be reconstructed on the screen just the way it was before it was saved.

The metric conversion table can be expanded to include other conversion equivalents. You can use the /INSERT command to add new rows, or you can simply append additional rows at the bottom of the table given here.

## AN INCOME TAX RETURN TABLE

In this example we can learn how to use the /REPLICATE command with the adjust option. Suppose we construct an income tax return table like the one shown in Figure 5-4. This table is to be used to compute the amount of income tax due on the adjusted gross income displayed in cell B1. See Screen Display 5-3.

```
E4  /FG   (V)   +C4+(D4*(B1-A4)/100)                                          C
                                                                             33
```

| | A | B | C | D | E | F | G |
|---|---|---|---|---|---|---|---|
| 1 | Gross $ | 55000 | | | | | |
| 2 | Over-- | Not over-- | Taxes | % | Tax Due | | |
| 3 | ----------|-----------|----------|------|----------|-------|--- |
| 4 | 3200 | 4200 | 0 | 14 | 7252 | | |
| 5 | 4200 | 5200 | 140 | 15 | 7760 | | |
| 6 | 5200 | 6200 | 290 | 16 | 8258 | | |
| 7 | 6200 | 7200 | 450 | 17 | 8746 | | |
| 8 | 7200 | 11200 | 620 | 19 | 9702 | | |
| 9 | 11200 | 15200 | 1380 | 22 | 11016 | | |
| 10 | 15200 | 19200 | 2260 | 25 | 12210 | | |
| 11 | 19200 | 23200 | 3260 | 28 | 13284 | | |
| 12 | 23200 | 27200 | 4380 | 32 | 14556 | | |
| 13 | 27200 | 31200 | 5660 | 36 | 15668 | | |
| 14 | 31200 | 35200 | 7100 | 39 | 16382 | | |
| 15 | 35200 | 39200 | 8660 | 42 | 16976 | | |
| 16 | 39200 | 43200 | 10340 | 45 | 17450 | | |
| 17 | 43200 | 47200 | 12140 | 48 | 17804 | | |
| 18 | 47200 | 55200 | 14060 | 50 | 17960 | | |
| 19 | 55200 | 67200 | 18060 | 53 | 17954 | | |
| 20 | 67200 | 79200 | 24420 | 55 | 17710 | | |
| 21 | 79200 | 91200 | 31020 | 58 | 16984 | | |

**Screen Display 5-3.** A tax worksheet.

```
Gross $           55000
Over--      Not over--        Taxes         %   Tax Due
-----------------------------------------------------------
      3200         4200           0          14      7252
      4200         5200         140          15      7760
      5200         6200         290          16      8258
      6200         7200         450          17      8746
      7200        11200         620          19      9702
     11200        15200        1380          22     11016
     15200        19200        2260          25     12210
     19200        23200        3260          28     13284
     23200        27200        4380          32     14556
     27200        31200        5660          36     15668
     31200        35200        7100          39     16382
     35200        39200        8660          42     16976
     39200        43200       10340          45     17450
     43200        47200       12140          48     17804
     47200        55200       14060          50     17960
     55200        67200       18060          53     17954
     67200        79200       24420          55     17710
     79200        91200       31020          58     16984
     91200       103200       37980          60     16260
```

**Figure 5-4.** An income tax table.

## Building The Tax Table

Figure 5-4 was obtained from the formulas shown in Figure 5-5. We obtained Figure 5-5 by setting the "global column" width to 10 characters.

/GLOBAL C 10

Then the following command was selected.

/SS
LPT1:

The formulas in column E are all very similar. The pattern is the same in all of them, for example let i be the row number, then the general formula is shown below.

$$Ci + Di * (B1 - Ai) / 100$$

This formula is valid for i equals 4 to i equals 22.

Rather than repeat this formula for all cells in column E, we can do the following. Enter the formula into cell E4 as shown in Figure 5-5. Then replicate this formula with Relative Adjustment.

/REPLICATE E4 . . . E4, E5 . . . E22

```
    !     A     ! !      B       ! !     C    ! !E! !        G             !
  1 !Gross Income 55000
  2 !Over--          But not over--        Taxes                      Tax due
  3 !--------------------------------------------------------------  ------------
  4 !  3200           4200                     0+ 14%   C4+E4*(B1-A4)/100
  5 !  4200           5200                   140+ 15%   C5+E5*(B1-A5)/100
  6 !  5200           6200                   290+ 16%   C6+E6*(B1-A6)/100
  7 !  6200           7200                   450+ 17%   C7+E7*(B1-A7)/100
  8 !  7200          11200                   620+ 19%   C8+E8*(B1-A8)/100
  9 ! 11200          15200                  1380+ 22%   C9+E9*(B1-A9)/100
 10 ! 15200          19200                  2260+ 25%   C10+E10*(B1-A10)/100
 11 ! 19200          23200                  3260+ 28%   C11+E11*(B1-A11)/100
 12 ! 23200          27200                  4380+ 32%   C12+E12*(B1-A12)/100
 13 ! 27200          31200                  5660+ 36%   C13+E13*(B1-A13)/100
 14 ! 31200          35200                  7100+ 39%   C14+E14*(B1-A14)/100
 15 ! 35200          39200                  8660+ 42%   C15+E15*(B1-A15)/100
 16 ! 39200          43200                 10340+ 45%   C16+E16*(B1-A16)/100
 17 ! 43200          47200                 12140+ 48%   C17+E17*(B1-A17)/100
 18 ! 47200          55200                 14060+ 50%   C18+E18*(B1-A18)/100
 19 ! 55200          67200                 18060+ 53%   C19+E19*(B1-A19)/100
 20 ! 67200          79200                 24420+ 55%   C20+E20*(B1-A20)/100
 21 ! 79200          91200                 31020+ 58%   C21+E21*(B1-A21)/100
 22 ! 91200         103200                 37980+ 60%   C22+E22*(B1-A22)/100
```

**Figure 5-5.** Formulas in the tax table.

This causes the formula to be searched for all cell names. Each time a cell name is found, VisiCalc waits for an "R" (relative), or "N" (no-change). Hence, we entered the following "R" and "N" responses to each cell name:

$$\begin{array}{ll} \text{C4} & \text{"R"} \\ \text{D4} & \text{"R"} \\ \text{B1} & \text{"N"} \\ \text{A4} & \text{"R"} \end{array}$$

Thus, all cell names are adjusted except B1. The results are shown in Figure 5-5.

If we change the value of B1, all entries in partial column E4 . . . E22 are recalculated. These values give the amount of income tax that would be charged in each income bracket. But suppose we modify this worksheet slightly by adding the formula below to cell B23.

## A Modified Tax Table

Suppose we move column E to a new column B as shown below.

/MOVE From . . . To
E4 . . . B4

This command is entered by first positioning the cursor at cell E4 and typing /M. The cursor is then moved to cell B4, thus causing "E4 . . . B4" to be displayed on the VisiCalc edit line.

All formulas are automatically adjusted as shown in Figure 5-6. The cells in old columns B, C, etc. have been shifted right one column. This

```
>B23:@LOOKUP(C1,A4...A22)
>A23:"Tax due =
>E22:60
>D22:37980
>C22:103200
>B22:/FG+D22+(E22*(C1-A22)/100)
>A22:91200
>E21:58
>D21:31020
>C21:91200
>B21:/FG+D21+(E21*(C1-A21)/100)
>A21:79200
>E20:55
>D20:24420
>C20:79200
>B20:/FG+D20+(E20*(C1-A20)/100)
>A20:67200
>E19:53
>D19:18060
>C19:67200
>B19:/FG+D19+(E19*(C1-A19)/100)
>A19:55200
>E18:50
>D18:14060
>C18:55200
>B18:/FG+D18+(E18*(C1-A18)/100)
>A18:47200
>E17:48
>D17:12140
>C17:47200
>B17:/FG+D17+(E17*(C1-A17)/100)
>A17:43200
>E16:45
>D16:10340
>C16:43200
>B16:/FG+D16+(E16*(C1-A16)/100)
>A16:39200
>E15:42
>D15:8660
>C15:39200
>B15:/FG+D15+(E15*(C1-A15)/100)
>A15:35200
>E14:39
>D14:7100
>C14:35200
>B14:/FG+D14+(E14*(C1-A14)/100)
>A14:31200
>E13:36
>D13:5660
>C13:31200
>B13:/FG+D13+(E13*(C1-A13)/100)
>A13:27200
>E12:32
>D12:4380
>C12:27200
>B12:/FG+D12+(E12*(C1-A12)/100)
>A12:23200
>E11:28
```

**Figure 5-6.** Formulas and formats for modified tax table.

```
>D11:3260
>C11:23200
>B11:/FG+D11+(E11*(C1-A11)/100)
>A11:19200
>E10:25
>D10:2260
>C10:19200
>B10:/FG+D10+(E10*(C1-A10)/100)
>A10:15200
>E9:22
>D9:1380
>C9:15200
>B9:/FG+D9+(E9*(C1-A9)/100)
>A9:11200
>E8:19
>D8:620
>C8:11200
>B8:/FG+D8+(E8*(C1-A8)/100)
>A8:7200
>E7:17
>D7:450
>C7:7200
>B7:/FG+D7+(E7*(C1-A7)/100)
>A7:6200
>E6:16
>D6:290
>C6:6200
>B6:/FG+D6+(E6*(C1-A6)/100)
>A6:5200
>E5:15
>D5:140
>C5:5200
>B5:/FG+D5+(E5*(C1-A5)/100)
>A5:4200
>E4:14
>D4:0
>C4:4200
>B4:/FG+D4+(E4*(C1-A4)/100)
>A4:3200
>F3:"----------
>E3:"----------
>D3:"----------
>C3:"----------
>B3:"----------
>A3:"----------
>E2:/FR"%
>D2:/FR"Taxes
>C2:/FR"Not over-
>B2:/FR"Tax Due
>A2:"Over--
>C1:55000
>A1:"Gross $
/W1
/GOC
/GRA
/GC10
/X>A1:>A3:/TH
/X>A1:>A1:
```

**Figure 5-6.** continued.

means the formulas in new column B must be adjusted to have the same meaning.

## Searching the Tax Table

Look at cell B23 of Figure 5-6. The LOOKUP function has been used to compute the tax amount due on the $55000 shown in cell C1.

LOOKUP (C1, A4 . . . A22)

This function uses the value stored in C1 (55000) as a search value. It then searches down column A4 . . . A22 looking for the last number less than 55000. The last number less than 55000 is 47200 in cell A18. The value returned by LOOKUP is the value in cell B18. Hence, 17960.00 is shown in cell B23 (see Figure 5-7).

The modification shown here uses the LOOKUP function to search the worksheet. We had to move column E to column B because LOOKUP uses the column to the immediate right side. Hence, we moved the "tax due" column so it would be used by LOOKUP.

LOOKUP works on rows, too. If we specify a partial row as the row to be searched, then the value returned will be below the value found.

The VisiCalc Tax Table makes computing your income tax easier to do. The hard part is paying the IRS!

```
Gross $                      55000
Over--        Tax Due Not over-        Taxes         %
----------------------------------------------------------------
        3200      7252       4200           0         14
        4200      7760       5200         140         15
        5200      8258       6200         290         16
        6200      8746       7200         450         17
        7200      9702      11200         620         19
       11200     11016      15200        1380         22
       15200     12210      19200        2260         25
       19200     13284      23200        3260         28
       23200     14556      27200        4380         32
       27200     15668      31200        5660         36
       31200     16382      35200        7100         39
       35200     16976      39200        8660         42
       39200     17450      43200       10340         45
       43200     17804      47200       12140         48
       47200     17960      55200       14060         50
       55200     17954      67200       18060         53
       67200     17710      79200       24420         55
       79200     16984      91200       31020         58
       91200     16260     103200       37980         60
Tax due =         17960
```

Figure 5-7. The modified income tax table.

# AN INSTALLMENT PAYMENT SPREADSHEET

VisiCalc is most useful for "what if" types of calculations. We can build a numerical model of a financial situation and then ask "what if" questions. This concept is demonstrated by the installment payment worksheet shown in Figure 5-8.

```
Installment Payment  Worksheet         !       Scratchpad
-----------------------------------!       Calculations
Amount borrowed   $          60000.00      1.0100585666(annuity)
Annual interest   %                16      .013333333333(per month)
Months to repay   =               348      100.41774326(present)
-----------------------------------------------------------
Monthly payment   $            808.05
Total payment     $         281200.30
Total interest    $         221200.30
-----------------------------------------------------------
```

**Figure 5-8.** Installment payment model.

## Building The Installment Model

The financial model we used to construct the worksheet shown in Figure 5-8 is based on the annuity formulas below:

Payment = (Amount) * (Interest Rate) * (Annuity)
Annuity = V / (V-1)
V = (Interest Rate + 1) $^\wedge$ Months

Therefore, cell C5 contains V and cell C3 contains (Annuity) and so forth. The model depends on values stored in cells B3 . . . B5. For example, if we change any one of these numbers, all the calculations must be redone to reflect the single change. This means we can ask "what if" questions.

## What If Questions

Let's ask some questions. What if we borrow $60,000 at 16% for 348 months (29 years)? The resulting values are shown in Figure 5-9.

| | | |
|---|---|---|
| Monthly Payment | $ | 808.05 |
| Total Payment | | $281,200.30 |
| Total Interest | | $221,200.30 |

In short, we learn that it will cost almost a quarter of a million dollars to borrow $60,000 for 29 years!

But, what if we change the interest rate to 15%? This changes the

```
>C10: "--------------------
>B10: "--------------------
>A10: "--------------------
>B9: /F$(B8-B3)
>A9: "Total interest    $
>B8: /F$(B7*B5)
>A8: "Total payment     $
>B7: /F$(C4*C3*B3)
>A7: "Monthly payment   $
>C6: "--------------------
>B6: "--------------------
>A6: "--------------------
>D5: "(present)
>C5: (C4+1)^B5
>B5: /FI348
>A5: "Months to repay   =
>D4: "(per month)
>C4: +B4/1200
>B4: /FG16
>A4: "Annual interest   %
>D3: "(annuity)
>C3: +C5/(C5-1)
>B3: /F$60000
>A3: "Amount borrowed   $
>C2: "         Calculations
>B2: "-------------------!
>A2: "--------------------
>C1: /FR"Scratchpad
>B1: "   Worksheet         !
>A1: /FL"Installment Payment
/W1
/GOR
/GRA
/GC19
/X>A1:>A1:
```

**Figure 5-9.** Formulas and formats for installment payment model.

value stored in cell C4, and in turn changes the values in cells C5, B7, B8, and B9. Notice a very subtle problem here, however.

Cell C3 depends on the value in cell C5. But since VisiCalc recalculates everything from top-to-bottom (by row in this case) the value of C5 used in cell C3 is "old." That is, C5 is not recalculated before it is used in cell C3. This means that C3 is incorrect! We can repair the damage using the recalculation command:

!

For example, we entered 15% in place ot 16% in cell B4. The incorrect values obtained were:

Monthly Payment $ 757.54
Total Payment $263,625.29
Total Interest $203,625.29

We command VisiCalc to recalculate everything just to make sure:

!

The correct values were obtained. We know they were correct because subsequent ! commands did not cause changes.

Monthly Payment $ 760.08
Total Payment $264,507.25
Total Interest $204,507.25

Here are some other "what if" questions we can ask using this financial model. What if we change the length of the repayment period? What if we change the amount borrowed? In each case we make sure the answers are correct by commanding VisiCalc to recalculate all values using !.

In some cases like the one demonstrated here, the recalculation can be avoided by changing the order of the calculation. For example, if a column-by-column sweep of the worksheet leads to correct values, then change the order to column-major calculation.

/GLOGAL O C

Now, all formulas are evaluated in column A followed by column B, column C, etc. until all columns have been calculated. This is called column-major, then, because the formulas in each column are evaluated first. In row-major order, all formulas in each row are evaluated, first (row 1, row 2, 3, . . . etc.).

Just to make sure, however, use ! to recalculate the entire worksheet in either order. If no change occurs, you know that the order is not important.

Finally, you might want to suspend calculations altogether by making recalculation manual, that is, only after a ! command. This is done by toggling the /GR switch:

/GLOBAL R M

This causes all recalculation to cease until a ! command is entered by the user. Thus, all values will remain unchanged until the manual recalculation command is given.

This example demonstrated several useful implementations of Visi-Calc and shows how to enter a worksheet with a minimum of typing effort. In the next two examples we show you some more VisiCalc features that should be useful in your own worksheet work.

# A DATA REDUCTION SPREADSHEET
# FOR EXPERIMENTERS

Scientists, psychologists, agricultural extension agents, engineers, and statisticians all need to perform a variety of statistical data reduction calculations on their data. VisiCalc is an ideal way to perform these calculations in a hurry. In this section we study one example of the way you can use VisiCalc to do data reduction on a list of observed values.

In statistician terms a list of observed values is any collection of measurements taken from an experiment. Suppose, for example, that we try to determine the number of inches in a yardstick experimentally. We can do this by measuring the yardstick many times using another tape measure or whatever. Each measurement is called an observation, and as you might expect, each observation consists of the true value plus or minus a small error.

Figure 5-10 shows an experimenter's table of 5 observations. Each observation is different because of a (small) experimental error.

The average value (36.306) is an estimate of the true length of the yardstick (see Figure 5-10). However, we know that each observation used to compute the average value contained a certain (unknown) error. Therefore, the average value contains a certain error. We hope the plus and minus deviations will cancel one another so that the average value is a better estimator than any single observation. In fact, as the number of observations is increased without bound, the plus and minus deviations in the observed measurements would tend to cancel one another. Therefore, a very large collection of observed values yields a "better" average. This is the "law of large numbers" used by statisticians to estimate the probable error in any average value calculation.

```
Number Observations =                   5
                                  Observed                    Diff^2
--------------------------------------------------------------------
                                    36.75          .19713600003
                                    35.55          .57153599994
                                    34.67         2.6764960006
                                    39.23         8.5497759649
                                    35.33          .95257599296
--------------------------------------------------------------------
Sum of Observed      =             181.53         12.9475199583
Avg of Observed      =              36.306         1.2135152903=probable error
```

**Figure 5-10.** An experimenter's data reduction table.

Figure 5-10 contains a number labeled "probable error." This value is the "most likely" plus or minus deviation in the average value. Thus the length of a yardstick is estimated as the average value plus or minus the probable error. In the example of Figure 5-10 we get an answer as follows:

$$1 \text{ yd} = 36.306 + \text{or} - 1.214 \text{ inches}$$

The "most likely" length of a yardstick is somewhere between 35.092 and 37.520 inches. Here is how we compute this interesting experimental result.

## Building The Experimenter's Table

The average value of the column of observations is computed using the AVERAGE function of VisiCalc. This is computed in cell B11 (see Figure 5-11).

$$@AVERAGE (B4 \ldots B8)$$

```
>D11:"=probable error
>C11:.6745*@SQRT(C10)/@SQRT(B1-1)
>B11:@AVERAGE(B4...B8)
>A11:"Avg of Observed      =
>C10:@SUM(C3...C8)
>B10:@SUM(B4...B8)
>A10:"Sum of Observed      =
>E9:"----------------------
>D9:"----------------------
>C9:"----------------------
>B9:"----------------------
>A9:"----------------------
>C8:(B8-B11)^2
>B8:35.33
>C7:(B7-B11)^2
>B7:39.23
>C6:(B6-B11)^2
>B6:34.67
>C5:(B5-B11)^2
>B5:35.55
>C4:(B4-B11)^2
>B4:36.75
>C3:"----------------------
>B3:"----------------------
>A3:"----------------------
>C2:/FR"Diff^2
>B2:/FR"Observed
>B1:/FI5
>A1:"Number Observations =
/W1
/GOC
/GRA
/GC21
/X>A1:>A1:
```

**Figure 5-11.** Formulas and formats for experimenter's table.

The average value is used to estimate the size of each "plus or minus" deviation from the true value. Thus, column C contains the squared value of the difference:

$$(B4 - B11)^{\wedge}2$$

The /REPLICATE command is used to copy this formula into the remaining cells and at the same time adjust the B4 to B5, B6, B7, and B8.

$$/REPLICATE\ C4\ .\ .\ .\ C4,\ C5\ .\ .\ .\ C8$$

You may notice that the average value stored in B11 is used in every difference calculation of column C. But B11 is calculated after column C instead of beforehand if we use row-major order of calculation. Suppose we change the order of calculation. This is done by switching to column-major order:

$$/GLOBAL\ O\ C$$

Now, the sum and average in B10, B11, are calculated first. The differences in column C are calculated next, and the probable error is calculated last.

The formula for probable error is given as follows:

$$0.6745 * @SQRT\ (@SUM\ (C3\ .\ .\ .\ C8))\ /\ @SQRT\ (N - 1)$$

Here, N is the total number of observations, 5. The value 0.6745 comes from the statistical fact that the error most likely differs by plus or minus 0.6745 times the @SQRT expression.

## Modifying The Table

The experimenter's table can be extended by inserting additional rows (#9) into the table used in this example. If you do this be sure to modify block expressions in the other formulas to reflect the addition. Hence, B8 would be changed to B9, etc.

You might want to use this approach to analyze experimental data collected from any experiment. Here are some suggestions:

windmill data
gasoline mileage
personal weight gain/loss

## VISICALC GRAPHICS

As a final example of the usefulness of VisiCalc suppose we examine how to use it to display numerical data in bar-chart form. This feature is provided in the /FORMAT command using the * option.

To display a bar-chart instead of a numerical value use the following format command:

/FORMAT *

This is placed in cell C2 of the worksheet, and then replicated into the column C2 . . . C18:

/REPLICATE C2 . . . C2, C3 . . . C18

Figure 5-12 illustrates how a bar-chart might appear in a VisiCalc worksheet. Column A contains an age, and column B contains the number of deaths per 1000 population in the United States in 1958. Column C contains a formula for computing the number of characters to be displayed. The number of asterisks corresponds to the number in column B. In Figure 5-12 one * equals 2 deaths per 1000 population.

```
Age      Deaths    1 * equals 2
       0       7.08 ***
       5       1.35
      10       1.21
      15       1.4
      20       1.8
      25       1.9
      30       2.1 *
      35       2.5 *
      40       3.5 *
      45       5.4 **
      50       8.3 ****
      55        13 ******
      60      20.3 *********
      65      31.8 *********
      70      49.8 *********
      75      73.4 *********
      80       110 *********
```

**Figure 5-12.** Bar chart worksheet.

# Building The Mortality Table

Figure 5-13 shows what was entered into each cell in order to produce the mortality bar-chart. Column C computes the ratio of column B cell values to the values of cell D1.

Actually, the worksheet is split into two halves. The split screen command was used to divide the screen into a left-half and a right half:

/WINDOW V

The screen will appear as shown in Screen Display 5-4. Be sure to position the cursor in column C before entering this command. Once en-

```
>C18:/F*+B18/D1
>B18:110
>A18:80
>C17:/F*+B17/D1
>B17:73.4
>A17:75
>C16:/F*+B16/D1
>B16:49.8
>A16:70
>C15:/F*+B15/D1
>B15:31.8
>A15:65
>C14:/F*+B14/D1
>B14:20.3
>A14:60
>C13:/F*+B13/D1
>B13:13
>A13:55
>C12:/F*+B12/D1
>B12:8.3
>A12:50
>C11:/F*+B11/D1
>B11:5.4
>A11:45
>C10:/F*+B10/D1
>B10:3.5
>A10:40
>C9:/F*+B9/D1
>B9:2.5
>A9:35
>C8:/F*+B8/D1
>B8:2.1
>A8:30
>C7:/F*+B7/D1
>B7:1.9
>A7:25
>C6:/F*+B6/D1
>B6:1.8
>A6:20
>C5:/F*+B5/D1
>B5:1.4
>A5:15
>C4:/F*+B4/D1
>B4:1.21
>A4:10
>C3:/F*+B3/D1
>B3:1.35
>A3:5
>C2:/F*+B2/D1
>B2:7.08
>A2:0
>D1:/FL2
>C1:/FR"1 * equals
>B1:/FL" Deaths
>A1:/FL"     Age
/W1
/GOC
/GRA
/XV23
/GC10
/X>A1:>A1:;/GC40
/X>C1:>C3:;
```

**Figure 5-13.** Formulas and formats for the bar chart.

```
C2 /F*  (V)  +B2/D1                                          C
                                                            34

        A        B                        C
  1    Age     Deaths    1                           1 * equals
  2         0     7.08    2 ***
  3         5     1.35    3
  4        10     1.21    4
  5        15     1.4     5
  6        20     1.8     6
  7        25     1.9     7
  8        30     2.1     8 *
  9        35     2.5     9 *
 10        40     3.5    10 *
 11        45     5.4    11 **
 12        50     8.3    12 ****
 13        55      13    13 ******
 14        60    20.3    14 *********
 15        65    31.8    15 ***************
 16        70    49.8    16 ************************
 17        75    73.4    17 *************************************
 18        80     110    18 *******************************************
 19                      19
 20                      20
 21                      21
```

**Screen Display 5-4.** The split-screen bar chart.

tered, you must use the ; command to flip back and forth between the
left and right halves.

;

Now, notice that the width of the right screen is much greater than the
width of the left screen. The /GLOBAL C 50 command was used to expand the right-half (column C), while leaving the left-hand alone. This
is one of the advantages of the /WINDOW feature. Thus, the column
widths of column C are 50 characters and the column widths of all other
columns are 10 characters.

We have set the width of Column C at 50 and the display format to
"asterisk." We also forced all text to be right-justified, (R) and the bar-
chart to be left-justified (L). The split window feature has made it possible to set different formats and column widths in a single worksheet.

You can create a MORT.PRF file for display purposes by using the /P
command. Be sure to position the cursor at the upper-right-hand cell of
the block you want to display:

/PRINT F
A1 . . . C18

This causes the block A1 . . . C18 to be saved in file MORT.PRF. But,
as you will notice, the .PRF file is stored in the format set up by the left
screen. Thus, it is printed in narrow format. To overcome this unfortu-
nate limitation, you must change the global format of the left screen to
50 also. This may result in a worksheet that is too wide to display on
your printer, however. To partially get around this, use the PRTSC key
to print the contents of the screen. This will produce Screen Display 5-4.

# COMMON QUESTIONS

Q. Can a formula in a VisiCalc cell modify another formula in another cell?

A. No. But you can use the IF function to conditionally use one formula or another, depending on the value stored in another cell.

Q. What is the maximum width of a cell?

A. 77 characters. In general, it is the width of the screen minus 3. The minimum is 3.

Q. If you make a mistake and put something in a cell that you want to be empty, how do you reset it to an empty cell?

A. /BLANK it. Move the cursor to the cell and type /B (ENTER)

Q. What is the difference between /COPY and /REPLICATE?

A. The /COPY command makes a one-for-one copy. The /REPLICATE command makes many replicates of one cell into many other cells.

Q. What is the difference between a /MOVE and a /COPY command?

A. The /MOVE command always adjusts its formulas, and it erases the source row or column. The /COPY does not erase the original row or column.

Q. Does /INSERT destroy the inserted column or row if it already contains data?

A. No. It moves everything to one side, and automatically adjusts the formulas.

Q. How can you "patch" two or more worksheets together to make a bigger one?

A. Use /STORAGE S to write them to diskette, then use /STORAGE L to superimpose one on top of another.

Q. How do you strip the column and row labels from the border of a worksheet?

A. You cannot do this on the worksheet directly. However, the .PRF file obtained from /PRINT does not have a border, so you can use this instead.

Q. How is an entire worksheet erased to start all over again?

A. Use /CLEAR Y.

Q. How can you cancel an incorrect entry line?

A. Several ways. The CTRL + Z cancels a line before it is put into the current cell. The /EDIT command can be used to change a cell after it has been written.

Q. How do you print a worksheet?

A. Use /PRINT F or /PRINT P to print the values only. Use the /S# command to print the formulas and formats.

Q. What is the purpose of /TITLE?

A. To conveniently keep a heading from scrolling off the screen.

Q. What does the "memory" message in the upper right-hand of the screen mean?

A. It tells you how much RAM you have left (measured in 1K units). The smaller this number, the more memory used by the worksheet.

Q. Is there some way to display the file names on diskette when using the /STORAGE Load command?

A. Yes, press SL and the right arrow (numeric pad key 6). Each time you press the arrow, another file name is displayed. Use ENTER to fetch the one you want. For example,

/SL

B:

Now, press the right arrow, and watch the file names from drive B appear in the edit line. When the one you want shows up there, press the (ENTER) key and it will be loaded.

# Chapter 6

# How To Write Your Own Programs

The two archaeologists moved slowly and carefully among the ruins. The light of day was about gone when one of them stumbled over a large cellulose cube. She picked it up, but it began to crumble under its own weight. Quickly now, her companion beamed the matter recorder on the decayed artifact. The ancient finding was instantly recorded for analysis back in the ship.

The lab tests revealed the source and approximate date of the rare book. It belonged to an ancient civilization that lived on the planet's surface in the 21st century. The strange language could not be understood, however. For example, what does this mean, "BASIC Payroll Program. Written by Scotty Moore?"

## SOFTWARE TOOLS

Chapter 1 showed how computer programmers use abstraction and planning to solve a variety of problems. The levels of abstraction discussed were:

Requirements definition
Design specification
Coding specification
Implementation (the subject of this chapter)
Testing
Documentation

Each level is refined into the next lower level in simple steps leading to a completed program. This is known as **structured design** because it is a disciplined method of producing correctly functioning programs.

In this chapter we study various methods of actually writing a computer program. We will assume that the reader has mastered the structured design methodology and concentrate only on the implementation level of abstraction.

Furthermore, we will restrict our discussion in this chapter to two language translators: advanced BASIC and Pascal. Recall from Chapter 2 (and 8) that BASIC is an interpretive language whereas Pascal is a compiled language.

Computer programmers are generally undecided about which language is "best." BASIC is simple to learn and easy to use. It is directly translated and executed without a time-consuming compilation step in between. This makes it more responsive than Pascal for quick results.

On the other hand, Pascal is "structured" and easy to read. Therefore, a Pascal program can be easily maintained and modified, and Pascal programs can be incorporated into other programs. This makes Pascal ideal for large systems where many separate parts must be maintained and perhaps enhanced at some later time.

Which is better then, BASIC or Pascal? This is probably a personal decision, one that you can make for yourself. Generally, BASIC should be used to write small programs so you can get quick results, and Pascal should be used to write large programs that will be used for a long time.

Computer programming in either BASIC or Pascal can be a difficult task unless proper tools are used. The software tools provided by the IBM Personal Computer include the following:

**Editors.** DOS command EDLIN, and the EDIT command in BASICA are all text editors that can be used to enter and modify a program.

**Filers** DOS commands COPY, TYPE, RENAME, ERASE, and the SAVE/LOAD/FILES commands in BASICA are all filer systems that can be used to move stored programs around on diskette.

**Language Processors** BASICA is an interpreter for BASIC which is typically used to implement and test a new program. PAS1 is a compiler for Pascal which is typically used to translate a working program into a faster-running binary machine code program.

These tools are used only after you have refined the abstract levels of a program into a concrete source program. Then you can enter your source program into the computer and "run" it.

If you are not familiar with the terms used here, please review Chapter 8 before continuing. Otherwise, you are now ready to learn the details of writing your own programs. But first, you need some software tools.

## USING AN EDITOR

There are two ways to edit a program:

1. BASICA entry and EDIT command
2. DOS EDLIN editor program

The first method is typically used to enter and modify BASIC programs, and the second is typically used to enter and modify Pascal programs. However, it is possible to use the BASICA editor in place of the EDLIN editor, or vice-versa, if you remember to SAVE the BASICA text in ASCII mode. For example, you can save a program in file SOURCE and then retrieve it with EDLIN:

SAVE "SOURCE", A

Later, when using EDLIN, retrieve the text in SOURCE as shown below:

A > EDLIN SOURCE.BAS

Conversely, you can create a program using EDLIN and load it prior to execution as follows:

LOAD "SOURCE"

Be sure you use the extension type .BAS from EDLIN, though, because BASICA will expect the file name to be SOURCE.BAS, above.

The second method is typically used to create Pascal source text. In fact, at the time this was written, it was the only practical editor for entering Pascal source text. But since EDLIN is a line editor and the editor that is built into BASICA is a screen editor, we will write a program called "stripper" that converts programs entered through BASICA into programs that the Pascal compiler will accept.

In summary, a program can be entered and modified as follows:

**BASICA edit mode** You can enter and edit any BASIC program using this "screen" editor. Also, you can enter and edit any Pascal program using this editor if you do two additional things: (a) SAVE the file in ASCII mode, and (b) use the "stripper" program given in the next section before you attempt to compile your Pascal program using PAS1.

**EDLIN** You can enter and edit any BASIC or Pascal program using this "line" editor. If you use this program to enter a BASIC program, be sure to put line numbers in front of every statement.

If you decide to use EDLIN for all of your work, turn to the section which describes the EDLIN commands. However, if you decide to use the screen editor built into BASICA (and the IBM Personal Computer keyboard/screen), then continue to the next section.

## BASICA Screen Editor

To activate BASICA from DOS, simply type the following command:

A > BASICA

This will cause the BASICA interpreter to be loaded into RAM and begin to execute. When it responds with OK, you can use the following screen editor commands.

| | |
|---|---|
| AUTO | Automatic line-numbers |
| DELETE | Erase certain lines |
| EDIT | Edit a certain line |
| LIST | Display certain lines |
| LLIST | Print certain lines |
| MERGE | Merge together pieces of a program |
| RENUM | Renumber the program lines |

In addition to these commands, the keyboard contains the screen editing functions described below.

**Arrows:** The four arrow keys can be used to move the cursor to any line displayed on the screen.

**Ins:** This key will allow you to insert text before the character above the cursor. When the text has been entered, strike the ENTER key, one of the arrow keys, or the END key.

**DEL:** The delete key causes the character above the cursor to be erased. You will notice that a character disappears each time the DEL key is pressed.

**END:** This key causes the cursor to jump to the end of the current line.

**LEFT ARROW:** This key deletes in reverse.

Suppose we illustrate the BASICA screen editor with an example. Use the AUTO command to start entering the following program:

AUTO 100,10

This causes line numbers to be automatically displayed in increments of 10 each.

```
100 INPUT A,B,C
110 PRINT A + B, A + C
120 STOP
```

You will use CTRL + C to terminate the automatic line-numbering command. Now, to see what you have entered, use the LIST command:

LIST

This causes the entire program to be displayed on the screen.

Next, use the arrow keys to move the cursor underneath any character displayed. Suppose we want to change A + B in line 110 to A − B. Move the cursor underneath the + and strike the DEL key. The + disappears. Now strike the INS key followed by the − character. The line now has A − B in place of A + B. Move the cursor back down the screen and list the modified program a second time:

LIST

Now, two copies of the program are shown on the screen. What happens if we screen-edit both of them? The latest change will take effect if you make contradictory changes.

You can also use the EDIT command to screen-edit a line. Type EDIT followed by the line number and the line will be displayed on the following line. The line can now be edited in the same way as described above.

If you attempt to run your program and a syntax error is detected by BASICA, then the incorrect line is displayed just as if you had entered the EDIT command. You can correct the line by screen-editing it on the spot!

## Function Keys

You will also notice the function keys displayed in line 25 (at the bottom of the screen). This line tells you the meaning of the F1 through F10 keys located on the left side of the keyboard. You can change the meanings of these keys using the KEY command. For example, to define F1 as the EDIT key, enter the following.

KEY 1, "EDIT"

Now, pressing F1 will cause EDIT to be displayed. This will save you typing time.

Another method of increasing your typing speed is through the ALT key. If you hold the ALT key down at the same time that you type the first letter of certain key words in BASICA, the interpreter will complete the spelling for you. Here are a few of the key words that you can abbreviate. For a complete listing, see the BASIC manual.

ALT + A = AUTO
ALT + F = FOR
ALT + G = GOTO
ALT + I = INPUT
ALT + K = KEY
ALT + N = NEXT
ALT + P = PRINT
ALT + R = RUN

Finally, remember to save your program on disk using the SAVE command (or F4):

SAVE "TAXES", A

This saves the current program in a file called TAXES.BAS in ASCII format. To retrieve it, use the LOAD command:

LOAD "TAXES"

To erase the current program from RAM, use the NEW command:

NEW

To see what program files might be on the diskette use the FILES command:

FILES

or

FILES "B:*.*"

This last example displays all files on drive B.

## EDLIN Line Editor

To activate the line editor from DOS, simply type the command followed by the name of the file you want to create or edit:

A > EDLIN TEST.PAS

This will cause a new file called TEST.PAS (containing a Pascal source language program) to be created and stored:

A > EDLIN B:TEST.PAS

The EDLIN program creates a new file if none existed before, or it reads the old file into RAM if it exists.

After you have entered, modified, or examined the file, you can exit the line editor. This will cause the previous file to be renamed with the extension .BAK. Thus, a backup copy always exists which you can use to recover from an editing error. (This file must be renamed before it can be read by EDLIN.)

EDLIN is a typical line editor. That is, it can only "point at" a single line at a time. The "current line" is the line that is currently being singled out by EDLIN. The current line is marked with an * in column one.

The editor commands of EDLIN operate on the current line cursor. To move the cursor to another line, all you have to do is enter the line number followed by an ENTER key. The current line is displayed on one line and its line number is displayed on a second line. You can use the arrow keys to move over the current line, and as described before, you can edit the current line.

The current line can be edited by using the arrow keys, the INS (insert), and DEL (delete) keys. If you move over the current line using the arrow keys, the current characters in the line will be displayed. If you insert new text, then the new text will be inserted at the position indicated by the screen cursor. Similarly, text is deleted at the position indicated by the screen cursor each time the DEL key is used.

To begin entering text, or to insert an entire line or lines of text, use the insert command:

li

9i

These commands cause a new line of text to be inserted immediately before line 1 and 9. Similarly, you can delete entire lines as shown below:

10,15d

This causes lines 10 through 15 to be deleted. The remaining lines are renumbered to "fill the gap" left by these departing lines.

All commands that move the current line cursor are entered by specifying the line or lines affected, followed by the command letter:

⟨number of line⟩     ⟨command letter⟩

Thus, the following commands use one or more line numbers, L# followed by a single command letter.

## EDLIN COMMANDS

| | |
|---|---|
| L# A | Append L# lines to the text by reading them from disk. This is used in files that are too large to fit into RAM. |
| L#, L# D | Delete lines L# to L#. If one of these is missing, start from line 1, or end on the last line. |

L#                              Edit line number L#.

L# I                            Insert new lines beginning with line
                                number L#. If line L# already exists,
                                move it down to make room.

L#, L# L                        List lines L# through L# on the
                                screen.

L#, L# ? R s1 (F6) s2           This is the search and replace com-
                                mand. It operates on all lines from L#
                                to L#. The ? means to ask for permis-
                                sion to do the replace each time a
                                match is found. The pattern in s1 is
                                found and replaced by s2. The function
                                key F6 is used to separate the two
                                strings. If ? is omitted, the replace-
                                ments are done without your permis-
                                sion. If (F6)s2 is omitted, the string s1
                                is deleted from every line containing
                                it.

L#, L# ? S s1                   Search for a line containing the pattern
                                s1. If ? is omitted, the first match halts
                                the command. If ? is included, then the
                                search continues if you want it to. The
                                line containing s1 becomes the current
                                line.

L# W                            Write L# lines to diskette. This is used
                                with L# A to edit files that will not fit
                                into RAM.

Finally, to exit from EDLIN use one of the following commands that
do not modify the current line cursor.

E                               End edit and save text in RAM.

Q                                                   Quit edit, but do not save text.


   To illustrate some of the most useful EDLIN commands, consider the
following examples.


1,L                                                 This displays a full page of text on the
                                                    screen.

5L                                                  This causes line 5 to be displayed and
                                                    edited. It makes line 5 the current line.

,5D                                                 Delete all lines from the current line
                                                    through 5.

1I                                                  Begin inserting text at line #1. This is
                                                    used to build a new file, or insert lines
                                                    at the top of an existing file. To exit
                                                    this mode, use the CTRL + C or
                                                    CTRL + BREAK key pair.

10,20 ? R cat (F6) dog                              Replace all occurrences of cat in lines
                                                    10 through 20 with dog.

   Now you should be ready to enter either a BASIC or Pascal program
into a file prior to processing it with a language translator. If you plan to
use BASICA as language translator, then read the next section for an
overview of BASIC. If, however, you are eager to learn about Pascal,
then review the EDLIN commands given here, and then turn to the section that reviews the Pascal compiler.

## THE BASICA INTERPRETER

   Many excellent manuals and textbooks exist that teach the elements of
BASIC programming. Therefore, we are not going to repeat the topics
that are easily obtainable somewhere else. Instead, we will present a
collection of program segments for doing a variety of useful things on
your IBM Personal computer. If you are a novice programmer, then you
can learn to program in BASIC by reading the following program segments. If you are an experienced programmer, then you can learn a variety of programming techniques that will help you to use BASIC more

effectively. But before beginning, what can you do with the BASICA interpreter?

## Commands

These commands are accessible to you while in the BASICA interpreter program. This program is started by typing BASICA while in the DOS command level. Once the BASICA program begins to execute, you can type any one of the following commands to the BASICA interpreter, and they will be immediately carried out.

| | |
|---|---|
| AUTO | line numbers generated, automatically |
| BLOAD | get and load into RAM a binary program |
| BSAVE | save a machine language program |
| CLEAR | set program variables to zero, and empty strings |
| CONT | continue an interrupted program |
| DELETE | delete one or more lines of BASIC program |
| EDIT | edit a line of BASIC program |
| FILES | display file names on diskette |
| KILL | erase files from diskette |
| LIST | display part or all of a BASIC program |
| LLIST | print part or all of a BASIC program |
| LOAD | copy a program from diskette into RAM |
| MERGE | combine two BASIC programs |
| NAME | rename a diskette file |
| NEW | erase current program from RAM |
| RENUM | renumber current program in RAM |
| RESET | close all diskette files |
| RUN | run the current program or load and run. |
| SAVE | copy RAM program onto diskette |
| SYSTEM | leave the interpreter and get back to DOS |
| TRON | turn on trace (debug) option |
| TROFF | turn off trace option |

Remember, these commands can be performed from the keyboard prior to running a program, or during a program's execution. The next collection of commands are actually BASICA statements that you must use in order to write a program. We will show many examples of their use, but first, what are they?

## Statements

The following is a complete list of the statements that BASICA directly interprets. These statements are discussed in greater detail in the examples below. They are also explained in depth in the IBM Personal Computer BASIC Programming Manual.

| | |
|---|---|
| BEEP | sound a "beep" on the internal speaker |
| CALL | execute a machine language subprogram |
| CHAIN | execute another BASIC program from the diskette |
| CIRCLE | draw a circle, ellipse, wedge, pie. |
| CLOSE | close a diskette file |
| CLS | clear (erase) screen |
| COLOR | select foreground, background colors |
| COM | enable/disable communications interrupts |
| COMMON | passed variables between chained programs |
| DATA | list of input data values |
| DATE$ | set the calendar date |
| DEFFN | define a function |
| DEFSEG | define a segment of memory |
| DEFUSR | define starting address for USR call |
| DIM | define size of arrays |
| DRAW | draw from a graphics command, as follows: |

GRAPHIC COMMANDS FOR DRAW

| | |
|---|---|
| Un | move up $n$ steps |
| Dn | move down $n$ steps |
| Ln | move left $n$ steps |
| Rn | move right in $n$ steps |
| En | move diagonally (NE) $n$ steps |
| Fn | move diagonally (SE) $n$ steps |
| Gn | move diagonally (SW) $n$ steps |
| Hn | move diagonally (NW) $n$ steps |
| Mn,m | move to point (n,m) or add (n,m) to position |
| Bn,m | same as M, but no point is painted |

| | |
|---|---|
| Nn,m | same as M, but return to original point when done |
| An | set angle in multiples of 90 degrees |
| Cn | set color to *n* |
| Sn | set step size (scale factor) *n* |
| Xs$ | execute substring s$ containing graphic commands |
| | |
| END | end program |
| ERASE | reclaim memory from unused arrays |
| ERROR | set-off simulated error condition |
| FIELD | define file record format |
| FOR | FOR loop to repeat section of program |
| GET | get a record from direct access file |
| GET | get graph from screen |
| GOSUB | execute a subprogram |
| GOTO | jump to another statement |
| IF | IF-THEN-ELSE selection of next statement |
| INPUT | enter data from keyboard or file |
| KEY | display, redefine, or trap on key press |
| LET | assign a value to a variable |
| LINE | draw a line, box, or solid box |
| LINE INPUT | enter an entire line at keyboard |
| LOCATE | position screen cursor to a screen position |
| LPRINT | print a line on the printer |
| LPRINT USING | formatted line printer output |
| LSET | left-justify a string into a file buffer |
| MID$ | substring insert or extract |
| MOTOR | control cassette motor |
| NEXT | end a FOR loop |
| ON | enable interrupt conditions or multiway branch |
| OPEN | prepare disk file or communications line for data |
| OPTION BASE | start array subscripts at 0 or 1 |
| OUT | output a byte to a port |
| PAINT | fill-in area on graphics screen with color |
| PEN | enable/disable light pen |

| | |
|---|---|
| POKE | put a value in a byte in RAM |
| PRINT | output to screen or file |
| PRINT USING | formatted print |
| PRESET | plot a point in background graphics color |
| PSET | plot a point in given color |
| PUT | write a record to direct file |
| PUT | display an image on screen |
| RANDOMIZE | start a random number sequence |
| READ | get data from a DATA statement |
| REM | remark |
| RESTORE | reset DATA statements |
| RESUME | return from an error trap routine |
| RETURN | return from a normal subroutine |
| RSET | right-justify string into file buffer |
| SCREEN | select text or graphics screen for display |
| SOUND | generate sound from speaker |
| STOP | stop program execution |
| STRIG | enable/disable joystick button |
| SWAP | exchange values of two variables |
| TIME$ | set clock |
| WAIT | delay |
| WEND | end of WHILE statement loop |
| WHILE | loop as long as a condition is true |
| WRITE | display or output data to screen or file |

These commands are used to process data that are stored in RAM or in a diskette file. Data are stored in a variety of forms, however, and before it can be processed, we must know its **type.** This is the topic of the next section.

## BASICA Data Types

A *type* is a collection of values. Thus, a value in BASICA belongs to one type. An integer value, for example, belongs to the *type integer* because it is encoded like all other integer values in the computer memory.

Typed variables are used in programming to save memory space, decrease execution time, and make programs more understandable. We can think of a type as a kind of a unit of measurement. For example, to add 15 inches to 3 feet, we must convert all units of measurement into the same "type." We could convert feet into inches and then add 15 inches to 36 inches to get 51 inches. We must convert the data into identical units of measurement before a meaningful addition can be done.

BASICA uses the following types as a means of storing data:

**Integer (%)** Integer values from −32,768 to +32,767.

**Single-precision (!)** Real values up to 7 digits in length.

**Double-precision (#)** Real values over 7 digits in length.

**String variables ($)** Character string values up to 255 characters in length.

**Buffer variables ($)** Disk file buffer storage up to 128 characters in length.

**Array variables** A group of values all of identical type, but accessible through the same variable name.

Obviously it is necessary to be able to convert from one type to another in order for a program to perform arithmetic and so on. This is done using a set of type conversion rules similar to the inches-to-feet rule in the example, above.

**Rule #1** String ($) and buffer ($) values are converted into numbers using special functions: CVI, CVS, CVD which return integers, single-precision, and double-precision, respectively.

Numbers are converted into strings using special functions MKI\$, MKS\$, MKD\$ which convert from integers, single-precision, and double-precision numbers into string equivalents.

**Rule #2** Constants are always converted into the type corresponding to the variable which contains them. For example, the single-precision number 35.8 is converted into 35 when stored in variable I% because I% is an integer variable.

**Rule #3** Expressions are always evaluated in the most precise type, where the most precise type is double-precision, followed by single-precision, and then integer last. For example, I% + A! + B# is evaluated in two stages: I% + A! is done in single-precision and then converted into double-precision so that B# can be added to the sum.

**Rule #4** Logical operators convert their operands to integers and return integer results (real numbers are rounded). Thus, A% AND B# is evaluated by converting the values in A% and B# into 16-bit integers (rounded). If they will not round off to 16-bits, an error occurs.

Here are some examples of types and type conversion in BASICA.

A = I%               Convert the integer stored in I% into a single-
                     precision number stored in A!

I% = A!              Convert (round) the single-precision value stored
                     in A! into an integer stored in I%.

I$ = MKI$(I%)        Convert the integer value in I% into a 2-character
                     string stored in I$

I% = CVI (I$)        Convert the two-character string I$ into an in-
                     teger.

A# = I% − B!         Evaluate I% − B! in single-precision, then con-
                     vert to double-precision to store in variable A#.

The list of types above includes two kinds of strings. A **buffer variable** is a special string that contains characters waiting to be transferred between diskette and RAM. The buffer variable defines a region of RAM that holds diskette information. During an input operation, the buffer is the place where the diskette information is recorded as a string. During an output operation, the buffer is treated like a string by the program. When this string is written to disk, it is copied from RAM onto diskette. We will discuss this in greater detail in a subsequent section.

An **array** is simply a collection of values, all of the same type. Hence it is possible to define an array in BASICA as a block of integer, single-, double-precision, or string values. This is done using the DIM statement:

$$\text{DIM } A\%(10), B!(20), C\#(15), D\$(8)$$

In this DIM statement we have set aside 11 integers corresponding to A%, twenty-one single-precision real numbers corresponding to B!, sixteen double-precision real numbers corresponding to C#, and nine strings corresponding to D$.

In order to select one of the values from an array of values, we must use an integer valued **subscript.** Hence, A%(3) selects the third integer in A%, D$(5) selects the fifth string from D$, and C#(0) selects the zero-th number in C#.

Arrays are very useful data structures because they enable you to write a program that can repeat identical operations on different values within an array by simply changing the value of a subscript. Indeed, a subscript can be computed from an expression as illustrated, below:

$$A\%(I\% + 2) = A\%(I\% * J\% - 3)$$

The minimum value of an array subscript is zero, and the maximum value is limited by the amount of memory available or 32767. Hence, A%(0) refers to the zero-th integer value stored in A%, and A%(5280) refers to the 5280th integer value stored in A%.

An array may also have up to 255 subscripts. Thus,

$$DIM\ X(35,\ 10,\ 3)$$

is a three-dimensional array of size 36*11*4 equals 1584 numbers. To select one number from these we must specify three subscripts:

$$X(I\%,\ J\%,\ K\%)$$

This selects one number at position

$$I\% * 11 * 4 + J\% * 4 + K\%$$

That is, X(0,0,0,) is stored at position zero, and X(35,10,3) is stored at position 1583 in X.

## Console I/O Statements

There are two classes of I/O statements you can use to do I/O at the keyboard, CRT and line printer. The unformatted statements are simple to use, but do not give you control over formatting. The formatted statements are more sophisticated, and allow you to format output to the screen and line printer.

$$PRINT\quad or\quad LPRINT$$
$$INPUT$$

These are used to send the values of variables to the screen (PRINT), printer (LPRINT), or accept values as input from the keyboard (INPUT). Double-quoted strings can be used in the PRINT and LPRINT statements in order to prompt or label values as shown in the examples below:

```
100 PRINT "Enter size =" ; : INPUT S%
200 LPRINT "Enter size ="; S%
```

This sequence causes the prompt

$$Enter\ size\ =$$

to be displayed on the screen. Since a semicolon follows this prompt in statement 100, the input value is taken from the same line as the prompt. The colon is used to separate two lines of BASICA.

The value of S% is accepted and line 200 prints the prompt as well as the value of S% on the printer.

We can also use formatted I/O in order to tidy up the display/printed page. The following statements are used for formatted I/O:

PRINT USING   or   LPRINT<br>
LINE INPUT   or   INPUT

The LINE INPUT statement is used only for string-valued inputs. For example, to enter the value of Y$, use LINE INPUT with a prompt as shown below:

1400   LINE INPUT "Do you want more data?" ; Y$

The LINE INPUT statement cannot be used to enter numerical values, though. The following illustrates what you must do to enter both string and numeric data:

```
100 LINE INPUT "Strike RETURN when ready" ; Y$
200 PRINT "Enter size =" ; : INPUT S%
300 LINE INPUT "Is this correct?" ; Y$
400 LINE INPUT "Enter name =" ; N$
500 LINE INPUT "Is this correct?" ; Y$
```

The PRINT USING and LPRINT USING statements let you decide how many columns each output value may consume. The most common use of PRINT USING is to format numeric values. Here are some examples.

```
100 PRINT USING "##.###"; A
200 PRINT USING "+##.##"; B
300 PRINT USING "$$ ###. ##"; C
```

The ##.### pattern in line 100 causes a total of six columns to be reserved for the output value. The decimal point is placed as shown (3 decimal digits to the right of the decimal point).

Line 200 reserves a column for a plus or minus sign. Line 300 shows how to force a leading $ sign to be printed. Both lines force the output value to be rounded to two decimal digits.

The following is a brief list of format control symbols for use in a PRINT USING or LPRINT USING statement.

| | |
|---|---|
| ! | Print first character of a string only |
| \ n spaces\ | Print n + 2 characters of string |
| & | Variable-length string |
| # | Digit position or blank |
| . | Decimal point |
| + | Sign |
| − | Minus sign after number (on the trailing right end of number) |
| ** | Fill with asterisks |

| $$ | Print dollar sign |
| ∧∧∧ | Leave room for exponent part, E + XX |
| % | Print % if number too large. |

## Control Statements

A BASICA program normally executes one statement after another. However, programs of much greater flexability and power can be written using a handful of control statements. A **control statement** is any statement that governs the flow of control through a program. A control statement determines which statement is to be executed next.

The following control statements govern the flow of control through BASICA.

**STOP,END** The program stops, all files are closed, and returns to the user.

**FOR-NEXT, WHILE-WEND** The program loops (repeats) over a segment of statements.

**IF-THEN, IF-THEN-ELSE** Control flows along one of two possible paths. Either the THEN clause or the ELSE clause is executed next.

**GOTO, ON-GOTO, GOSUB, ON-GOSUB** The program executes the statement indicated by the GO statement next.

These statements are illustrated in the following examples.

Read An Array of Values

```
100 DIM DATA (100)
200 FOR I% = 1 to 100
210     INPUT DATA (I%)
220 NEXT I%
```

Another way to do the same operation using the WHILE-WEND statement is shown below:

```
100 DIM DATA (100)
200 I% = 1
210 WHILE I% <= 100
220 INPUT DATA (I%)
230 I% = I% + 1
240 WEND
```

We can make a segment of program into a **subroutine** by adding a RETURN statement to it. For example,

```
900 FOR I% = 1 TO N%
910    PRINT DATA (I%)
920 NEXT I%
930 RETURN
```

The GOSUB statement is used to "call" this segment whenever the values in DATA are to be printed. For example,

```
100 GOSUB 900
```
. . .
```
550 GOSUB 900
```
. . .
```
750 GOSUB 900
```

Each time a GOSUB 900 is executed, statements 900–930 are executed and then control returns to the statement following the GOSUB. Hence, the next statements executed after a RETURN in the example above are 101, 551, and 751 respectively.

The GOTO and ON-GOTO statements branch to another statement, but do *not* return from the branch. Hence, the GOTO and ON-GOTO cause flow of control to permanently move to a different part of the program.

Here are several useful examples showing how to apply these control statements.

### Menu Handler

```
140 FOR I% = 1 to 24: PRINT : NEXT I% ' Clear CR
150 PRINT " [1]. Enter Accounts"
160 PRINT " [2]. Print Checks"
170 PRINT " [3]. Print Bills"
180 PRINT "Enter selection 1,2,or 3 "; : INPUT N%
190 IF (1 <= N%) AND (N% >= 3) THEN 200 ELSE 140
200 ON N% GOTO 2000, 3000, 4000
```

The menu handler prints a menu of options on the CRT. The user enters a number corresponding to the desired selection. This number is stored in N%, and then used to GOTO 2000, 3000, or 4000 depending on the value of N%. Notice in line 190 how N% is tested for a valid N%. If N% does not contain 1, 2, or 3, the menu is repeated.

## File I/O Statements

There are two kinds of files in BASICA:

1. Sequential (opened as I or O)
2. Random (opened as R)

The sequential file is accessed sequentially beginning with the first record of the file. To read the N-th record of a sequential file, a program must access and read the first (N-1) records of the file.

A random access file is much like an array, because to access the N-th record, a program must set up a buffer string and perform a get or put operation, and the N-th record is immediately retrieved. For more information on file structures turn to Chapter 7. The following examples illustrate the ideas.

## Sequential File Output

```
1020 OPEN "O", 2, "HEADER.DAT" 'Open #2 for output
1025 PRINT #2, ST$; ","; ROOT%; LNG%; M$
1030 CLOSE 2
```

This outputs a single record to disk file HEADER.DAT. The record contains string ST$, integers ROOT%, and LNG%, and string M$. Notice how the semicolons are used to separate values in the record, and in particular notice the "," inserted between ST$ and ROOT%. This comma is necessary to terminate the ST$ string.

You can write a program that outputs many records by simply repeating the PRINT statement. Thus, file number 2 above can hold many records as shown below.

```
1000 OPEN "0", 2, "HEADER.DAT"
1020 FOR I% = 1 TO N%
1025    PRINT #2, ST$(I%); ","; ROOT%(I%);
                 LNG%(I%); M$(I%); ","
1030 NEXT I%
1040 CLOSE 2
```

Similarly, to input the array of values as indicated above, you must repeatedly execute an INPUT # statement.

## Sequential File Input

```
2025 OPEN "I",2,"HEADER.DAT"
2025 FOR I% = 1 TO N%
2030 INPUT #2, ST$(I%), ROOT%(I%), LNG%(I%), M$(I%)
2040 NEXT I%
2050 CLOSE 2
```

This segment of program differs from the output segment because no semicolons or "," characters are needed in line 2030. These are used strictly for separating strings and numbers from one another in each record. The input segment relies on them to separate strings and numbers.

## Random Access Output

A random access file must be formatted as a collection of fixed-length records, each record containing character strings alone. No numeric values are allowed in a random file! This means we must convert every number into a string before writing it to disk, and then convert the strings back into numbers after reading a random file record.

The random file statements include an OPEN and CLOSE statement as before plus a FIELD statement for formatting each record (buffer variable), and GET/PUT statements for transmitting the buffer from/to disk.

```
1135 OPEN "R",1,FNAME$
1140 FIELD 1, 127 AS R$
```

These two statements establish a file as random (R), number one (1), and named FNAME$. The FIELD statement defines a buffer variable R$ as a 127 character long string. The buffer variable will be used by the program to move data between the disk and the program. For example, suppose FLAG%, array ARC(10), and a string array KEY$(10) are to be output as a single record. String REC$ receives the converted output:

```
180 FOR IN% = 1 TO 10
181   CH% = SIZE% * (IN% − 1)
182   FLAG$ = "E"
183   MID$(REC$, CH% + 1, 1) = FLAG$
184   MID$(REC$, CH% + 2,SIZE%) = KEY$(IN%)
185   MID$(REC$, CH% + SIZE% + 2,4) = MKS$(ARC(IN%))
186 NEXT IN%
190 LSET R$ = REC$
195 PUT 1, P%
199 RETURN
```

This subroutine builds a string called REC$ from a one-character FLAG$ value, an array of two-character integers called ARC, and an array of SIZE% character strings called KEY$. The MID$ function inserts the converted values into REC$ at intervals of CH% characters. Note the use of MKS$ to convert from numeric to character form.

The LSET statement in line 190 copies the string in REC$ into the field buffer called R$. LSET means to left-justify the string.

Next, the buffer R$ is sent to record number P% in line 195. File number 1 is written in position P% by transmitting the buffer to the diskette.

## Random File Input

Assuming we have opened file #1 as an "R" file, and assuming we have stored each record as shown above, the following causes the data to be read back into the program:

```
130 GET 1, P%
131 LSET REC$ = R$      'put into string
132 FOR IN% = 1 to 10
133   CH% = SIZE% * (IN% − 1)
134   FLAG$ = MID$(REC$, CH% + 1, 1)
136   KEY$(IN%) = MID$(REC$, CH% + 2, SIZE%)
137   ARC(IN%) = CVS(MID$(REC$, CH% + SIZE% + 2, 4)
138 NEXT IN%
140 RETURN
```

Notice how the LSET is used to copy the buffer into REC$. The MID$ and CVS functions are used to extract a part of the string from the buffer and then convert back to the proper type.

## Program Debugging

Once you have designed and written a program, the next step is to enter it and see if it works. Most likely it will not function correctly the first time. Therefore, you must locate and correct all errors before your program is completed.

Two BASICA commands are useful for debugging a new program. They are listed below.

**TRON** Turn on trace. This causes the statement number of every statement that is executed to be displayed on the CRT screen as your program runs.

**TROFF** Turn off trace.

In some cases an error cannot be anticipated. Thus, it is possible for an error to occur much later (after you think your program works). This situation can be handled by putting an error recovery subroutine in the program itself.

```
10 ON ERROR GOTO 3999
```

This statement causes the subroutine at statement 3999 to be executed whenever any error occurs during program execution. To turn the ERROR trap above off:

```
99 ON ERROR GOTO 0
```

This disables the error trap, so subsequent errors cause the program to terminate, as before.

## LIST OF BUILT-IN FUNCTIONS

| Name | Meaning and Example |
| --- | --- |
| ABS | Absolute value, ABS (X) |
| ASC | ASCII value, ASC(X$) |
| ATN | Arctangent in radians, ATN(X) |
| CDBL | Convert to double-precision, CDBL(X) |
| CHR$ | ASCII character, CHR$ (X) |
| CINT | Convert to integer, CINT(X) |
| COS | Cosine in radians, COS(X) |
| CSNG | Convert to single-precision, CSNG(X) |
| CSRLIN | Row number of the cursor position |
| CVI,CVS,CVD | Convert string to number, CVS(X$) |
| EOF | End of file, EOF(2) |
| ERL,ERR | Line number, and error code of an execution error |
| EXP | Raise e to power X, EXP(X) |
| FIX | Truncate to integer, FIX(X) |
| FRE | Amount of RAM remaining, FRE(O) |
| HEX$ | Convert to hexidecimal as a string, HEX$(X) |
| INKEY$ | Input a character from keyboard, INKEY$ |
| INP | Read a byte from part I, INP(I) |
| INPUT$ | Read a string from keyboard, INPUT$(X) |
| INSTR | Search stringX$ for Y$, INSTR(X$,Y$) |
| INT | Integer part of X, INT(X) |
| LEFT$ | Left-most I characters of X$, LEFT$(X$,I) |
| LEN | Length of X$, LEN(X$) |
| LOC | Return next record number of file I,LOC(I) |
| LOF | Length of file extent, LOF(1) |
| LOG | Natural logarithm of X, LOG (X) |
| LPOS | Position of line printer, LPOS (O) |
| MID$ | Return J character beginning at character position I, from X$, MID$(X$,I,J) |

| | |
|---|---|
| MKI$,MKS$,MKD$ | Convert from numbers to character strings, MKI$(X%) |
| OCT$ | Return octal value as string, OCT$(X) |
| PEEK | Read RAM, directly, PEEK(X%) |
| PEN | Read light pen |
| POINT | Read color number from graphics screen |
| POS | Return CRT cursor position, POS(O) |
| RIGHT$ | Extract right-most I characters from string X$, RIGHT$(X$,I) |
| RND | Return random number between 0 and 1, RND(X) |
| SGN | Return sign of number, SGN(X) |
| SIN | Sine in radians, SIN(X) |
| SPACE$ | Return a string of spaces, space$(X) |
| SPC | Print I blanks on CRT, SPC(1) |
| SQR | Square root, SQR(X) |
| STR$ | Convert X to string, STR$(X) |
| STRING$ | Return a string of identical characters, STRING$ (I,X$) |
| TAB | Space I places, TAB(I) |
| TAN | Tangent in radians, TAN(X) |
| USR | Call machine language routine, USR (X) |
| VAL | Convert X$ to number, VAL(X$) |
| VARPTR | Return address of a variable, VARPTR(X) |

## A Complete Example: Disk Sorter

Figure 6-1 contains a complete program for building a random file containing words and phrases of up to WIDE% characters each. This program is a useful piece of software for entering long lists of names, dictionary words, etc. and then sorting them into ascending (alphabetical) order. The list of words can be printed out at any time.

The main purpose of this program, however, is to illustrate BASICA. Therefore, the following descriptions should be carefully read along with the program itself in Figure 6-1. The line numbers below correspond to the line numbers of the program.

**10–35** This is a program heading for documentation purposes. The name of the file containing this program is FILESORT.BAS. The method used is called "quickersort."

**50** The quickersort method for sorting a list uses an array called STACK% to hold the record numbers (beginning and ending) of subjects yet to be sorted. Since this is a first-in-last-out kind of array, it is called a pushdown stack. If very large lists (greater than 100) are sorted, it may be necessary to increase this array to 50, 100, etc in length.

**60–85** This is the menu which prompts the user. If J% is entered as a 1, then control passes to statement 100, J% equals 2 causes control to pass to statement 300, etc. If J% is greater than 4, control falls through to STOP (line 90).

**100–105** The heading for the input routine. This routine is used to enter the original (unordered) list and store it on diskette.

**110–128** The user must enter the name of the list and the maximum length of a word. This name becomes the filename. The size of records in the file is equal to WIDE%.

**129–135** This is an example of opening a file named F$ for random access. The file number is 1, and the size of each record in the file is set to WIDE%. The field statement establishes REC$ as the buffer string for file number 1.

**140** P% is the record number used to access the random file.

**145–153** Each word is entered (up to WIDE% characters) and stored in K$.

**155** The string in K$ is copied into the string buffer, REC$.

**160** Stop the input program if no string is entered by the user.

**165–170** Increment the record pointer and write the string buffer REC$ to disk file number 1.

**175** Return to 153 to get another word, K$

**240–250** This routine is executed when all processing is done and the files are updated and closed.

**260–265** Close the file containing the word list and open another file named H$ to update the header file. The header file simply contains an integer which is equal to the length of the list, and an integer which is equal to the record size.

**270–275** Write the length of the list to sequential file number 1, and then close the file.

**280** Return to the main menu.

**300–325** The quickersort method of sorting. It works as follows. Select a middle word initially, and use it to divide the list into two (roughly) equal parts. The "left" side sublist must be rearranged so that it contains only words less than the middle word. The "right" side sublist must be rearranged so that it contains only words greater than the middle word. Search the left list for a word out of place, and exchange it with a right sublist word that is out of place. When quickersort cannot find any more words to exchange, it cuts the sublists into two sublists and saves the start and stop locations of one sublist in STACK%. The other sublist is processed in the same way as before: select a middle word and exchange words between the left and right sublists. This process continues until all sublists have been put into order. The overall list is sorted when all of its sublists are sorted.

**330–345** Get the name of the file containing the list to be sorted and make sure that it is correct. The name of the header file has an extension .HED, and the name of the list has an extension .DAT.

**350** Initially the pushdown stack is empty, thus, TOS% is zero.

**355** Input the length of the random file. N%, and size of records, WIDE%.

**360–365** Open the random file containing the list.

**370–375** Allocate WIDE% characters of memory space to each of the working variables.

**380–450** This is the quickersort method. It stores the beginning and ending record numbers (L%, RIGHT%) in STACK% until they are needed. Subroutine 1000 stores (L%, RIGHT%), and subroutine 1100 fetches them back as (LEFT%, RIGHT%). Subroutine 1200 does the actual exchanging needed to place words in their proper sublists.

**460–470** When the sorting is done, close the file and return to the main menu.

**500–525** The print routine allows you to output the list anytime before or after it is sorted.

**530–570** Get the file names, open the files, and read the length N%, and width, WIDE%.

**575–580** Initially allocate space for K$, and wait for the printer to be turned on.

**585–610** Print the list. Access each record of file number 1, directly.

**615–625** Close the file and return to the menu.

**700–780** Add to the list. Similar to input routine.

**1000–1035** The push routine for saving the record locations (L%, RIGHT%)

**1100–1135** The pop routine for restoring record locations (LEFT%, RIGHT%) when it is time to sort them.

**1200-1215** The exchange subroutine locates all words in the left sublist which are larger than MIDL$, and swaps them with words in the right sublist.

**1220-1230** Initialize variables and get the middle element from the random file.

**1235** Repeat the exchange until all candidates for swapping have been exchanged.

**1240-1255** Find a word in the left sublist that is too big. Save it in S$.

**1300-1315** Find a word in the right sublist that is too small. Save it in R$.

**1322-1350** Exchange S$ and R$. Also increment the record number pointers so we don't find the same pair again.

**1400** If the two searches (up from the left, and down from the right) meet each other, then the exchange is done.

**1410** Return to statement 420.

```
10  REM  -----------------------------------
15  REM
20  REM            FILESORT.BAS
25  REM            Enter, sort, and print
30  REM            a list of words using
35  REM            the Quickersort method
40  REM
45  REM  -----------------------------------
50  DIM STACK%( 100 )     'pushdown stack
55  REM -------- restart here ----------
60  CLS: PRINT"[ 1]. Enter a list of words."
65  PRINT"[ 2]. Sort the list of words."
70  PRINT"[ 3]. Print the list of words."
72  PRINT"[ 4]. Add to existing list."
75  PRINT"[ 5]. Stop"
80  PRINT : PRINT"Enter 1... to 5 :"; : INPUT J%
85  ON J% GOTO 100, 300, 500, 700
90  STOP
100 REM  -----------------------------------
101 REM          Input a random file of
102 REM          words.Width% = max length
103 REM  -----------------------------------
104 REM
110    CLS: LINE INPUT"Enter name of list : "; F$
115    LINE INPUT"Correct(Y/N) ?"; Y$
120    IF Y$ <> "Y" AND Y$<>"y" THEN 110
125 H$ = F$ + ".hed" : F$ = F$ + ".dat"
126    INPUT"Enter max. word length: ";WIDE%
127    LINE INPUT"Correct(Y/N) ? ";Y$
128    IF Y$ <> "Y" AND Y$ <> "y" THEN 126
```

**Figure 6-1.** File sort program.

Figure 6-1 continued.

```
129 REM --------open, initialize file ---
130   OPEN "R",1,F$,WIDE%
135   FIELD 1, WIDE% AS REC$
140   P% = 0
141 REM ------------------------------
145   CLS: PRINT"Enter ENTER key to stop."
150   PRINT"Enter up to";WIDE%;" characters : "
152 REM ---- repeat until k$ is null ---
153   LINE INPUT">"; K$
155   LSET REC$ = K$          'fill buffer
160   IF LEN( K$ ) = 0 THEN 250
165   P% = P% + 1 'direct access location
170   PUT 1, P%    'write to file
175 GOTO 153      'get another word
240 REM ----------------------------------
245 REM           Write header file
250 REM ------------------------------
255 PRINT"Done. Writing header file."
260 CLOSE 1
265   OPEN "O",1,H$
270   PRINT #1,P%;WIDE% 'save length
275   CLOSE 1
280 GOTO 55                 'restart menu
300 REM -----------------------------
305 REM
310 REM           Quickersort
315 REM
320 REM -----------------------------
325 REM
330   LINE INPUT"Enter name of list : "; F$
335   LINE INPUT"Correct(Y/N) ? "; Y$
340   IF Y$ <> "Y" AND Y$ <> "y" THEN 330
345 H$ = F$ + ".hed": F$ = F$ + ".dat"
350 TOS% = 0             'initial stack
352 REM ---read header file ----------
355   OPEN "I",1,H$ : INPUT #1,N%,WIDE% : CLOSE 1
358 REM ---open word list file --------
360   OPEN "R",1,F$,WIDE%
365   FIELD 1,WIDE% AS REC$
366 REM ---allocate string space ------
370   R$=SPACE$(WIDE%):S$=SPACE$(WIDE%)
375   K$=SPACE$(WIDE%):MIDL$=SPACE$(WIDE%)
378 REM
380 REM ---- start quickersorting -----
382 REM
385 L% = 1: RIGHT%=N%: GOSUB 1000 'push
390 REM ------- loop here -----------
395 REM
400 GOSUB 1100               'pop left%,right%
405 REM ------------inner loop--------
410 GOSUB 1200              'exchange
```

(Continued on next page)

Figure 6-1 continued.

```
420 IF NEWL% < RIGHT% THEN L% = NEWL% : GOSUB 1000
430 RIGHT% = NEWR%
440 IF LEFT% < RIGHT% THEN 410
442 REM --- keep user informed --------
445   PRINT TOS%/2;" lists to do"
447 REM
450 IF TOS% <> 0 THEN 400          'end loop
455 PRINT F$; " is sorted."
460 CLOSE 1
470 GOTO 55                        'restart menu
500 REM ------------------------------
505 REM
510 REM          Print list
515 REM
520 REM ------------------------------
525 REM
530   LINE INPUT"Enter name of list : "; F$
535   LINE INPUT"Correct(Y/N) ? ";Y$
540   IF Y$<> "Y" AND Y$ <>"y" THEN 530
545 H$ = F$ + ".hed": F$ = F$ + ".dat"
547 REM ---get file length and width ---
550   OPEN "I",1,H$
555   INPUT #1,N%,WIDE%
557 REM ---open direct access file -----
560   CLOSE 1
565   OPEN "R",1,F$, WIDE%
570   FIELD 1, WIDE% AS REC$
571 REM ------------------------------
575 K$ = SPACE$( WIDE% )
580 LINE INPUT"Printer ready ? ";Y$
585 LPRINT"List = ";F$
590 LPRINT : LPRINT
592 REM --access, fetch, and print -----
595 FOR I% = 1 TO N%
600   GET 1, I% : LSET K$ = REC$
605   LPRINT K$
610 NEXT I%
615 CLOSE 1
620 LINE INPUT"Ready ?";Y$
625 GOTO 55                        'restart menu
700 REM ------------------------------
705 REM
710 REM          Add to list
715 REM
720 REM ------------------------------
725 REM
730   CLS : LINE INPUT"Enter name of list : ";F$
735   LINE INPUT"Correct(Y/N) ? ";Y$
740   IF Y$ <> "Y" AND Y$ <> "y" THEN 730
745 H$ = F$ + ".hed" : F$ = F$ + ".dat"
746 REM ---get length and width of list-
750 OPEN "I",1,H$
```

Figure 6-1 continued.

```
755  INPUT #1,N%,WIDE%
760  CLOSE 1
762 REM ---prepare to append to list---
765    OPEN "R",1,F$,WIDE%
770    FIELD 1,WIDE% AS REC$
775    P% = N%
780 GOTO 145              'append
1000 REM -----------------------------
1005 REM          Push
1010 REM -----------------------------
1015 REM
1020 TOS% = TOS% + 2
1025 STACK%( TOS%-1 ) = L%
1030 STACK%( TOS% ) = RIGHT%
1035 RETURN
1100 REM -----------------------------
1105 REM          Pop
1110 REM -----------------------------
1115 REM
1120 RIGHT% = STACK%( TOS% )
1125 LEFT% = STACK%( TOS% - 1 )
1130 TOS% = TOS% - 2
1135 RETURN
1200 REM -----------------------------
1205 REM          Exchange
1210 REM -----------------------------
1215 REM
1220 NEWL% = LEFT%: NEWR% = RIGHT%
1225 MIDL% = ( LEFT% + RIGHT% ) \ 2
1230 GET 1, MIDL%: LSET MIDL$ = REC$
1235 REM ----------repeat-------------
1240 REM -----------while------------
1242 REM search for k$ > midl$
1245   GET 1, NEWL% : LSET K$ = REC$
1250   IF K$ < MIDL$ THEN NEWL% = NEWL% + 1 : GOTO 1240
1255 LSET S$ = K$        'save k$ for later
1300 REM -----------while------------
1303 REM search for k$ < midl$
1305   GET 1, NEWR% : LSET K$ = REC$
1310   IF K$ > MIDL$ THEN NEWR% = NEWR% - 1 : GOTO 1300
1315 LSET R$ = K$
1320 IF NEWL% <= NEWR% THEN 1325 ELSE 1400
1322 REM ---exchange file records ------
1325 LSET REC$ = S$
1330 PUT 1, NEWR%        'put left in rt.
1335 LSET REC$ = R$
1340 PUT 1, NEWL%        'put right in lt
1345 NEWL% = NEWL% + 1
1350 NEWR% = NEWR% - 1
1400 IF NEWL% <= NEWR% THEN 1235
1410 RETURN
1420 REM ---end of filesort -----------
```

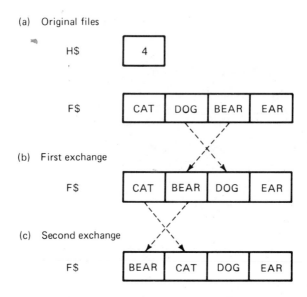

(a) Original files

H$

F$

(b) First exchange

F$

(c) Second exchange

F$

**Figure 6-2.** Quickersort a simple list in File F$.

Figure 6-2 shows what this program does to a very simple list stored on diskette. The middle word is initially DOG ((1 + 4)/2). The first exchange ends up with a sublist on the left containing CAT, and another sublist on the right containing BEAR, DOG, and EAR. The second exchange ends up with ordered sublists, hence the exchanges cease.

The author uses this program to prepare index pages for books on computers (like this one). The words and their page numbers are entered into a diskette file in the order they occur in the manuscript. Then they are sorted into alphabetical order and the ordered file is printed. All duplicate words appear together in the ordered output, and so it is an easy task to eliminate them.

The length of time it takes to sort a list of length N is approximately

$$(0.0876) \ N \ (\log_e N) \text{ seconds}$$

on the IBM computer. For example, 52 single-letter words were sorted in 18 seconds. The performance will vary with the length of the words and the number of words to be sorted.

This program illustrates many of the features of BASICA. Remember, BASICA is an interpreter language (directly executed) as opposed to a compiler language. In the next section we take a look at Pascal, which is a compiled language.

# THE PASCAL COMPILER

The Pascal compiler* is a program that translates Pascal language source files into IBM Personal Computer object files. Recall that a source file is any high level language text file, and an object file is any machine language (binary) file.

Unlike BASIC, a program written in Pascal must be translated into a machine language program before it can be "run." This is done in three distinct stages on the IBM Personal Computer, because the Pascal compiler is too large to fit on a single diskette.

In step one, the PAS1 diskette is used to translate your Pascal program into an inefficient object code program. This step will find syntax errors that may be in your Pascal program. Syntax errors, of course, are caused by incorrect use of Pascal.

Step two uses the program on PAS2 to optimize the inefficient object code generated by PAS1. If you have a correct program, and it successfully compiles through both PAS1 and PAS2, then the resulting machine language program will reside in a file with extension type of .OBJ. This file must be linked with other "run time" programs before it can run by itself, however.

Step three uses the LINK program and the PASCAL.LIB diskette to combine your machine language file with the run-time support routines in PASCAL.LIB. This step is done for the purpose of linking the machine code routines that do READs, WRITEs, file input/output, etc.

The three steps and the files created by them are summarized below. Assume that MYPROG.PAS is the name of the Pascal program you want to compile into machine code.

**Step 1** Use PAS1 to translate MYPROG.PAS into a binary file called MYPROG.BIN

**Step 2** Use PAS2 to optimize MYPROG.BIN and produce the optimized object code file called MYPROG.OBJ

**Step 3** Use the LINK program of DOS and the library routines on PASCAL.LIB to combine MYPROG.OBJ with the necessary run time support routines. The resulting file is MYPROG.EXE. This is the file that can be executed. In fact, to run this program, enter the "command" shown below:

A > MYPROG

The three steps described above generate other files as well, but they are not important at this point.

---

* Requires 128k RAM and two disk drives.

Obviously, the three steps cause a lot of uncertainty and confusion when using the Pascal compiler. We can reduce some of this confusion by constructing several help files to make the job of translation automatic. This is the purpose of the following batch file.

## The PASCAL.BAT File

Suppose we make compiling a Pascal program as simple as possible by creating the following environment. You can use EDLIN or the COPY command to create these files.

**First** Be sure the editor, EDLIN, is copied onto the PAS1 diskette. Also, for the purposes of the following .BAT file, copy MODE from DOS to PAS1 also.

**Second** Format and load a program diskette in drive B. Put either DOS or PAS1 in drive A.

**Third** Execute the following batch file.

A > B:PASCAL MYPROG LPT1:

This will cause the program named MYPROG.PAS to be executed and listed on the line printer. But how does PASCAL get put on drive B?

To make things easy, create the PASCAL.BAT file on drive B as follows. This file will use another file called LINKPARM discussed below.

```
a:mode 80
Rem Compile, Link, and Run a Pascal program
Rem PASCAL SOURCE LISTING is command line
Pause. Put PAS1 in drive A, and your program diskette in B.
B:
A:PAS1 %1,,%2;
Pause. Put PAS2 in drive A, and leave your program diskette in B.
A:PAS2
rename %1.obj result.obj
Pause. Put PASCAL.LIB in A, and leave your program diskette in B.
a:link b:linkparm
rename result.obj %1.obj
rename result.exe %1.exe
Pause. Running your program, now.
%1
```

This batch file does the following:

1. Changes screen width to 80 columns.

2. Changes the logged drive to B.

3. Runs PAS1 on the source file (%1) and outputs a listing to the listing file (%2).

4. Runs PAS2.

5. Temporarily changes the file names to RESULT in order to fool the LINK program.

6. Uses LINKPARM as inputs to the LINK program.

7. Changes the names of the RESULT files back to %1.

8. Runs the translated program

The LINKPARM file contains the following input values for the LINK program.

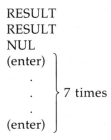

```
RESULT
RESULT
NUL
(enter)  ⎤
     .   ⎥
     .   ⎬ 7 times
     .   ⎥
(enter)  ⎦
```

This file tells LINK that the RESULT.OBJ is to be linked with the routines in PASCAL.LIB and the resulting RESULT.EXE file produced. The map file, NUL, is not used. The seven blank lines cause all other LINK parameters to assume default values.

When both the PASCAL.BAT and LINKPARM files are placed on the program diskette you can compile any program by simply executing PASCAL.BAT.

## An Example of Pascal

Pascal was invented by Niklaus Wirth to teach people how to program in a language that promotes "good" style. Actually, the purpose of good style is to make programs easy to understand by someone who did not write the program. This can be accomplished by clear thinking and simple structure.

Pascal programs are not as easy to write as BASIC programs. But they are much easier to read and understand. Comprehension is much more important than coding when programs are to be maintained and modified for years.

In fact, since Pascal is easy to read and understand, it is appropriate to begin our survey of the language by reading a complete program. Figure 6-3 contains a small Pascal program that is not only useful for introducing the language, but also useful for converting a program entered in BASICA into an acceptable input file to PAS1.

The program of Figure 6-3 is used to strip off line numbers from program statements. Suppose you use the BASICA screen editor to enter a Pascal program. The BASICA screen editor requires that each line of program be preceded by a line number. You could use AUTO, for example, to automatically number each line as you enter it. The statements must be Pascal statements, however, instead of BASIC statements.

Next, use the BASICA screen editor discussed in the section on editors to modify your numbered Pascal program. Once you have edited your program, save it in ASCII format.

SAVE "MYPROG", A

This causes the numbered program to be saved as a file of text.

Leave the BASICA interpreter and execute the program shown in Figure 6-3). This program strips the leading line numbers from every line, thus leaving only the acceptable Pascal statements behind. How is this done?

In Figure 6-3 every line has a line number (from 1 to 34). These line numbers were placed on the listing by the compiler as it printed the listing. The PAS1 compiler will not accept line numbers as shown in the figure. However, we will refer to each Pascal statement by the listing line number.

**Line 1 program stripper (input, output)** This is the program header. It tells what the program name is, and what is allowed as "input" and "output." This program is called "stripper." It uses the keyboard as an input device (input), and the screen as an output device (output).

**Lines 2-7** The var statement contains a list of all variables that the program will use. This is where the variable data values are declared. Notice in Pascal that *all* variable names must appear in a single var statement. In fact, since every variable must take on a value of a certain *type,* the variables must be "typed" here.

The two file names, diskout and diskin, are defined as "text" files in line 3. A text file is a collection of characters organized as screen lines. Each line can actually be up to 127 characters long.

The two text files, diskin and diskout, are going to be used in stripper as the input file obtained from BASICA, and the output file generated by stripper, respectively. File diskout will be the file that is input to the Pascal compiler.

```
JG IC  Line#    Source Line         IBM Personal Computer Pascal Compiler V1.00
   20     1     program stripper(input,output);
   10     2     var
   10     3       diskin,diskout : text;
   10     4       infile, outfile : string(15);
   10     5       ch : char;
   10     6       line    : lstring(80);
   10     7       i : integer;
   10     8     begin
   11     9      page;
   11    10      repeat
   12    11        write('Enter source file name=');
   12    12        readln( infile);
   12    13        write('Enter destination file name = ');
   12    14        readln( outfile );
   12    15        write('Ok --Y/N ? ' );
   12    16        read( ch );
   11    17      until (ch='Y') or (ch='y');
   11    18      assign( diskin, infile ) ;
   11    19      reset( diskin );
   11    20      assign( diskout, outfile );
   11    21      rewrite( diskout );
   11    22      while not eof( diskin ) do
   11    23        begin
   12    24          readln(diskin,line );
   12    25          i:=1;
   12    26          while line[i] in ['0'..'9']
   12    27            do i := i+1;
   12    28          delete( line, 1, i );
   12    29          writeln( diskout, line )
   11    30        end;
   11    31      close( diskin );
   11    32      close( diskout );
   11    33      writeln( infile,'-->',outfile )
   00    34     end.

Symtab  34     Offset Length    Variable
                    0   1392     Return offset, Frame length
                    2    636     DISKIN                      :File     Static
                 1306      1     CH                          :Char     Static
                 1390      2     I                           :Integer Static
                 1308     82     LINE                        :Array    Static
                  638    636     DISKOUT                     :File     Static
                 1274     16     INFILE                      :Array    Static
                 1290     16     OUTFILE                     :Array    Static
```

STRIPPER

**Figure 6-3.** A Pascal program for converting text obtained from BASICA into text acceptable to PAS1.

In line 4 we have declared infile and outfile to be strings of characters. A character string is any string of keyboard characters. The string (15) type limits the length of each string to 15 characters. Of course, the string variables infile and outfile may contain fewer than 15 characters. These two strings will be used to hold the name of the input and output files.

The next variable to be typed in line 5 is a character called CH. CH will be used to hold responses Y or N. You can see this in lines 16–17.

Line 6 declares variable line to be a "length-string." In IBM Pascal, lstring is a string that can be operated on by string functions. These functions will be used to insert, delete, and concatenate characters. In a sense, lstrings are elastic. This variable will be used to hold one line at a time while its line number is being deleted.

Line 7 shows how to declare i an integer. This will be used to index line in order to access a single character at a time.

The var statement defines what variables are to be used by the program as well as their types. It does not, however, supply the values that are associated with the variables. Assigning values to variables is the responsibility of the "executable part" of a Pascal program.

**Lines 8-34** In Figure 6-3, the executable part is shown in lines 8 through 34. This is where the instructions are placed. Every Pascal program has at least one pair of "begin-end" delimiters that designate a "compound statement" containing executable program statements.

In line 9 you can see an example of a PAGE procedure for clearing the screen (and ejecting the line printer page).

PAGE is an example of many built-in functions and procedures that are part of the PASCAL.LIB routines. We call these the intrinsic functions, because they are built into the language.

Lines 10-17 form a loop in the program. This loop is repeated until either an upper or lower case Y is entered as the character value of ch. The purpose of this loop is to correctly capture the names of the input and output files.

Lines 11-12, for example, cause the prompt "Enter source file name =" to appear on the screen. This is followed by READLN (infile) which accepts a string of up to 15 characters as input. The string of characters is stored in string variable infile. This is the directory name of a file on diskette.

Lines 18-21 cause the text files diskin and diskout to be opened for input and output. The ASSIGN procedure is an intrinsic procedure that associates the directory file name stored in infile with the file called diskin. The use of diskin here is important, but subtle. What happens is as follows.

Whenever a file is accessed by a program, only a small piece of it is read into RAM. This small piece is stored in the file variable. In this example, the file variables are diskin and diskout. These are sometimes called "windows" in Pascal, because they are windows into a portion of a file.

The RESET intrinsic causes the file assigned to diskin to be prepared for input (see line 19). RESET resets an existing file, whereas REWRITE creates an entirely new file. In fact, line 21 will cause an existing file to be erased in the process of creating another file of the same name.

The purpose of lines 18-21 is to open an existing file containing the BASICA generated text, and to create and open an output file that will be used to hold the stripped lines of text. At this point in Figure 6-3 we are ready to get a single line at a time, remove its line numbers, and store the stripped line in the output file.

Lines 22–30 show a while-loop in Pascal. This loop is executed over and over again for as long as "not EOF" is true. That is, this loop executes once for each line of text in file diskin. The EOF intrinsic computes TRUE as soon as the end-of-file is reached. Thus, each time the loop finishes one of its passes over the "begin-end" compound statement shown in lines 23–30, the "not EOF" test is performed. As soon as it is FALSE, the loop terminates and the statement at line 31 is executed.

Lines 23–30 contain a "begin" and "end" keyword pair. This means that all statements between the pair are considered a single statement. In Pascal, a compound statement formed with a begin-end pair like this is considered a single statement. A compound statement can go anywhere a simple statement is allowed. Thus, the entire compound statement is executed each time the while-loop is executed.

Lines 24–29 get a line of text from file diskin, and store it in string variable line. Then the number of digits at the beginning of the line is counted and stored in variable i. Lines 26–27 show how this is done in an elegant fashion using a while-loop test. The test is as follows.

$$\text{line}[i] \text{ in } ['0'..'9']$$

This means to compare the i-th character in line[i] with each character in the set '0' through '9'. The square brackets around the digits '0'..'9' mean to form a set. The elements of this set are taken from the consecutive characters '0' through '9'. The two dots mean "through."

In line 27 a single simple statement is executed each time the loop is executed. The value of i is simply incremented by one.

Line 28 shows the use of a string intrinsic that deletes characters 1 through i from lstring line. This is where the line numbers are removed.

Line 29 writes the stripped line to file diskout. This causes the string stored in line to be copied into the file window, diskout. Subsequent outputs to diskout cause the current string to be "forced out" of the window onto the disk.

The two CLOSE intrinsics shown in lines 31–32 force out the last string in the two windows, and mark the files as closed. Finally, line 33 displays the name of the input file and output file on the screen so that the user knows the stripped file is in place.

Line 34 shows how every Pascal program is terminated. The period following the "end" keyword is required.

Figure 6-3 also shows some statistics about the program. This is the symbol table showing all variables and their types. In addition, you can see how much RAM each variable occupies while in the machine.

## The Form of a Pascal Program

Several generalizations can be made from the example in Figure 6-3. First, what is the general form of a Pascal program? Every Pascal program is made up of a data section containing constants, labels, types, and variables, a procedure and function section containing subprograms, and an executable instructions section.

```
program ANYNAME (input, output);
    (* optional labels *)
    (* optional constants *)
    (* optional types *)
    (* optional variables *)
    (* optional procedure and/or function *)
begin
    (* optional executable statements *)
end.
```

The (* and *) pair enclose comments anywhere they appear in a Pascal program. Furthermore, all of the optional sections are selectable by the programmer. For example, here is a program with a constant and a variable, but no executable part.

```
program NULL (input, output);
    const
        X = 5; (* constant integer *)
    var
        Y: integer; (* variable integer *)
    begin
    end.
```

This is a perfectly correct Pascal program even though it does nothing! Notice how constants and variables may belong to the same type, but one will be allowed to vary over a range of values, while the other (constant) takes on only a single value.

We can restrict the range of values that an integer variable can take on using the subrange notation. The smallest value and largest value in the range are separated by two periods.

```
var
    Y: -15 .. 25; (* subrange *)
```

This types Y as an integer, but furthermore, it restricts Y to only the integers from -15 to 25, inclusively.

Pascal would not be very interesting if it restricted programmers to only a limited number of data types. Therefore, Pascal uses concatenation and nesting of a few basic data types to construct more elaborate data structures. This is probably the most elegant concept in programming to come along in 25 years.

## Data Structures in Pascal

Pascal defines four basic data types. These are called the base types because all other types can be derived from these four.

| | |
|---|---|
| **boolean** | (* collection of values either TRUE or FALSE *) |
| **integer** | (* collection of integer values*) |
| **real** | (* collection of real number values *) |
| **char** | (* collection of single character values *) |

In addition, the IBM Pascal compiler accepts the following nonstandard type:

Word (* 16-bit integer values, no type *)

This is used to do systems programming in Pascal. In a sense, this removes the strongly typed restriction of Pascal. Any operation on a word produces a 16-bit result.

Here are examples of variables of base type.

```
var A,B,C  : integer;
    X,Y    : word;
    T1,U,W : real;
    CH,CA  : char;
    T,F    : boolean;
```

The next step up from base types is the structured type. Structured types may be constructed from base types.

| | |
|---|---|
| **array** | (* array of values of the same type *) |
| **record** | (* collection of values of different types *) |
| **set** | (* collection of values as a set *) |
| **file** | (* disk file window *) |
| **( )** | (* scalar enumeration of base type *) |

Here are some examples of structured types.

```
var
  A : array [1..10] of char;
  B : array [1..5, 0..10] of integer;
  C : record
        X : real;
        Y : integer;
        Z : char
      end
```

Notice that arrays can be single, or two-dimensional. The subscripts on an array can change over a specified subrange as designated by 1..10, etc.

The record structure above contains three values, a real, integer, and a character. To access one or the other you must use the dot notation of Pascal:

C.X
C.Y
C.Z

In addition, IBM Pascal extends the structured types for the purpose of systems programming and string processing.

**string (n)**    (* string of characters *)
**lstring (n)**    (* string of characters *)
**adv**    (* the address of a value *)
**ads**    (* segment address in 8086 processor *)

IBM Pascal includes pointers and dynamic memory allocation, also. However, we will not summarize this feature of Pascal here.

One interesting language extension included in IBM Pascal is the so-called super array. This type allows differing arrays to be passed to procedures and functions. For example, the super array defined by SR can ´ be used to define one or more other arrays of various lengths.

```
type
  SR = SUPER ARRAY [1..*] of REAL;
var
  M : SR(10);    (* of length 10*)
  N : SR(3) ;    (* of length  3*)
```

Let's examine another complete example that incorporates many of these ideas. Remember, Pascal is designed for readability, hence you should gain a better understanding of the language through careful study of examples.

## Another Complete Example

Figures 6-4 and 6-5 contain one program each that, taken together, form a small database system. The DATAENTRY program of Figure 6-4 is used to enter information into an employee file. The RETRIEVE program of Figure 6-5 is used to retrieve the information through the last name of an employee. You can discover how these programs work, and learn about Pascal by following the detailed analysis below.

First, suppose we study the DATAENTRY program shown in Figure 6-4. This program takes a user's inputs and stores them in a file on diskette.

**Line 1** This is the usual program heading.

**Line 2–31** This is a separate file containing the data structures for this and the RETRIEVE program. The $INCLUDE metacommand says to insert the text from B:DATA into the program as shown. The text occupies lines 1 through 31 (as renumbered in the figure).

The const statement declares N and NDEP as integer constants. They are used in the subsequent data structures.

The type statement declares new types that were invented to hold the data. A type is a collection of values, remember. So the type statement informs the Pascal compiler what is to be expected. A type statement is a "template" of a data structure. It does not hold any data, but instead, tells what data can be held later on.

The three new types shown on $INCLUDE lines 5–7 are for real numbers and character strings. The dates (string (*)) will hold up to 8 characters. The names will hold up to N characters, where N is a constant defined previously as 16.

The new type called employees is an aggregation of other types. The first three "components" of employees is "first", "last", and "middle" names. These tell Pascal to hold names in these components later on. The component shown in $INCLUDE line 13 is actually another aggregate. This is an example of data structure nesting. The payroll and history components are nested within the employee type. These in turn each contain additional nested components.

Notice $INCLUDE line 17 has a component of type (married, single, head). These are called scalars of ordinal type. That is, we reference these values by using their names instead of their values. Thus, the "value" of an mstatus is married, single, or head. No other "values" are allowed.

The actual variables of type employees, names, and other base types are shown in $INCLUDE lines 26–31. The file window for the database is called dbase. Thus, the file contains data in the format defined by type "employees." Of course, there will be many file records in the file, and each record will conform to the structure defined by "employees."

A working variable called temp is also needed by DATAENTRY to hold values of type employees.

Variables fname (file name), I, j (working counters), and ms (working character), are all used in both programs.

**Lines 3–46** These are the program statements that actually carry out the actions of data capture and storage.

**Lines 4–8** The name of the file is entered, the file is assigned a file window (dbase), and the file is opened for output. In line 8 the screen is cleared by writing 24 blank lines.

**Lines 9–44** This repeat loop is executed over and over again until the user decides to stop adding new employees to the database.

The most important feature to observe in this program is the method of data structure access. Notice the "dot" notation:

> temp.first
> temp.last
> temp.payroll.rate

Each dot indicates one level of nesting within a data structure. Therefore, temp.first refers to the "first" component of structure temp. Since components can themselves contain components, it may be necessary to use two or more dots in order to "index" into the structure at the proper level.

In lines 10–12 the dot notation is used to index into temp only one level deep. The values of first, last, and middle are captured and stored in temp.

In line 13–14 we are doing something new and different. The "with" statement is a shorthand method of eliminating the redundant dot notation. Thus, in place of the following notation, we can use the shorthand shown in Figure 6-4.

> temp.payroll.rate
> temp.payroll.hours
> temp.payroll.depends
> temp.payroll.mstatus

Furthermore, you will notice in lines 21–31 a combination of things going on. First of all, the repeat-until construction is used to capture a correct input value for mstatus. Secondly, notice that the scalar (married, single, head) cannot be entered directly because scalars cannot be input or output. Therefore, the character codes m, s, or h (or the capitalized versions) must be used instead.

**Lines 23–30** This is an example of an extended Pascal case statement. The value of ms is used to decide which one of the cases to perform. If ms is equal to either "m" or "M", then the first case clause is executed and all other clauses are skipped. Similarly, the other clauses are executed if the value of ms matches the labels on the clauses. If no match occurs, then the statements in the OTHERWISE clause are executed.

**Lines 33–39** The components of temp.history are entered one at a time. The with statement is used again here to abbreviate the dot notation that would have been needed otherwise.

Line 41 is interesting because it shows how to copy the entire contents of temp into the file window designated by dbase ↑ . Notice the "up-arrow" following dbase. This signifies that dbase is a file window rather than an entire file. A window holds a single record. A file holds many records.

Line 42 shows how to put the value of a window to the disk file. The PUT intrinsic outputs the file record in dbase ↑ , and then increments the file record pointer to the next record position in the file. Thus, the next time PUT is executed, the next file record is output in sequence.

Line 45 closes the file after all records have been entered. The employee information is permanently saved on diskette.

Figure 6-5 shows how to write a Pascal program that sequentially searches the file named fname and finds one or more file records with matching last name strings. Figure 6-5 uses the same $INCLUDE file to define its data structures as the previous program. We will skip $IN-CLUDE lines 1–31 in the details below.

**Lines 4–6** Again, the name of the employee file is read into fname, and this name is associated with the file window called dbase. The repeat-until statement in lines 7–37 causes looping until the user is done retrieving employee records by last name. Each time a record is retrieved, the file is closed and then reopened. The RESET intrinsic differs from the REWRITE intrinsic in that it is used to open an existing file.

In the case of a sequential file (DBASE.MODE : = SEQUENTIAL is automatic, here), the RESET also pre-fetches the first file record. Hence, line 9 opens and retrieves the first record in fname.

Lines 11–32 loop while the EOF (End-Of-File) is not TRUE. The EOF intrinsic returns TRUE when the end of a file has been reached.

Line 13 compares the last name stored in the file window with the last name entered into temp.last by the user. If they are equal, then the complete record is displayed by lines 14–31. Notice the use of "with", again, to abbreviate the lengthy dot notation.

Lines 20–24 show how to use a case statement (without the optimal OTHERWISE clause) to "decode" the scalar value stored in payroll.mstatus.

Lines 14 and 32 illustrate how the Pascal compiler aids in error detection by printing warnings. In line 14 the compiler is worried that you might change something in the file window (like GET or PUT different values). This would lead to an error, but as used here, it will not cause an error. Line 32 shows how the computer has inserted a semicolon following the END. The author forgot to follow the rules of Pascal which state that concatenation of two statements is done using a semicolon. The compiler was "smart" enough to make the correction for the programmer.

This example illustrates Pascal data structures, sequential file input/output, the case, repeat, while, and if-then-else statements. This is by no means a complete treatment of the language. For a complete coverage the reader should consult one of many books that cover Pascal in greater depth.

To get an idea of the power and flexibility of IBM Pascal, consider the following list of features, intrinsic functions, and statements. You will notice that IBM Pascal has been extended to include systems programming, application programming, and communications control.

```
                                                         Page    1
                                                         00-00-80
                                                         02:31:33
JG IC  Line#    Source Line          IBM Personal Computer Pascal Compiler V1.00
   20      1    program DATAENTRY( input, output );
           2    {$include:'b:data'}
           1    { Data section for DATAENTRY and RETRIEVE  }
   10      2    const  N=16;   { string lengths }
   10      3           ndep=10;   { maximum dependents }
   10      4    type
   10      5      dollars = real ;
   10      6      dates    = string(8);
   10      7      names    = string(N);
   10      8      employees
   10      9              = record
   20     10                  first : names;
   20     11                  last  : names;
   20     12                  middle: char;
   20     13                  payroll : record
   30     14                    rate : dollars;
   30     15                    hours: integer;
   30     16                    depends:0..ndep;
   30     17                    mstatus:(married, single, head );
   20     18                  end; ( payroll )
   20     19                  history : record
   30     20                    hired  : dates;
   30     21                    boss   : names;
   30     22                    dept   : names;
   30     23                    title  : names;
   30     24                  end ( history )
   10     25              end  ;( employees )
   10     26    var
   10     27      dbase    : file of employees;
   10     28      temp     : employees;
   10     29      fname    : names;
   10     30      I,j      : integer;      ( working variables )
   10     31·     ms       : char;
   10      3    begin  ( enter an employee record one at a time )
   11      4      write('Enter Employee Information File Name: ');
   11      5      readln( fname );
```

**Figure 6-4.** DATAENTRY program for the employee database.

```
11    6    assign( dbase, fname );
11    7    rewrite( dbase );
11    8    for I := 1 to 24 do writeln;  { clear screen }
11    9    repeat
12   10      write('Enter first name: '); readln( temp.first );
12   11      write('Enter last name: '); readln( temp.last );
12   12      write('Enter middle initial: ' ); readln( temp.middle );
12   13      with temp.payroll do
22   14        begin
23   15          write('Enter rate of pay: '); readln( rate );
```

DATAENTRY

```
JG IC  Line#   Source Line        IBM Personal Computer Pascal Compiler V1.00
   23    16        write('Enter hours per week: '); readln( hours );
   23    17        repeat    { get correct dependents }
   24    18          write('Enter number dependents( 0..', ndep:2, '): ');readl
   24    18  n( j );
   23    19        until ( 0<=j ) and ( j<=ndep );
   23    20        depends := j;    { correct subrange }
   23    21        repeat    { get correct ms }
   24    22          write('Enter marital status (m,s,h): '); readln( ms );
   25    23          case ms of
   25    24          'm','M': mstatus := married;
   25    25          's','S': mstatus := single;
   25    26          'h','H': mstatus := head;
   25    27          otherwise
   25    28            write('Incorrect input, try again.');
   25    29            ms :='?';
   25    30          end  { case }
   23    31        until ms <>'?' ;
   22    32        end;   { with }
   12    33      with temp.history do
   22    34        begin
   23    35          write('Enter date hired (mm/dd/yy): '); readln( hired );
   23    36          write('Enter supervisor''s last name: '); readln( boss );
   23    37          write('Enter department name: '); readln( dept );
   23    38          write('Enter position title:' ); readln( title );
   22    39        end;  { with }
   12    40      writeln('Thankyou');
   12    41      dbase^ := temp ;  { load buffer with record }
   12    42      put( dbase ) ;    { write to disk file }
   12    43      write('Are you done (Y/N) ?'); readln( ms ) ;
   11    44    until (ms='Y') or (ms='y');
   11    45    close( dbase );
   00    46  end.
```

```
Symtab  46    Offset Length    Variable
                  0    854      Return offset, Frame length
                848      2      I                               :Integer Static
                850      2      J                               :Integer Static
                852      1      MS                              :Char    Static
                734     98      TEMP                            :Record  Static
                  2    732      DBASE                           :File    Static
                832     16      FNAME                           :Array   Static


              Errors  Warns   In Pass One
                 0       0
```

Figure 6-4 continued.

```
                                                            Page    1
                                                            00-00-80
                                                            04:24:48
JG IC  Line#   Source Line         IBM Personal Computer Pascal Compiler V1.00
   20     1    program RETRIEVE( input, output );
          2    {$include:'data'}
          1    { Data section for DATAENTRY and RETRIEVE  }
   10     2    const  N=16;  { string lengths }
   10     3              ndep=10;  { maximum dependents }
   10     4    type
   10     5     dollars = real ;
   10     6     dates    = string(8);
   10     7     names    = string(N);
   10     8     employees
   10     9              = record
   20    10                  first : names;
   20    11                  last  : names;
   20    12                  middle: char;
   20    13                  payroll : record
   30    14                    rate : dollars;
   30    15                    hours: integer;
   30    16                    depends:0..ndep;
   30    17                    mstatus:(married, single, head );
   20    18                  end; { payroll }
   20    19                  history : record
   30    20                    hired  : dates;
   30    21                    boss   : names;
   30    22                    dept   : names;
   30    23                    title  : names;
   30    24                  end { history }
   10    25                  end  ;{ employees }
   10    26    var
   10    27     dbase   : file of employees;
   10    28     temp    : employees;
   10    29     fname   : names;
   10    30     I,j     : integer;     { working variables }
   10    31     ms      : char;
   10     3    begin
   11     4     write('Enter Employee Information File Name:' );
   11     5     readln( fname );
   11     6     assign( dbase, fname );
   11     7     repeat
   12     8      for I := 1 to 24 do writeln;
   12     9      reset( dbase );
   12    10      write('Enter last name of employee to find :'); readln( temp.
   12    10    last );
   12    11      while not EOF( dbase ) do
   12    12       begin
   23    13        if dbase^.last = temp.last
   13    14        then with dbase^ do
```

```
                                                            Page    2
                                                            00-00-80
RETRIEVE                                                    04:25:38
JG IC  Line#   Source Line         IBM Personal Computer Pascal Compiler V1.00
         14    ---------------------^Warning 208 File Dereference Considered Ha
         14    rmful
   23    15         begin
   24    16          writeln( first,' ',middle,' ', last );
   24    17          writeln('Rate $', payroll.rate:8:2 );
   24    18          writeln('Hours #', payroll.hours:8 );
   24    19          writeln('Dependents #', payroll.depends:3 );
   25    20          case payroll.mstatus of
   25    21           married : writeln( 'Married' );
   25    22           single  : writeln( 'Single' );
   25    23           head    : writeln( 'Head-of-household' );
   24    24          end;   { case }
   24    25          with history do
   34    26           begin
   35    27            writeln('Date hired : ', hired );
   35    28            writeln('Supervisor : ', boss );
```

**Figure 6-5.** RETRIEVE a database record.

```
35    29              writeln('Department :  ', dept );
35    30              writeln('Position   :  ', title );
35    31            end   ( with history )
34    32          end ( with dbase )
      32    ---------^Warning 164 Insert ;
13    33          get( dbase );
12    34          end;  ( while not EOF )
12    35          close( dbase );
12    36          write('Are you done (Y/N) ? ' ); readln( ms );
11    37          until (ms='Y') or ( ms='y' );
11    38          write('Thanks' );
00    39      end.

Symtab  39    Offset Length    Variable
                   0    854    Return offset, Frame length
                 848      2    I                        :Integer  Static
                 850      2    J                        :Integer  Static
                 852      1    MS                       :Char     Static
                 734     98    TEMP                     :Record   Static
                   2    732    DBASE                    :File     Static
                 832     16    FNAME                    :Array    Static


              Errors  Warns  In Pass One
                   0      2
```

Figure 6-5 continued.

# Metacommands

Metacommands are imbedded in comments and direct the compiler,
itself. They are used for toggle debugging, error handling, listing format, and conditional compile parameters. A + sign following a meta-
command causes it to be turned on, and a − sign causes it to be turned
off. The default toggle condition is listed only, below.

| | |
|---|---|
| $BRAVE + | Display compiler errors and warnings |
| $DEBUG + | Turn on debug checking |
| $ENTRY − | Generate code for telling where an error oc- curred in a procedure/function |
| $ERRORS:n | Set upper limit n of number of errors |
| $GOTO − | Warning goto considered harmful |
| $IF$THEN$ELSE | Conditional compile |
| $INCLUDE:'name' | Merge name with current file |
| $INDEXCK + | Check array subscripts |
| $INITCK − | Initialize integers to − 32,768 |
| $LINE − | Generate source line numbers for debugging |
| $LINESIZE:n | Set width of screen (default 79) |
| $LIST + | Generate source code listing |
| $MATHCK | Detect arithmetic errors |

| | |
|---|---|
| $MESSAGE:text | Display message during a compile |
| $NILCK + | Detect pointer dereferencing |
| $OCODE + | Generate disassembled object code |
| $PAGE:n | Page number set to n |
| $PAGEIF:n | Skip to next page if fewer than n lines left |
| $PAGESIZE:n | Sets page length (default 53) |
| $PAGESIZE:n | Sets/restores metacommand values |
| $PUSH/$POP | Saves/restores metacommand values |
| $RANGECK + | Check subrange values |
| $RUNTIME − | Run time error checking |
| $SKIP:n | Skip n lines |
| $STACKCK + | Check for stack overflow |
| $SUBTITLE:'text' | Set page subtitle |
| $SYMTAB + | List the program variables, types, etc. |
| $TITLE:'text' | Set page title |
| $WARN + | Give warning messages |

## Data Types

| | |
|---|---|
| boolean | TRUE or FALSE |
| char | character |
| real | floating point |
| integer | − 32,768 .. 32,767 |
| word | 16-bit |
| byte | 8-bit |
| address | ADR, ADS pointers |
| super arrays | STRING, LSTRING for character strings, and SUPER ARRAY for arrays that are to be passed as parameters |
| pointers | ↑ , NEW, DISPOSE for linked list processing |
| set | Sets |
| file | I/O devices |
| text | special text files |
| enumerated | scalar, e.g. (RED,WHITE,BLUE) |
| subrange | range, e.g. 100 .. 200 |

## Miscellaneous Intrinsics

| | |
|---|---|
| ABORT | abnormal program termination |
| BYWORD | concatenate two bytes into one word |
| DECODE | Character-to-ASCII conversion |
| ENCODE | ASCII-to-character conversion |
| EVAL | Procedure parameter evaluation only |
| LOBYTE,HIBYTE | Returns byte of word |
| LOWER,UPPER | Lower/upper bounds of a structure |
| RESULT | Return function result, not function evaluation |
| SIZEOF | Return size of a structure |
| RETYPE | Change the type of a structure |
| MOVEL,MOVER | Move characters from left or right end of a string. |
| FILLC | Fill a string with character |

## String Intrinsics

| | |
|---|---|
| CONCAT | Append string |
| DELETE | Delete substring |
| INSERT | Insert substring |
| COPYLST | Copy string |
| SCANEQ | Search string (equal) |
| SCANNE | Search string (not equal) |
| COPYSTR | Copy string |
| POSITN | Position of a substring |

## Clock Intrinsics

| | |
|---|---|
| TIME | Assign a time-of-day |
| DATE | Assign a calendar date |
| TICS | Return clock value of 18.2 ticks per second (0.055 sec), increments. |

## File Intrinsics

| | |
|---|---|
| GET/PUT | File I/O (binary) |
| RESET/REWRITE | File open |
| EOF/EOLN | End-of-file, End-of-line sensor |
| PAGE | Next page |
| READ/READLN | Input of text |
| WRITE/WRITELN | Output of text |
| ASSIGN | Assign a file window to a file name |
| CLOSE/DISCARD | Close and discard a file |
| SEEK | Direct access |

## File Modes

| | |
|---|---|
| TERMINAL | Interactive display/keyboard |
| SEQUENTIAL | Sequential access mode |
| DIRECT | Random access mode |

## Special Control Structures

| | |
|---|---|
| BREAK | Exit from (nested) loop(s) |
| CYCLE | Exit and cycle back to beginning of loop |
| RETURN | Leave a procedure/function |
| OTHERWISE | Default clause of a case statement |
| AND THEN | Delayed evaluation of AND |
| OR ELSE | Delayed evaluation of OR |

These control structures merit further explanation since they are un-usual extensions to Pascal (and cannot be found in books on Pascal).
Here is an example of loop control.

```
OUT : for I := 1 to N do
        for J := 1 to M do
          begin
                . . .
            if . . . then BREAK OUT
          end
```

This shows how you would terminate both loops using the BREAK statement.
Here is the same example with the cycle statement.

```
OUT : for I := 1 to N do
         for J := 1 to M do
         begin
             . . .
             if . . . then CYCLE OUT
         end
```

This time, the two loops are terminated, but control branches back to OUT where the two loops are restarted again.

Here is an example of the AND THEN test.

**while** (Y < = N) AND THEN (S[Y] <> KEY) **do**

The expression (Y < = N) is evaluated and if it is TRUE, the second expression is evaluated. However, if (Y < = N) evaluates to FALSE, the second expression is not evaluated. This is useful because evaluation of (S[Y] <> KEY) may cause a range error when Y > N. The AND THEN operation avoids this inconvenience.

## COMMON QUESTIONS

Q. What editors can be used to write a program?

A. EDLIN and BASIC EDIT.

Q. Why is the ASCII option important when saving a file in BASICA?

A. Only ASCII files can be merged together, and only ASCII files can be understood by EDLIN.

Q. Why does the IBM Personal Computer use both BASICA and Pascal?

A. BASICA is good for developing new programs quickly, and Pascal is good for programs that need extra speed or more RAM.

Q. What is the difference between variable I% and I?

A. I% is an integer valued variable and takes on only integer values. I is a real valued variable and takes on real values (with a decimal point).

Q. How is output to the line printer done?

A. In BASICA use LPRINT, and in Pascal use WRITELN (PRINTER, . . .), where PRINTER is a TEXT file, and use ASSIGN(PRINTER,'LPT1') to define PRINTER to the system.

Q. What is a string?

A. A row of characters instead of a number.

Q. How is a number stored in a random file in BASICA?

A. First it must be converted into a string using the MKI$, MKS$, or MKD$ functions. Then it must be LSET or RSET into the buffer string. Finally, you can PUT it.

Q. How is "IF A = O THEN 1010" rewritten in Pascal?

A. If A = O THEN BEGIN .. END ELSE BEGIN . . . END.

Q. How is a new file opened in Pascal?

A. USE REWRITE instead of RSET to create and open.

Q. What is an array?

A. A collection of elements or values all of the same type. For example, a string array is a collection of strings.

Q. Are line numbers required in Pascal?

A. In general, no. Only use line numbers whenever a GOTO or CYCLE references a line.

Q. Why are there so many ways to do the same thing on the IBM Personal Computer?

A. Each subsystem, e.g. DOS, BASIC, etc., was developed independently. Thus, each subsystem is able to do some of the same things as other subsystems.

Q. Where must a compiler directive appear in a program?

A. In Pascal the $LIST + etc., directives (called metacommands by IBM) must be placed in the source file at the start of a comment.

Q. What is the difference between LSET and RSET in BASICA?

A. LSET left-justifies, RSET right-justifies a string.

Q. Why are there different types of data in a program?

A. The different types are there for reliability, flexibility, and speed. Integer arithmetic is faster than real arithmetic, for example.

# Chapter 7

# An Introduction to Database Processing

He had thought of everything. The System started with a big bang and then kept on expanding. Soon there were clumps of matter here and there; some of it too hot, and some of it too cold. But then a few "clumps" became just right, and life began.

Business was so good he had trouble managing it. As soon as one part of the System settled down the creatures in some other part would evolve into a problem. If only there was a way to simplify it all. Perhaps something like a data management system . . .

## WHAT IS A DBMS?

In Chapter 1 we defined a database management system DBMS as a computer with software for entering, retrieving, modifying, and outputting information stored on disks. The main goal of a DBMS is to simplify a user's access to the database information by assuming a simplified **user's view** of data.

Chapter 1 illustrates three user's views:

Network,
Hierarchical, and
Relational.

The second and third views above are the most common in use, but we will describe only the relational model in this chapter. In fact, we will show you how to build and use a very simple relational database system. The BASIC program listing for this simple relational DBMS is given in the third section of this chapter.

177

A relational DBMS assumes that all data in the system can be stored as a collection of tables. Each table contains rows and columns as shown below.

| Qty | Part No. | Price | Date |
|-----|----------|-------|---------|
| 5 | NC-875 | 5.95 | 9/1/81 |
| 3 | NC-501 | 0.35 | 9/30/81 |
| 0 | NC-450 | 1.95 | 9/9/81 |

The columns are called relational **domains** and the rows are called **tuples.** A tuple in the PARTS relation above is:

tuple

| 3 | NC-501 | 0.35 | 9/30/81 |

for example, and contains values for each domain of PARTS. A domain in the PARTS relation above is:

Part No.

NC-875
NC-501
NC-450

for example, and contains values for each tuple of PARTS.

As you can see from the examples above, it is necessary to designate one or more domains as an **access key** in order to select a particular row or column from the relation. Thus, suppose we designate "Part No" as an access key in PARTS. Then, a database retrieval is made by specifying a certain value of the access key. For example, suppose we retrieve all tuples with "Part No" equal to NC-501. This would cause the tuple below to be retrieved.

tuple with Part No = NC-501

| 3 | NC-501 | 0.35 | 9/30/81 |

A more sophisticated retrieval request might cause more than a single row to be retrieved. For example, we might ask for all "Part No" values greater than "NC-500" to be retrieved. In this case, two tuples are returned.

tuples with "Part No" > NC-500

| 5 | NC-875 | 5.95 | 9/1/81 |
| 3 | NC-501 | 0.35 | 9/30/81 |

This collection of tuples should look familiar because it is also a relation. Hence, in a relational database system all **queries** (requests for information) operate on a set of relations and return a set of relations. The idea in a relational DBMS is to simplify the user's view of data by producing relations from other relations. This idea is called a **relational algebra.** Operations are performed in a relational DBMS by writing relational algebra statements in a high level **query language.** Most microcomputer systems, however, use DBMS's with a menu-driven query language instead of a high-level query language based on the algebra of relations. Thus, in the IBM Personal Computer it is most likely that you will employ a database system similar to the one described in the remainder of this chapter.

## The Parts of a DBMS

Most DBMSs consist of a collection of programs for doing the following things:

**Physical Database Management.** A DBMS must manage a unified collection of files. These programs insert, modify, and delete data per the user's requests.

**Logical Database Management.** A DBMS must present a simplified view of the physical database to the user. Thus, in a relational DBMS the user views the database as a collection of tables. Each table is actually stored in some more complicated file structure, but the user need not be aware of this. Hence the tables, query algebra, menus, and so forth give the user a logical view of the database.

**Query Language Processor.** A DBMS must allow a user to browse, retrieve, change, process, and discard information somehow. Typically, a menu-driven query language is supplied with a DBMS to support a user's queries.

**I/O Control.** A DBMS must include a collection of report generator programs that allows the user to format and display retrieved information.

These parts of a DBMS are illustrated in the next section which describes the simple relational DBMS included in this book. The program for the simple DBMS can be entered into your IBM Personal Computer and directly interpreted using BASIC*. The last section of this chapter describes the physical level file structure used by the simple relational DBMS.

# A SIMPLE RELATIONAL DBMS

The simple relational DBMS described here has the following features:

**Physical Database Management.** The system uses a B-tree index file substructure to build a unified collection of files. Programs are included to insert, modify, and delete tuples from a relation per a user's request. A backup facility maintains the files.

**Logical Database Management.** The system uses relations defined by a CRT screen form to simplify its use. The CRT form is entered by a user. This form defines the domains of each relation, and is used to enter, retrieve, and output information stored as a tuple.

**Query Language Processor.** The system uses a very simple query menu. A tuple is retrieved on the basis of a single access key (domain value). Once the tuple is retrieved, the user can delete it, change it, or leave it alone.

**I/O Control.** The simple DBMS system can be modified (by the reader) to print a tuple and its screen form on the printer. However, there is no provision for formatting the output in any other format.

Screen Display 7-1 illustrates the capabilities of the simple DBMS. When in BASIC, you can obtain this menu by loading and running the DBMENU.BAS file.

ok

LOAD "DBMENU", R

The main menu will appear as shown in Screen Display 7-1.

The first task that you must perform in order to construct a relation is illustrated in Screen Display 7-2. Here is an explanation of Screen Display 7-2.

BTREE.DAT     This is the name given for the index file to be used during a query to find a tuple. See the final section that describes the physical level model for more information on how this file is used.

---

* A diskette for the IBM Personal Computer containing these programs may be purchased separately from Reston Publishing Company.

```
[ 1 ]. Create a database system. or
[ 2 ]. Add new records. or
[ 3 ]. Lookup/Modify existing records. or
[ 4 ]. Backup file and index. or
[ 5 ]. Build screen form ( for input ). or
[ 6 ]. Quick dump index file. or
[ 7 ]. Stop. Exit DBMS system.


Enter a number : ? 1_
```

**Screen Display 7-1.** Main menu of database retrieval system.

```
            Create Index File Header


Enter index file name : BTREE.DAT
       Correct ( Y/N ) ? Y
How many characters per search key ? 16
       Correct ( Y/N ) ? Y
Enter screen form file name : SCREEN.DAT
       Correct ( Y/N ) ? Y
Enter number screen lines in form : ? 6
       Correct ( Y/N ) ? Y
Enter data file name : MASTER.DAT
       Correct ( Y/N ) ? Y
Enter number fields in screen form : ? 8
       Correct ( Y/N ) ? Y_
```

**Screen Display 7-2.** Example of creating a database system of files.

| | |
|---|---|
| 16 | One domain will be used as an access key. This domain is stored in the database and the index file BTREE.DAT. Its length, therefore, must be known in advance. Here we have limited an access key value to 16 or fewer characters in length. |
| SCREEN.DAT | The CRT form which defines a relation (including the domains) is saved in this file. |
| 6 | The CRT form in SCREEN.DAT has 6 lines. |
| MASTER.DAT | This is where the relation is stored. Each tuple corresponds to a record of the file. |

8                    The SCREEN.DAT file contains a definition of a relation with 8 domains in it. Each domain value occupies a single field on the relation file. Hence each record of MASTER.DAT holds 8 values.

Once a relation is created using selection 1 of the main menu, you can design the CRT form and then enter, modify, delete, and retrieve any tuple desired in the relation. Suppose we examine an example.

## Defining a Relation's Screen Form

Screen Displays 7-3 and 7-4 show how to define a relation by entering a screen form. Main menu selection five causes the DBMS to respond as shown in Screen Displays 7-4.

A **relation** is defined as a collection of tuples (rows), each **tuple** is defined as a collection of domain values. Hence, in Screen Displays 7-4 each domain value is defined as a blank field (minus sign) beginning with a special character.

*     This field holds an access domain value
:     This field holds a normal domain value
—     This is a character position for a value

The relation corresponding to Screen Display 7-4 might look as follows.

### ACCOUNTS

| Id | Last | First | Street | City | State | Zip | Balance |
|-----|-------|-------|--------|-------|-------|-------|---------|
| L01 | Lewis | Ted | Oak | Corv | OR | 97330 | 10.50 |
| S01 | Smith | Joe | Main | San F | CA | 97560 | 0.0 |
| S01 | Smith | Mary | Park | San F | CA | 97660 | 3.50 |

Figure 7-1 shows the printed output obtained from answering "Y" in Screen Display 7-4. Notice also that changes to a line may be performed by entering the line number to be re-defined. In this illustration, no changes were made, so a zero was entered.

This CRT form defines the relation stored in MASTER.DAT. All subsequent references to the relation must use this form. Therefore, data entry, information retrieval, and DBMS processing all use this form.

```
[ 1 ]. Create a database system. or
[ 2 ]. Add new records. or
[ 3 ]. Lookup/Modify existing records. or
[ 4 ]. Backup file and index. or
[ 5 ]. Build screen form ( for input ). or
[ 6 ]. Quick dump index file. or
[ 7 ]. Stop. Exit DBMS system.


  Enter a number : ? 5_
```

**Screen Display 7-3.** Selection of screen forms builder.

```
Enter form a line at a time. remember :
            * = keyed value
            : = begins a field
            - = field designation
         6  = lines per screen
1 Id :----
2 Last * ---------------- First : ----------
3 Street : ----------------------------------
4 City   : ------------- State :---
5                    Zip :---------
6 Balance : --------

Enter 0 to stop. or line number to change : ? 0

Do you want hard copy ? y_
```

**Screen Display 7-4.** Example of a screen form for a database retrieval system.

```
              Screen Form SCREEN.DAT


1 Id :----
2 Last * ---------------- First : ----------
3 Street : ----------------------------------
4 City   : ------------- State :---
5                    Zip :---------
6 Balance : --------
```

**Figure 7-1.** A relation defined as a screen format.

## Data Entry into a Relation

The next step in this example is to enter data into the relation. Each tuple of the relation corresponds to a screen full of values. The screen full of values is obtained via the CRT form, of course.

Screen Displays 7-5 and 7-6 show how to enter information into the relation. The screen form is redisplayed as shown in Screen Display 7–6 for each tuple as it is supplied with values.

In Screen Display 7-6 each field is entered under control of the screen form prompt. Thus, for example, line 4 contains two prompts: one for CITY and another for STATE. Notice in line 2 that entry of a last name results in an indexing operation:

Indexing by LEWIS

This means that the tuple is indexed so it can be retrieved at a later time by this access value. The LAST domain is an access domain because it was defined as such in Screen Display 7-4. (Observe the * in line 2 of Screen Display 7-4.)

After all fields of the tuple have been entered the tuple is stored in the database. In this case the database manages a file (MASTER.DAT) containing the relation, and another file (BTREE.DAT) containing the values of the access domain (LEWIS,etc.). Subsequent queries will use the access domain to fetch one or more tuples and display both their CRT form and their domain values.

## Database Query Processing

Now, suppose you have entered hundreds of tuples into the relation illustrated by the previous examples. You might want to retrieve one of the tuples and change a domain value. This is done by using the lookup program. The lookup program takes a search key value like "LEWIS" and uses it to find a tuple. The CRT screen form and corresponding values are displayed as shown in Screen Display 7-7.

Once a tuple is retrieved you can perform one of the following operations on it:

M   Modify the tuple by changing one or more domain values.

L   Lookup another tuple

D   Delete the current tuple. This causes the tuple to be inaccessible, and during a backup operation all deleted tuples are erased.

E   Exit the lookup operation and return to the main menu level.

```
[ 1 ]. Create a database system, or
[ 2 ]. Add new records, or
[ 3 ]. Lookup/Modify existing records, or
[ 4 ]. Backup file and index, or
[ 5 ]. Build screen form ( for input ), or
[ 6 ]. Quick dump index file, or
[ 7 ]. Stop, Exit DBMS system.



      Enter a number : ? 2_
```

**Screen Display 7-5.** Example of selecting data entry option.

```
     1.   Id :L01
     2.   Last •LEWIS
   Indexing by LEWIS
     First :TED
     3.   Street :2812 MONTEREY
     4.   City   :CORVALLIS
     State :OR
     5.   Zip :97330
     6.   Balance :10.95
   Inputs stored in file : MASTER.DAT
   Do you want to enter more (Y/N) ? Y_
```

**Screen Display 7-6.** Example of data entry under screen format control.

Screen Display 7-7 illustrates what happens if M is selected. Entering zero causes the modify mode to be terminated. If you want to modify domain 6, for example, then enter number 6. The query processor responds with a prompt:

Change OR to ?

In the example, ORE is the new value of domain 6 (STATE). The new value is placed in the relation, and if no other modifications are requested, the query processor again asks for a command to modify, lookup, delete, or exit.

## Database Backup

After many modifications and deletions a database should be backed up in order to create a copy just in case the system fails. The backup copy can be stored until a subsequent backup copy is made. This process guarantees that you always have "most of the database" on another diskette.

```
Enter search key value : LEWIS
        Correct ( Y/N ) ? Y
1.Id :L01
2.Last •LEWIS                First :TED
3.Street :2812 MONTEREY
4.City   :CORVALLIS          State :OR
5.Zip :97330
6.Balance :10.95


Enter M=modify. L=lookup. D=delete. E=exit M
Enter 0=quit. = field to change : ? 6
Change OR to ? ORE
Are you sure ? Y
Enter 0=quit. = field to change : ? 0
Enter M=modify. L=lookup. D=delete. E=exit L_
```

**Screen Display 7-7.** Example of information retrieval using screen format.

```
[ 1 ]. Create a database system. or
[ 2 ]. Add new records. or
[ 3 ]. Lookup/Modify existing records. or
[ 4 ]. Backup file and index. or
[ 5 ]. Build screen form ( for input ). or
[ 6 ]. Quick dump index file. or
[ 7 ]. Stop. Exit DBMS system.



    Enter a number : ? 4


Enter name of backup data file : MASTER.CPY
    Correct ? Y
Enter name of backup index file : BTREE.CPY
    Correct ?Y_
```

**Screen Display 7-8.** Example of database backup operation.

A second reason to make a backup copy of the database periodically is to remove "garbage", i.e., information that is no longer needed. A deletion operation marks a tuple as unneeded information. Therefore, backup copies contain all but the deleted tuples. It is also possible to compress the information into a smaller file by rewriting it during the backup operation.

Screen Display 7-8 shows how to backup the relation described in the example of this section. MASTER.DAT is copied into MASTER.CPY, and BTREE.DAT is copied into BTREE.CPY. All tuples marked for deletion are skipped during the copy operation.

This example demonstrates the four main parts of a DBMS. The simple relational DBMS supports one relation using CRT screen forms and a single-access domain. In more sophisticated relational DBMS's multiple relations, multiple-access domains per relation, and powerful queries are supported.

## PROGRAM LISTING FOR THE SIMPLE RELATIONAL DBMS

Figure 7-2 contains a complete listing of the BASIC program for the simple relational DBMS used as an example in this chapter. An explanation of how this system works is given in the next section.

This program is written to work for beginning BASIC; however, to make it work for BASICA on your IBM Personal Computer, you must modify it slightly. This is necessary because of a minor flaw in BASICA. The reserved keywords cannot be used as variables in BASIC. Unfortunately, KEY$ conflicts with the keyword KEY in BASICA. To overcome this flaw, simply replace KEY$ with KEYS$ in the program shown here. (This flaw in BASICA will show up as a "syntax error.")

```
100 REM  -----------------------------------------------------------
105 REM
110 REM                    dbmenu.bas
115 REM    Root program of the DBMS demonstration program.
120 REM
125 REM  -----------------------------------------------------------
130 REM
135 NMAX% = 7
140 FOR I% = 1 TO 25: PRINT : NEXT I%
145 PRINT"       [ 1 ]. Create a database system, or"
150 PRINT"       [ 2 ]. Add new records, or"
155 PRINT"       [ 3 ]. Lookup/Modify existing records, or"
160 PRINT"       [ 4 ]. Backup file and index, or"
165 PRINT"       [ 5 ]. Build screen form ( for input ), or"
172 PRINT"       [ 6 ]. Quick dump index file, or"
174 PRINT"       [ 7 ]. Stop. Exit DBMS system."
175 PRINT : PRINT : PRINT
180 PRINT : PRINT"        Enter a number : "; : INPUT N%
185 PRINT : PRINT : PRINT
190 IF N% > NMAX% OR N% < 1 THEN 140
195 ON N% GOTO 200, 205, 210, 215, 220, 225, 230
200        RUN "CREATE"
205        RUN "INSERT"
210        RUN "LOOKUP"
215        RUN "BACKUP"
220        RUN "SCREEN"
225        RUN "DUMP"
230 STOP
250 END

100 REM  -----------------------------------------------------------
105 REM
110 REM                    create.bas
115 REM    Create a database from information about the files
120 REM
125 REM  -----------------------------------------------------------
```

**Figure 7-2.** Program listing for DBMS system. (Continued on pages 188–201.)

```
130 GOTO 340
140 REM ------------------------------------------------------------
150 REM            write ( p%, flag%, key$, arc%, link% )
160 REM ------------------------------------------------------------
170 REC$ = SPACE$ ( 127 )
180 FOR INDEX% = 1 TO N%
190  CH% = SIZE% * ( INDEX% - 1 )
200  ON FLAG% ( INDEX% ) + 1  GOTO 210, 230, 250
210        FLAG$ = "E" : GOTO 260
220        REM
230        FLAG% = "F" : GOTO 260
240        REM
250        FLAG% = "D"
260  MID$( REC$, CH%+1, 1 ) = FLAG$
270  MID$( REC$, CH%+2, SIZE%-3 ) = KEY$( INDEX% )
280  MID$( REC$, CH%+SIZE%-1, 2 ) = MKI$( ARC%( INDEX% ) )
290 NEXT INDEX%
300 MID$( REC$, 126, 2 ) = MKI$( LINK% )
310 LSET R$ = REC$
320 PUT 1, P%
330 RETURN
340 REM ------------------------------------------------------------
350 REM          create :  make header file for b-tree index
360 REM ------------------------------------------------------------
370 FOR I% = 1 TO 24 : PRINT : NEXT I%
380 PRINT"     Create Index File Header"
390 PRINT : PRINT : PRINT
395 LINE INPUT  "Enter index file name : "; INDEX$
400 LINE INPUT  "      Correct ( Y/N ) ? "; Y$
410      IF Y$ <> "Y" AND Y$ <> "y" THEN 395
420 PRINT"How many characters per search key "; : INPUT SIZE%
430 LINE INPUT  "      Correct ( Y/N ) ? "; Y$
440      IF Y$ <> "Y" AND Y$ <> "y" THEN 420
450 LINE INPUT  "Enter screen form file name : "; FSCREEN$
460 LINE INPUT  "      Correct ( Y/N ) ? "; Y$
470      IF Y$ <> "Y" AND Y$ <> "y" THEN 450
475 PRINT"Enter number screen lines in form : "; : INPUT LINS%
480 LINE INPUT "      Correct ( Y/N ) ? "; Y$
485      IF Y$ <> "Y" AND Y$ <> "y" THEN 475
490 LINE INPUT  "Enter data file name : "; MAST$
495 LINE INPUT  "      Correct ( Y/N ) ? "; Y$
500      IF Y$ <> "Y" AND Y$ <> "y" THEN 490
505 PRINT"Enter number fields in screen form : "; : INPUT AN%
510 LINE INPUT "      Correct ( Y/N ) ? "; Y$
515 IF Y$ <> "y" AND Y$ <> "Y" THEN 505
520 REM ------------------------------------------------------------
525 REM            write header file
530 REM ------------------------------------------------------------
535 SIZE% = SIZE% + 3
540 N% = INT ( 126/SIZE% )
545 OPEN "O", 2, "HEADER.DAT"
550 ROOT% = 1
555 LNF% = 1 : LNG% = 0
560 P% = ROOT%
565 PRINT #2,FSCREEN$;",";ROOT%;LNG%;LNF%;AN%;LINS%;N%;SIZE%;INDEX$;",";MAST$
570 CLOSE 2
575 REM ------------------------------------------------------------
580 REM            write first root node
585 REM ------------------------------------------------------------
590 DIM FLAG%( N%+1 ), KEY$( N%+1 ), ARC%( N%+1 )
595 ZERO$ = SPACE$( SIZE% - 3 ) :LSET ZERO$ = "0"
600 FOR IO% = 1 TO N%
605  KEY$( IO% ) = SPACE$( SIZE%-3 )
610  FLAG%( IO% ) = 0 : KEY$( IO% ) = ZERO$ : ARC%( IO% ) = 0
615 NEXT IO%
620 LINK% = 0
625 OPEN "R", 1, INDEX$
630 FIELD 1, 127 AS R$
635 GOSUB 140
640 CLOSE 1
645 REM ------------------------------------------------------------
```

**Figure 7-2.** Continued.

```
650 REM           all done, return to dbmenu.bas
655 REM ----------------------------------------------------------
660 RUN "DBMENU"
665 END

1   REM ----------------------------------------------------------------
2   REM
3   REM                         insert.bas
4   REM           add to the contents of a data file thru its index
5   REM
6   REM ----------------------------------------------------------------
10  REM
15  S0% = 20 : DIM STACK% ( S0% ) : GOTO 1100
20  REM
25  REM           Subroutines used :
30  REM             100, 150 : read, write a node of b-tree
35  REM             200, 250 : save, restore copy of b-tree node
40  REM             300, 350, 395 : push, pop, init the stack
45  REM             400 : shift items in node for splitting node
50  REM             500 : search down B-tree
55  REM             600 : allocate more space for B-tree
60  REM             700 : split B-tree node into left and right nodes
65  REM             800 : overflow B-tree node to root node
70  REM             900 : insert a new item into B-tree
75  REM             1000 : close all files and finish up
80  REM
85  REM
90  REM
100 REM ----------------------------------------------------------------
105 REM
110 REM                         read.bas
115 REM           input a b-tree node from disk file #1
120 REM
125 REM ----------------------------------------------------------------
130 GET 1, P%  : LSET REC$ = R$
131 FOR INDEX% = 1 TO N%
132     CH% = SIZE% * ( INDEX% - 1 )
133     FLAG$ = MID$( REC$, CH% + 1, 1 )
134     IF FLAG$ = "E" THEN FLAG%( INDEX% ) = 0
135     IF FLAG$ = "F" THEN FLAG%( INDEX% ) = 1
136     IF FLAG$ = "D" THEN FLAG%( INDEX% ) = 2
137     KEY$( INDEX% ) = MID$( REC$,CH%+2,SIZE%-3)
138     ARC%( INDEX% ) = CVI( MID$( REC$, CH% + SIZE% - 1, 2 ) )
139 NEXT INDEX%
140 ARC% ( N% + 1 ) = CVI( MID$ ( REC$, 126 , 2 ) )
145 RETURN
149 REM
150 REM ----------------------------------------------------------------
155 REM
160 REM                         write.bas
165 REM           output a b-tree node to file # 1
170 REM
175 REM ----------------------------------------------------------------
177 REC$ = STRING$( 127, " " )
180 FOR INDEX% = 1 TO N%
181     CH% = SIZE% * ( INDEX% - 1 )
182     ON FLAG%( INDEX% ) + 1  GOTO 183, 184, 185
183       FLAG$ = "E" : GOTO 186
184       FLAG$ = "F" : GOTO 186
185       FLAG$ = "D"
186     MID$( REC$, CH% + 1, 1 ) = FLAG$
187     MID$( REC$, CH% + 2, SIZE% - 3 ) = KEY$ ( INDEX% )
188     MID$( REC$, CH% + SIZE% - 1, 2 ) = MKI$( ARC%( INDEX% ) )
189 NEXT INDEX%
190 MID$( REC$, 126, 2 ) = MKI$( ARC%( N% + 1 ) )
195 LSET R$ = REC$ : PUT 1, P%
199 RETURN
200 REM ----------------------------------------------------------------
201 REM
202 REM                 save a b-tree node
203 REM ----------------------------------------------------------------
210 FOR INDEX% = 1 TO N% + 1
212     SFLAG%( INDEX% ) = FLAG%( INDEX% )
```

```
214     SKEY$( INDEX% ) = KEY$( INDEX% )
216     SARC%( INDEX% ) = ARC%( INDEX% )
218 NEXT INDEX%
220 RETURN
250 REM -----------------------------------------------------------------------
251 REM
252 REM                        restore a b-tree node
253 REM -----------------------------------------------------------------------
260 FOR INDEX% = 1 TO N% + 1
262     FLAG%( INDEX% ) = SFLAG%( INDEX% )
264     KEY$( INDEX% ) = SKEY$( INDEX% )
266     ARC%( INDEX% ) = SARC%( INDEX% )
268 NEXT INDEX%
270 RETURN
300 REM -----------------------------------------------------------------------
301 REM
302 REM                        push
303 REM -----------------------------------------------------------------------
304 REM
310 IF TS% <= S0% THEN 330
315     D$ = "Stack overflow"
320     RETURN
330 STACK%( TS% ) = A% : TS% = TS% + 1
340 D$ = "" : RETURN
350 REM -----------------------------------------------------------------------
351 REM
352 REM                        pop
353 REM -----------------------------------------------------------------------
360 TS% = TS% - 1
365 IF TS% > 0 THEN 380
370     D$ = "Stack underflow"
375     RETURN
380 A% = STACK%( TS% )
385 D$ = "" : RETURN
395 REM -----------------------------------------------------------------------
396 REM
397 REM                        initialize stack
398 REM -----------------------------------------------------------------------
399 TS% = 1 : RETURN
400 REM -----------------------------------------------------------------------
401 REM
402 REM                        shift B-tree node
403 REM
404 REM -----------------------------------------------------------------------
405 REM
410 SPLIT% = INT( (N%+1) / 2 )
415 I% = 1
420 IF SPLIT% + I% <= N% THEN 425 ELSE 450
425     ARC%( I% ) = ARC%( SPLIT% + I% )
430     KEY$( I% ) = KEY$( SPLIT% + I% )
435     FLAG%( I% )= FLAG%( SPLIT% + I% )
440     I% = I% + 1
445     GOTO 420
450 ARC%( I% ) = TEMP%
455 KEY$( I% ) = ZERO$
460 FLAG%( I% ) = 0
465 REM -----------------------------------------------------------------------
466 REM           zero out remaining items in node
467 REM -----------------------------------------------------------------------
470 FOR I% = I% + 1 TO N%
475     ARC%( I% ) = 0
477     KEY$( I% ) = ZERO$
480     FLAG%( I% ) = 0
485 NEXT I%
490 GOSUB 600     'allocate disk space at p2%
495 SWAP P% ,P2%
496 GOSUB 150     'write right son to disk
497 SWAP P%, P2%
499 RETURN
```

**Figure 7-2.** Continued.

```
500 REM -----------------------------------------------------------------
501 REM
502 REM            search b-tree for k$
503 REM
504 REM -----------------------------------------------------------------
505 REM
506 D$ = ""                       'message
510 GOSUB 395                      'initialize stack
515 P% = ROOT%
520 REM  repeat until found or not-in-file
525     I% = 1
530     GOSUB 100
535     IF KEY$( I% ) = ZERO$ THEN 545
540     IF KEY$( I% ) < K$ THEN 542 ELSE 545
542         I% = I% + 1 : GOTO 535
545     A% = P% : GOSUB 300        'push node number
550     A% = I% : GOSUB 300        'push item number
555 P% = ARC%( I% ) :IF P% <= 0 THEN RETURN
560 GOTO 520
600 REM -----------------------------------------------------------------
601 REM
602 REM            allocate more disk space for b-tree
603 REM
604 REM -----------------------------------------------------------------
605 REM
610 D$ = "" : LNF% = LNF% + 1
620 P2% = LNF%
630 RETURN
700 REM -----------------------------------------------------------------
701 REM
702 REM            split a b-tree node into lf and rt nodes
703 REM
704 REM -----------------------------------------------------------------
705 REM
710 GOSUB 200
715 GOSUB 400
720 GOSUB 250
725 K$ = KEY$( SPLIT% )
730 FOR I% = SPLIT% + 1 TO N%
731     KEY$( I% ) = ZERO$
732     FLAG%( I% ) = 0
733     ARC%( I% ) = 0
740 NEXT I%
745 ARC%( N% + 1 ) = P2%
750 GOSUB 150
790 RETURN
800 REM -----------------------------------------------------------------
801 REM
802 REM            overflow
803 REM
804 REM -----------------------------------------------------------------
805 REM
810 GOSUB 700 : P0% = P%
820 GOSUB 350 : ITEM% = A%
825 GOSUB 350 : P% = A%
830 IF D$ = "Stack underflow" THEN 835 ELSE 880
835     FLAG%( 1 ) = 1 : KEY$( 1 ) = K$ : ARC%( 1 ) = P0%
840     FLAG%( 2 ) = 0 : KEY$( 2 ) = ZERO$ : ARC%( 2 ) = P2%
845     FOR I% = 3 TO N%
850             FLAG%( I% ) = 0
851             KEY$( I% ) = ZERO$
852             ARC%( I% ) = 0
855     NEXT I%
860     ARC%( N% + 1 ) = 0
865     GOSUB 600 : P% = P2%
870     GOSUB 150 : ROOT% = P%
875     D$ = "Done" : RETURN
880 REM -----------------------------------------------------------------
885 GOSUB 100      'read parent node
890 ARC%( ITEM% ) = P2%
895 D$ = "Not done"
899 RETURN
```

```
900 REM --------------------------------------------------------------------
901 REM
902 REM          insert new item in b-tree
903 REM
904 REM --------------------------------------------------------------------
905 REM
910 GOSUB 500    'search
920 GOSUB 350 : ITEM% = A%        'pop
925 GOSUB 350 : P% = A%           'pop
930 IF K$ = KEY$( ITEM% ) THEN 931 ELSE 940
931     D$ = "Found" : PRINT"Already indexed"
932     LINE INPUT"Strike return to continue "; Y$
933     RETURN
940 REM --------------------------------------------------------------------
945 TEMP% = ARC%( N% )
950 FOR I% = N% TO ITEM% + 1 STEP (-1)
955     ARC%( I% ) = ARC%( I% - 1 )
960     KEY$( I% ) = KEY$( I% - 1 )
965     FLAG%( I% ) = FLAG%( I% - 1 )
970 NEXT I%
975 ARC%( ITEM% ) = PO%
976 KEY$( ITEM% ) = K$
977 FLAG%( ITEM% ) = 1
978 REM ------------------ insert done ------------------
980 IF KEY$( N% ) = ZERO$ THEN 990 ELSE 995
990      GOSUB 150 : RETURN                        're-write node
995 GOSUB 800 : IF D$ <> "Done" THEN 940           'ascend b-tree ?
999 RETURN
1000 REM --------------------------------------------------------------------
1001 REM
1002 REM          finish up
1003 REM
1004 REM --------------------------------------------------------------------
1005 REM
1010 FOR I% = 1 TO 24
1011     PRINT
1012 NEXT I%     'clear the screen
1015 CLOSE 1,2
1020 OPEN "O", 2, "HEADER.DAT"
1025 PRINT #2,FSCREEN$;",";ROOT%;LNG%;LNF%;AN%;LINS%;N%;SIZE%;INDEX$;",";MAST$
1030 CLOSE 2
1035 RETURN
1100 REM --------------------------------------------------------------------
1101 REM
1102 REM          capture data from screen form
1103 REM
1104 REM --------------------------------------------------------------------
1105 REM
1106 FOR I% = 1 TO 24 : PRINT : NEXT I%
1110 OPEN "I", 2, "HEADER.DAT"
1115     INPUT #2, FSCREEN$, ROOT%, LNG%,LNF%,AN%,LINS% ,N%, SIZE%, INDEX$, MAST$
1120 CLOSE 2
1125 NO% = N% + 1 : DIM FLAG%( NO% ), KEY$( NO% ), ARC%( NO% )
1130               DIM SFLAG%( NO% ), SKEY$( NO% ), SARC%( NO% )
1135 OPEN "I", 2, FSCREEN$
1140     FOR L% = 1 TO LINS% : INPUT #2, RW$( L% ) : NEXT L%
1145 CLOSE 2
1150 OPEN "R", 1, INDEX$
1155 FIELD 1, 127 AS R$
1160 REC$ = SPACE$( 128 ) : ZERO$ = SPACE$( SIZE% - 3 ) :   LSET ZERO$ = "O"
1165 K$ = SPACE$( SIZE% - 3 )
1170 OPEN "R", 2, MAST$
1175     FIELD 2, 127 AS MR$
1179 REM ------------------ forms input ------------------
1200 DIM AN$( AN% )                    'answers in an$
1210 K% = 0
1220 FOR L% = 1 TO LINS%
1225     SRW$ = RW$( L% )                       'save form prompt
1230     PRINT USING "##"; L% ; : PRINT ".";
1235     IF INSTR( LEFT$( RW$( L% ), 1 ), "-" ) = 1 THEN 1240
1236     IF INSTR( LEFT$( RW$( L% ), 1 ), " " ) = 0 THEN 1250
1240        RW$( L% ) = RIGHT$( RW$( L% ), LEN( RW$( L% ) ) - 1 )
```

**Figure 7-2.** Continued.

```
1245        GOTO 1235
1250     STAR% = INSTR( RW$( L% ), "*" )
1255     J% = INSTR( RW$( L% ), ":" )
1260     IF STAR% = 0 THEN 1270
1265       IF STAR% < J% THEN 1295
1270     IF J% = 0 THEN 1295
1275       PRINT " "; LEFT$( RW$( L% ), J% ) ;
1280       K% = K% + 1 : RW$( L% ) = RIGHT$( RW$( L% ), LEN( RW$( L% ) ) - J% )
1285       LINE INPUT AN$( K% )
1290       GOTO 1235
1295     J% = INSTR( RW$( L% ), "*" )
1300     IF J% = 0 THEN 1340
1305       PRINT " "; LEFT$( RW$( L% ), J% ) ;
1310       K% = K% + 1 : RW$( L% ) = RIGHT$( RW$( L% ), LEN( RW$( L% ) )- J% )
1315       LINE INPUT AN$( K% ) : K$ = ""
1320       K$ = LEFT$( AN$( K% ), SIZE% - 3 )
1325       LNG% = LNG% + 1 : PO% = - LNG%
1330       PRINT "Indexing by "; K$
1335       GOSUB 900        : GOTO 1235      'insert k$, pO% into b-tree
1340       RW$( L% ) = SRW$          'restore rw$
1342       IF D$ = "Found" THEN 1230        'try again
1345 NEXT L%
1350 TR$ = STRING$( 127, ":" ) : I1% = 1
1355 FOR I% = 1 TO AN%
1360   I2% = I1% + LEN( AN$( I% ) ) - 1
1365   MID$( TR$, I1%, I2% ) = AN$( I% )
1370   I1% = I2% + 2
1375 NEXT I%        'pack answers into tr$
1380 LSET MR$ = TR$
1385 PUT 2, LNG%          'write random record
1390 PRINT"Inputs stored in file : "; MAST$
1395 REM ----------- DO IT AGAIN ? --------------------------
1400 LINE INPUT"Do you want to enter more (Y/N) ? "; Y$
1405 IF Y$ ="y" OR Y$ = "Y" THEN 1210
1410 GOSUB 1000
1415 RUN"DBMENU"
1420 END


1    REM ---------------------------------------------------------------
2    REM
3    REM                    lookup.bas
4    REM            retrieve/change information in database
5    REM
6    REM ---------------------------------------------------------------
7    REM
10   GOTO 1100
20   REM ---------- subroutines --------------------------------------
30   REM
100  REM ---------------------------------------------------------------
105  REM
110  REM                         read.bas
115  REM            input a b-tree node from disk file #1
120  REM
125  REM ---------------------------------------------------------------
130  GET 1, P% : LSET REC$ = R$
131  FOR INDEX% = 1 TO N%
132     CH% = SIZE% * ( INDEX% - 1 )
133     FLAG$ = MID$( REC$, CH% + 1, 1 )
134       IF FLAG$ = "E" THEN FLAG%( INDEX% ) = 0
135       IF FLAG$ = "F" THEN FLAG%( INDEX% ) = 1
136       IF FLAG$ = "D" THEN FLAG%( INDEX% ) = 2
137     KEY$( INDEX% ) = MID$( REC$, CH% + 2, SIZE% - 3 )
138     ARC%( INDEX% ) = CVI( MID$( REC$, CH% + SIZE% - 1, 2 ) )
139  NEXT INDEX%
140  ARC% ( N% + 1 ) = CVI( MID$ ( REC$, 126 , 2 ) )
145  RETURN
149  REM
150  REM ---------------------------------------------------------------
155  REM
160  REM                         write.bas
165  REM            output a b-tree node to file # 1
170  REM
175  REM ---------------------------------------------------------------
177  REC$ = STRING( 127, " " )
```

```
180 FOR INDEX% = 1 TO N%
181     CH% = SIZE% * ( INDEX% - 1 )
182     ON FLAG%( INDEX% ) + 1  GOTO 183, 184, 185
183       FLAG$ = "E" : GOTO 186
184       FLAG$ = "F" : GOTO 186
185       FLAG$ = "D"
186     MID$( REC$, CH% + 1, 1 ) = FLAG$
187     MID$( REC$, CH% + 2, SIZE% - 3 ) = KEY$ ( INDEX% )
188     MID$( REC$, CH% + SIZE% - 1, 2 ) = MKI$( ARC%( INDEX% ) )
189 NEXT INDEX%
190 MID$( REC$, 126, 2 ) = MKI$( ARC%( N% + 1 ) )
195 LSET R$ = REC$ : PUT 1, P%
199 RETURN
500 REM ----------------------------------------------------------------------
501 REM
502 REM                   search for k$ in b-tree
503 REM
504 REM ----------------------------------------------------------------------
505 REM
515 P% = ROOT% : D$ = ""
520 REM ---------- repeat until found or not in file --------------------
525     I% = 1
530     GOSUB 100       'read node
535     IF KEY$( I% ) = ZERO$ THEN 545
540     IF KEY$( I% ) < K$ THEN 542 ELSE 545
542       I% = I% + 1 : GOTO 535
545     A% = P%
550     ITEM% = I%
552     P% = ARC%( I% )
555 IF P% <= 0 THEN 560 ELSE 520
560 IF KEY$( ITEM% ) <> K$ THEN 565
561 IF FLAG%( ITEM% ) <> 2 THEN 563       'may be deleted
562   PRINT"Key was deleted..cannot retrieve it.": GOTO 567
563 P% = A% : RETURN                       'found it !!!
565 PRINT"Key not found..cannot retrieve it."
567 D$ = "Not found"
570 RETURN
800 REM ----------------------------------------------------------------------
801 REM
802 REM           get and unpack data file
803 REM
804 REM ----------------------------------------------------------------------
805 REM
810 GET 2, -ARC%( ITEM% )
840 LSET TR$ = MR$ : I1% = 1
850 FOR I% = 1 TO AN%
860     I2% = INSTR( TR$, ":" )
865     AN$( I% ) = SPACE$( I2% - I1% )
870     LSET AN$( I% ) = MID$( TR$, I1%, I2% - 1 )
880     MID$( TR$, I1%, I2% ) = STRING$( I2% - I1% + 1 ," " )
890     I1% = I2% + 1
895 NEXT I%
899 RETURN
900 REM ----------------------------------------------------------------------
901 REM
902 REM                   pack and re-write data file record
903 REM
904 REM ----------------------------------------------------------------------
905 REM
920 TR$ = STRING$( 127,":" ) : I1% = 1
925 FOR I% = 1 TO AN%
930     I2% = I1% + LEN( AN$( I% ) ) - 1
935     MID$( TR$, I1%, I2% ) = AN$( I% )
940     I1% = I2% + 2
945 NEXT I%
950 LSET MR$ = TR$
955 PUT 2, -ARC%( ITEM% )
960 RETURN
1000 REM ---------------------------------------------------------------------
1001 REM                   finish
1002 REM ---------------------------------------------------------------------
```

**Figure 7-2.** Continued.

```
1003 REM
1010 CLOSE 1,2
1015 OPEN "O", 2, "HEADER.DAT"
1020  PRINT #2,FSCREEN$;",";ROOT%;LNG%;LNF%;AN%;LINS%;N%;SIZE%;INDEX$;",";MAST$
1025 CLOSE 2
1030 RUN "DBMENU.BAS"              'bail out.
1100 REM ----------------------------------------------------------------
1101 REM
1102 REM         retrieve data using screen form
1103 REM
1104 REM ----------------------------------------------------------------
1105 REM
1106 FOR I% = 1 TO 24 : PRINT : NEXT I%
1110 OPEN "I", 2, "HEADER.DAT"
1115    INPUT #2, FSCREEN$, ROOT%, LNG%,LNF%,AN%,LINS% ,N%, SIZE%, INDEX$, MAST$
1120 CLOSE 2
1125 NO% = N% + 1 : DIM FLAG%( NO% ), KEY$( NO% ), ARC%( NO% )
1130                 DIM SFLAG%( NO% ), SKEY( NO% ), SARC%( NO% )
1135 DIM AN$( AN% )
1137 OPEN "I", 2, FSCREEN$
1140    FOR L% = 1 TO LINS% : INPUT #2, RW$( L% ) : NEXT L%
1145 CLOSE 2
1150 OPEN "R", 1, INDEX$
1155 FIELD 1, 127 AS R$
1160 REC$ = SPACE$( 127 ) :ZERO$ = SPACE$( SIZE% - 3 ) :  LSET ZERO$ = "O"
1165 K$ = SPACE$( SIZE% - 3 ) : TR$ = SPACE$( 128 )
1170 OPEN "R", 2, MAST$
1175    FIELD 2, 127 AS MR$
1180 LINE INPUT "Enter search key value : "; KINP$ : LSET K$ = KINP$
1185 LINE INPUT "       Correct ( Y/N ) ? "; Y$
1190 IF Y$ = "y" OR Y$ = "Y" THEN 1192 ELSE 1180
1192 IF LEN( KINP$ ) = 0 THEN 1000
1195 GOSUB 500           'search
1196 IF D$ <> "" THEN 1180
1197 GOSUB 800
1199 REM --------------------------- forms display -------------
1200 REM
1210 K% = 0
1220 FOR I% = 1 TO LINS%
1225    SRW$ = RW$( I% )
1230    PRINT USING "##"; I% ; : PRINT ".";
1235    IF INSTR( LEFT$( RW$( I% ), 1 ), "-" ) = 1 THEN 1237
1236    IF INSTR( LEFT$( RW$( I% ), 1 ), " " ) = 0 THEN 1240
1237      RW$( I% ) = RIGHT$( RW$( I% ), LEN( RW$( I% ) ) - 1 )
1238      PRINT " "; : GOTO 1235
1240    J% = INSTR( RW$( I% ), ":" )
1242    JSTAR% = INSTR( RW$( I% ), "*" )
1243      IF JSTAR% = 0 THEN 1250
1245      IF JSTAR% < J% THEN 1300
1250    IF J% = 0 THEN 1300
1260      PRINT LEFT$( RW$( I% ), J% ) ;
1270      K% = K% + 1 : RW$( I% ) = MID$( RW$( I% ), J% + LEN( AN$( K% ))+1)
1280      PRINT AN$( K% );
1290      GOTO 1235
1300    J% = INSTR( RW$( I% ), "*" )
1310    IF J% = 0 THEN 1340
1311      K% = K% + 1 :  PRINT LEFT$( RW$( I% ), J% ) ;
1312      RW$( I% ) = MID$( RW$( I% ), J%+LEN( AN$( K% ) ) + 1 )
1313      PRINT AN$( K% );
1338      GOTO 1235
1340      PRINT : RW$( I% ) = SRW$
1345 NEXT I%
1400 REM ----------- modify, delete or what ----------------------------
1401 REM
1405 PRINT : PRINT
1410 LINE INPUT"Enter M=modify, L=lookup, D=delete, E=exit "; C$
1420 IF C$ = "E" OR C$ = "e" THEN 1000
1430 IF C$ = "D" OR C$ = "d" THEN 1450
1440 IF C$ = "M" OR C$ = "m" THEN 1500
1445 GOTO 1180
1450 REM ------------ delete data ---------------------------------------
1455 LINE INPUT "Are you sure you want to delete this information ?"; Y$
1460 IF Y$ <> "Y" AND Y$ <> "y" THEN 1410
```

```
1465 FLAG%( ITEM% ) = 2
1470 GOSUB 150           're-write b-tree node
1475 GOTO 1410
1500 REM ------------- change AN$ --------------------------------------------
1505 Y$ = "N"
1510 PRINT"Enter 0=quit, # field to change : "; : INPUT L%
1515 IF L% <= 0 OR L% > AN% THEN 1545
1520 PRINT"Change "; AN$( L% ); " to "; : INPUT C$
1525 LINE INPUT "Are you sure ? "; Y$
1530 IF Y$ <> "Y" AND Y$ <>"y" THEN 1510
1535 AN$( L% ) = C$
1540 GOTO 1510
1545 IF Y$ = "N" THEN 1410
1550 GOSUB 900 : GOTO 1410         're-write data
1599 END

1    REM --------------------------------------------------------------------
2    REM
3    REM                        backup.bas
4    REM          copy b-tree index file and master data file
5    REM          remove deleted items in the database
6    REM
7    REM --------------------------------------------------------------------
8    REM
10   GOTO 1100                     branch to main pgm
100  REM --------------------------------------------------------------------
105  REM
110  REM                        read.bas
115  REM          input a b-tree node from disk file #1
120  REM
125  REM --------------------------------------------------------------------
130  GET 1, PO%  : LSET REC$ = R$
131  FOR INDEX% = 1 TO N%
132      CH% = SIZE% * ( INDEX% - 1 )
133      FLAG$ = MID$( REC$, CH% + 1, 1 )
134       IF FLAG$ = "E" THEN FLAG%( INDEX% ) = 0
135       IF FLAG$ = "F" THEN FLAG%( INDEX% ) = 1
136       IF FLAG$ = "D" THEN FLAG%( INDEX% ) = 2
137      KEY$( INDEX% ) = MID$( REC$,CH%+2,SIZE%-3)
138      ARC%( INDEX% ) = CVI( MID$( REC$, CH% + SIZE% - 1, 2 ) )
139  NEXT INDEX%
140  ARC% ( N% + 1 ) = CVI( MID$ ( REC$, 126 , 2 ) )
145  LINK% = ARC%( N%+1 ) : RETURN
149  REM
150  REM --------------------------------------------------------------------
155  REM
160  REM                        write.bas
165  REM          output a b-tree node to file # 1
170  REM
175  REM --------------------------------------------------------------------
180  FOR INDEX% = 1 TO N%
181      CH% = SIZE% * ( INDEX% - 1 )
182      ON FLAG%( INDEX% ) + 1 GOTO 183, 184, 185
183        FLAG$ = "E" : GOTO 186
184        FLAG$ = "F" : GOTO 186
185        FLAG$ = "D"
186      MID$( REC$, CH% + 1, 1 ) = FLAG$
187      MID$( REC$, CH% + 2, SIZE% - 3 ) = KEY$ ( INDEX% )
188      MID$( REC$, CH% + SIZE% - 1, 2 ) = MKI$( ARC%( INDEX% ) )
189  NEXT INDEX%
190  MID$( REC$, 126, 2 ) = MKI$( ARC%( N% + 1 ) )
195  LSET NR$ = REC$ : PUT G%, LNF%
199  RETURN
250  REM --------------------------------------------------------------------
251  REM
252  REM                        restore a b-tree node
253  REM --------------------------------------------------------------------
260  FOR INDEX% = 1 TO N% + 1
262      FLAG%( INDEX% ) = SFLAG%( INDEX% )
264      KEY$( INDEX% ) = SKEY$( INDEX% )
266      ARC%( INDEX% ) = SARC%( INDEX% )
```

**Figure 7-2.** Continued.

```
268 NEXT INDEX%
270 RETURN
500 REM ---------------------------------------------------------------
501 REM
502 REM            search b-tree for left-most item, only
503 REM
504 REM ---------------------------------------------------------------
505 REM
510 D$ = "Found" : PO% = ROOT%
515 GOSUB 100            'read a node
520 IF ARC%( 1 ) = O THEN 525 ELSE 535
525     LINE INPUT"File is empty. Strike RETURN "; Y$
530     D$ = "Not Found" : RETURN
535 IF ARC%( 1 ) < O THEN 540 ELSE 545
540     ITEM% = 1 : RETURN
545 PO% = ARC%( 1 )
550 GOTO 515
700 REM ---------------------------------------------------------------
701 REM
702 REM                 read next sequential node
703 REM
704 REM ---------------------------------------------------------------
710 D$ = "" : PO% = LINK%
720 IF PO% = O THEN 725 ELSE 740
725     D$ = "Done" : RETURN
740 GOSUB 100 : ITEM% = 1 : RETURN
750 REM ---------------------------------------------------------------
751 REM
752 REM                 fill new index file node
753 REM
754 REM ---------------------------------------------------------------
755 FOR NI% = NI% TO N%
760     SKEY$( NI% ) = ZERO$
765     SFLAG%( NI% ) = O
770     SARC%( NI% ) = O
775 NEXT NI%
780 IF D$ = "Done" THEN SARC%( N%+1) = O ELSE SARC%( N%+1 ) = LNF% + 1
795 RETURN
1000 REM --------------------------------------------------------------
1001 REM
1002 REM                 finish up
1003 REM
1004 REM --------------------------------------------------------------
1005 REM
1015 CLOSE 1,2
1020 OPEN "O", 2, "HEADER.DAT"
1025 PRINT #2,FSCREEN$;",";ROOT%;NPTR%-1;LNF%-1;AN%;LINS%;N%;SIZE%;
1026 PRINT #2,INDEX$;MAST$
1030 CLOSE 2
1035 RETURN
1100 REM --------------------------------------------------------------
1101 REM
1102 REM         copy and garbage collect
1103 REM
1104 REM --------------------------------------------------------------
1105 REM
1110 OPEN "I", 2, "HEADER.DAT"
1115   INPUT #2, FSCREEN$, ROOT%, LNG%,LNF%,AN%,LINS% ,N%, SIZE%, INDEX$, MAST$
1120 CLOSE 2
1125 NO% = N% + 1 : DIM FLAG%( NO% ), KEY$( NO% ), ARC%( NO% )
1130             DIM SFLAG%( NO% ), SKEY$( NO% ), SARC%( NO% )
1150 OPEN "R", 1, INDEX$
1155 FIELD 1, 127 AS R$
1160 REC$ = SPACE$( 127 ) : ZERO$ = SPACE$( SIZE% - 3 ) :   LSET ZERO$ = "O"
1170 OPEN "R", 2, MAST$
1175     FIELD 2, 127 AS MR$
1200 REM --------------------------------------------------------------
1201 REM
1202 REM                 now that the files are open, etc.
1203 REM                 create backup copies...
1204 REM
1205 REM --------------------------------------------------------------
1210 REM
```

```
1270 LINE INPUT"Enter name of backup data file : "; NW$
1275 LINE INPUT"      Correct ? "; Y$
1280 IF Y$ <> "Y" AND Y$ <> "y" THEN 1270
1290 LINE INPUT"Enter name of backup index file : "; OUTDEX$
1300 LINE INPUT"      Correct ?"; Y$
1310 IF Y$ <> "y" AND Y$ <> "Y" THEN 1290
1320 PRINT"Busy working.."
1330 OPEN "R", 3, OUTDEX$
1340  FIELD 3, 127 AS NR$
1350 G% = 3
1360 OPEN "R", 4, NW$
1370  FIELD 4, 127 AS RR$
1380 GOSUB 500
1390 IF D$ = "Not Found" THEN 1395 ELSE 1400
1395   CLOSE 1,2,3,4 : RUN "DBMENU"
1400 REM -------------------- COPY FROM OLD MASTER TO NEW --------------
1470 NPTR% = 1 : LNF% = 1 : ITEM% = 1
1480 REM --------loop------------------
1490   FOR NI% = 1 TO N% - 1
1492     IF ITEM%'= N% THEN GOSUB 700
1496     IF D$ = "Done" THEN 1760
1500     MPTR% = -ARC%( ITEM% )
1505     IF MPTR% = 0 THEN 1506 ELSE 1510
1506        ITEM% = ITEM% + 1
1507        GOTO 1492
1510     IF FLAG%( ITEM% ) = 2 THEN 1506
1550     GET 2, MPTR%
1560     LSET RR$ = MR$
1570     PUT 4, NPTR%
1580 REM   copy index info
1590     SKEY$( NI% ) = KEY$( ITEM% )
1600     SFLAG%( NI% ) = 1
1610     SARC%( NI% ) = - NPTR%
1630 REM   update new master pointer
1650     NPTR% = NPTR% + 1
1700 REM   update old index info
1720        ITEM% = ITEM% + 1
1750 NEXT NI%
1751 PRINT"Calm down, Im still working on it .."
1755 IF ( KEY$( ITEM% ) = ZERO$ ) AND (LINK% = 0) THEN 1756 ELSE 1760
1756   D$ = "Done" : SARC%( N% + 1 ) = 0
1760 GOSUB 750 : GOSUB 250 : GOSUB 150
1770 LNF% = LNF% + 1
1780 IF D$ = "Done" THEN 1850 ELSE 1490
1850 REM ------------------------------------------------------------------
1855 REM       close files and redefine header file
1860 REM ------------------------------------------------------------------
1880 CLOSE 1,2,3,4
1890 INDEX$ = OUTDEX$
1900 MAST$ = NW$
1910 PRINT"Data file re-organized. Now for the index file..."
1930 REM ----------- Do b-tree tier by tier ----------------------------
1950 P0% = 1 : ROOT% = LNF%
1960 OPEN "R", 1, OUTDEX$
1965 G% = 1 : FIELD 1, 127 AS NR$
1980 REM ----------- Find last key and move it up ---------------------
2000 KOUNT% = 1 : D$ = ""
2010 FOR ITEM% = 1 TO N% - 1
2020    GOSUB 100 : SFLAG%( ITEM% ) = 1
2030    I% = 0
2031      I% = I% + 1
2032      SKEY$( ITEM% ) = KEY$( N% - I% )
2033      IF KEY$( N%-I% ) = ZERO$ THEN 2031
2060    SARC%( ITEM% ) = P0%
2070    P0% = LINK%
2080    IF P0% = 0 THEN 2100
2090 NEXT ITEM%
2100 REM ------------ Finish off node ----------------------------------
2105 PRINT"You are being so patient ..."
2130 IF P0% = 0 THEN 2140 ELSE 2250
2140    D$ = "Done" : NI% = ITEM% + 1 : GOSUB 750
```

**Figure 7-2.** Continued.

```
2150     GOSUB 250 : GOSUB 150
2155     PO% = ROOT% : ROOT% = LNF% + 1 : LNF% = ROOT%
2160     GOTO 2330
2200 REM ----------- More still to come ---------------------------------
2250     KOUNT% = KOUNT% + 1
2255     NI% = N%
2260     GOSUB 750 : GOSUB 250 : GOSUB 150
2270     LNF% = LNF% + 1 : GOTO 2010
2330 IF KOUNT% = 1 THEN 2340 ELSE 2000
2340 PRINT"Done, at last."
2390 ROOT% = ROOT% - 1 : GOSUB 1000
2400 RUN "DBMENU"
2500 END


1    REM -----------------------------------------------------------------
2    REM
3    REM                    dump.bas
4    REM         print contents of the entire b-tree
5    REM
6    REM -----------------------------------------------------------------
7    REM
10 GOTO 1100
100 REM -----------------------------------------------------------------
105 REM
110 REM                     read.bas
115 REM          input a b-tree node from disk file #1
120 REM
125 REM -----------------------------------------------------------------
130 GET 1, P%  : LSET REC$ = R$
131 FOR INDEX% = 1 TO N%
132     CH% = SIZE% * ( INDEX% - 1 )
133     FLAG$ = MID$( REC$, CH% + 1, 1 )
134      IF FLAG$ = "E" THEN FLAG%( INDEX% ) = 0
135      IF FLAG$ = "F" THEN FLAG%( INDEX% ) = 1
136      IF FLAG$ = "D" THEN FLAG%( INDEX% ) = 2
137     KEY$( INDEX% ) = MID$( REC$, CH% + 2, SIZE% - 3 )
138     ARC%( INDEX% ) = CVI( MID$( REC$, CH% + SIZE% - 1, 2 ) )
139 NEXT INDEX%
140 ARC% ( N% + 1 ) = CVI( MID$ ( REC$, 126 , 2 ) )
145 RETURN
149 REM
1100 REM -----------------------------------------------------------------
1101 REM
1102 REM          Quick read-out of b-tree index file
1103 REM
1104 REM -----------------------------------------------------------------
1105 REM
1110 FOR I% = 1 TO 24 : PRINT : NEXT I%
1115 OPEN "I", 2, "HEADER.DAT"
1120    INPUT #2, FSCREEN$, ROOT%, LNG%,LNF%,AN%,LINS% ,N%, SIZE%, INDEX$, MAST$
1125 CLOSE 2
1130 NO% = N% + 1 : DIM FLAG%( NO% ), KEY$( NO% ), ARC%( NO% )
1135 OPEN "R", 1, INDEX$
1140 FIELD 1, 127 AS R$
1145 REC$ = SPACE$( 128 ) :  LSET ZERO$ = "0"
1150 K$ = SPACE$( SIZE% - 3 )
1151 PRINT"Turn on printer, Strike RETURN :"
1152 PRINT"Printer ready (RETURN if it is)"; : INPUT Y$
1153 LPRINT"Quick dump of B-tree index file : "
1154 LPRINT : LPRINT
1155 P% = 0
1160 FOR II% = 1 TO LNF%
1165    P% = P% + 1 : GOSUB 100          'read a node
1170    LPRINT "--------------------- Node = ", P%, " -------------------"
1175    FOR I% = 1 TO N%
1180            IF FLAG%( I% ) = 0 THEN C$ = "Empty"
1185            IF FLAG%( I% ) = 1 THEN C$ = "Full"
1190            IF FLAG%( I% ) = 2 THEN C$ = "Deleted"
1195            LPRINT "Flag = "; C$;
1200            LPRINT " Key = "; KEY$( I% ) ;
1205            LPRINT " Arc = "; ARC%( I% )
1210    NEXT I%
1215    LPRINT "Link = "; ARC%( NO% )
```

```
1220 NEXT II%
1225 CLOSE 1
1230 REM ---------------- other stuff -----------------------------------
1240 LPRINT : LPRINT
1250 LPRINT "Root node = ", ROOT%
1260 LPRINT"Number items indexed = ", LNG%
1270 LPRINT"Number nodes(sectors)= ", LNF%
1280 LPRINT"Number fields per input form = ", AN%
1290 LPRINT"Number lines per input form  = ", LINS%
1300 LPRINT"Number items per node(sector)= ", N%
1310 LPRINT"Size(chars) of each node item= ", SIZE%
1320 LPRINT"Name of master(data) file    = ", MAST$
1330 LPRINT"Name of index file(b-tree)   = ",INDEX$
1400 RUN "DBMENU"
1499 END

100 REM ---------------------------------------------------------------
105 REM
110 REM                         screen.bas
115 REM         build a screen format for data entry
120 REM
125 REM ---------------------------------------------------------------
130 REM
135 OPEN "I", 2, "HEADER.DAT"
140   INPUT #2,FSCREEN$,ROOT%,LNG%,LNF%,AN%,LINS%,N%,SIZE%,INDEX$,MAST$
145 CLOSE 2
150 FOR I% = 1 TO 24 : PRINT : NEXT I%
155 PRINT" Enter form a line at a time, remember :"
160 PRINT"         * = keyed value"
165 PRINT"         : = begins a field"
170 PRINT"         - = field designation"
175 PRINT"       "; LINS%; " = lines per screen"
180 DIM RW$( LINS% )
185 FOR L% = 1 TO LINS%
190   PRINT USING "## "; L% ;
195   LINE INPUT RW$( L% )
200 NEXT L%
205 REM ---------------------------------------------------------------
210 REM          edit it
215 REM ---------------------------------------------------------------
220 PRINT
225 INPUT "Enter 0 to stop, or line number to change : "; L%
230 IF L% <= 0 OR L% > LINS% THEN 275
235   PRINT USING "## "; L% ;
240   PRINT RW$( L% )
245   PRINT USING "## "; L% ;
250   LINE INPUT RW$ ( L% )
255 GOTO 220
260 REM ---------------------------------------------------------------
265 REM          file it in fscreen$
270 REM ---------------------------------------------------------------
275 REM
290 PRINT : LINE INPUT "Do you want hard copy ? "; Y$
295 IF Y$ <> "y" AND Y$ <> "Y" THEN 310
300   GOSUB 360 : GOTO 290
305 REM ---------------------------------------------------------------
310 OPEN "O", 1, FSCREEN$
315   FOR L% = 1 TO LINS%
320        PRINT #1, RW$( L% )
325   NEXT L%
330 CLOSE 1
335 PRINT : PRINT"Form saved in "; FSCREEN$
340 RUN "DBMENU.BAS"
345 REM ---------------------------------------------------------------
350 REM          hard copy
355 REM ---------------------------------------------------------------
360 LPRINT : LPRINT "                    Screen Form "; FSCREEN$
365 LPRINT : LPRINT
370 FOR L% = 1 TO LINS%
375   LPRINT USING "## "; L%; : LPRINT RW$( L% )
```

**Figure 7-2.** Continued.

```
380 NEXT L%
385 LPRINT : LPRINT : LPRINT
390 RETURN


1100 REM ------------------------------------------------------------------
1101 REM
1102 REM          retrieve data using screen form
1103 REM
1104 REM ------------------------------------------------------------------
1105 REM
1106 FOR I% = 1 TO 24 : PRINT : NEXT I%
1110 OPEN "I", 2, "HEADER.DAT"
1115    INPUT #2, FSCREEN$, ROOT%, LNG%,LNF%,AN%,LINS% ,N%, SIZE%, INDEX$, MAST$
1120 CLOSE 2
1125 NO% = N% + 1 : DIM FLAG%( NO% ), KEY$( NO% ), ARC%( NO% )
1130                 DIM SFLAG%( NO% ), SKEY( NO% ), SARC%( NO% )
1135 OPEN "I", 2, FSCREEN$
1140    FOR L% = 1 TO LINS% : INPUT #2, RW$( L% ) : NEXT L%
1145 CLOSE 2
1150 OPEN "R", 1, INDEX$
1155 FIELD 1, 127 AS R$
1160 REC$ = SPACE$( 128 ) :   LSET ZERO$ = "0"
1165 K$ = SPACE$( SIZE$ - 3 )
1170 OPEN "R", 2, MAST$
1175    FIELD 2, 127 AS MR$
1179 REM ------------------ forms input --------------------------------
1200 DIM AN$( AN% )                    'answers in an$
1210 K% = 0
1220 FOR I% = 1 TO LINS%
1225    SRW$ = RW$( I% )                    'save form prompt
1230    PRINT USING "##", I% ;
1235    IF INSTR( LEFT$( RW$( I% ), 1 ), "-" ) = 0 THEN 1240
1236      RW$( I% ) = RIGHT$( RW$( I% ), LEN( RW$( I% ) ) - 1 )
1237      GOTO 1235
1240    J% = INSTR( RW$( I% ), ":" )
1250    IF J% = 0 THEN 1300
1260      PRINT LEFT$( RW$( I% ), J% ) ;
1270      K% = K% + 1 : RW$( I% ) = RIGHT$( RW$( I% ), LEN( RW$( I% ) ) - J% )
1280      LINE INPUT AN$( K% )
1290      GOTO 1235
1300    J% = INSTR( RW$( I% ), "*" )
1310    IF J% = 0 THEN 1340
1311      PRINT LEFT$( RW$( I% ), J% ) ;
1312      K% = K% + 1 : RW$( I% ) = RIGHT$( RW$( I% ), LEN( RW$( I% ) ) )
1313      LINE INPUT AN$( K% )
1320      K$ = LEFT$( AN$( K% ), SIZE% - 3 )
1325      LNG% = LNG% + 1 : PO% = - LNG%
1330      GOSUB 900         'insert k$ and pO% into b-tree index
1335      PRINT"Indexed by "; K$
1340      RW$( I% ) = SRW$           'restore rw$
1345 NEXT I%
1460 TR$ = STRING$( 127, ":" ) : I1% = 1
1465 FOR I% = 1 TO AN%
1470    I2% = I1% + LEN( AN$( I% ) ) - 1
1475    MID$( TR$, I1%, I2% ) = AN$( I% )
1480    I1% = I2% + 2
1485 NEXT I%                'pack answers into tr$
1490 LSET MR$ = TR$
1495 PUT 2, LNG%            'write random record
1500 PRINT"Inputs stored in file : "; MAST$
1510 REM ----------- DO IT AGAIN  ? --------------------------
1520 LINE INPUT"Do you want to enter more (Y/N) ? "; Y$
1530 IF Y$ ="y" OR Y$ = "Y" THEN 1210
1540 GOSUB 1000
1550 RUN "DBMENU"
1560 END
```

# HOW INDEX FILES WORK

In the previous example, main menu selection 6 will dump the entire contents of the index file to the printer. This file contains a clever file structure called a B-tree. The B-tree structure is at the heart of any high speed DBMS because it is the best way to store and retrieve information recorded on diskette. You do not need to understand B-trees to use a DBMS, but knowledge of a B-tree can be helpful to you in designing better DBMS's.

Here is the problem faced by anyone designing and implementing a DBMS. "How can information be quickly retrieved from a disk when it is indexed through one or more index values?" In fact, most DBMS's require that information be stored for fast retrieval in alphabetical order! This is the problem solved by the B-tree file structure.

## B-tree Structure

An **index file** is any file that contains keys and record numbers. A **master file** is any file containing information we want to store and retrieve. A relation can be stored in a master file, for example.

The purpose of an index file is to hold key values taken from the master file. The index file makes it possible to quickly access a certain record in a master file by first looking up the key to the record in an index file, and then, using the record number in the index file, to access the master record. Figure 7-3 illustrates this idea with two index files. Suppose the Name Index file holds all names stored in the master file, and suppose another index file called the Age Index holds all the ages stored in the master file. Now, to access a master file record by name, first search the Name Index and use the record number stored there to locate the master record. Figure 7-3 shows how access to "Adams" is made through the Name Index which contains the record number (4) of the record containing the name equal to "Adams". Similarly, the youngest entry in the master file is 18 years old. Thus, the Age Index is searched for a matching value of age (18). This value has a master record number associated with it (5), hence the master record containing 18 is accessed.

Notice in Figure 7-3 that the entries in either index file are stored in ascending alphabetical order. This means that we can retrieve all master records in alphabetical order by name using the Name Index, and we can retrieve them in order by age using the Age Index. Both index files maintain their keys in order regardless of the order of the records stored in the corresponding master file.

The example in Figure 7-3 illustrates two important properties of index files:

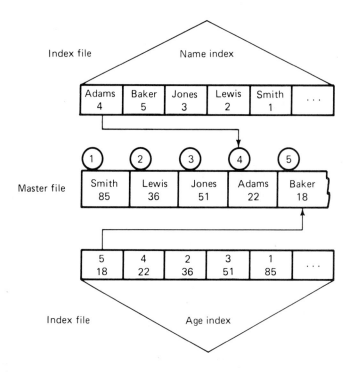

**Figure 7-3.** Example of two index files used to access by Name or Age. Arrows show how to get Adams or Age 18.

1. An index file must be organized so that lookup operations can be performed quickly.

2. An index file must be organized so that entries can be retrieved in order.

This is exactly what a B-tree structure does.

Figure 7-4 shows how to construct a B-tree to hold the letters of the alphabet. In Figure 7-4 we have entered the letters in reverse order. That is, Z is entered first, followed by Y, X, W, etc.

The boxes in Figure 7-4 correspond to a diskette sector (128 bytes). Each box has room for 4 keys and 5 record numbers. A negative record number is used to point to the location of a master file record. A positive record number is used to point to another sector in the B-tree index file.

Figure 7-4(a) shows the contents of the B-tree index file after Z has been entered into the B-tree. The (−1) points to record (+1) in the master file (not shown). Therefore, to retrieve the record containing key value "Z", we would search the B-tree first, and when Z is found, the

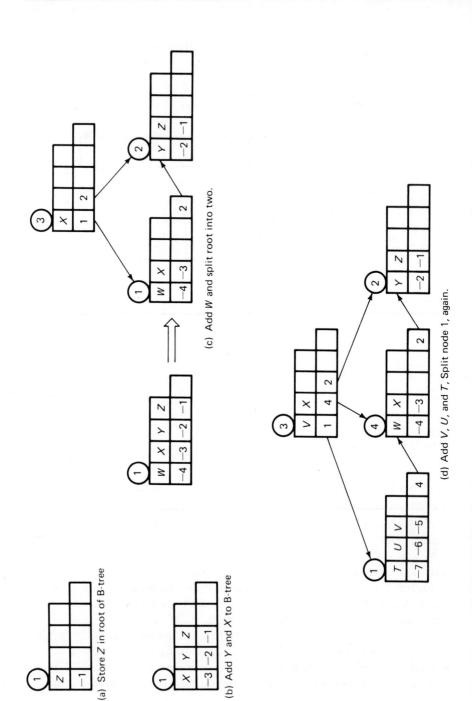

(a) Store Z in root of B-tree

(b) Add Y and X to B-tree

(c) Add W and split root into two.

(d) Add V, U, and T. Split node 1, again.

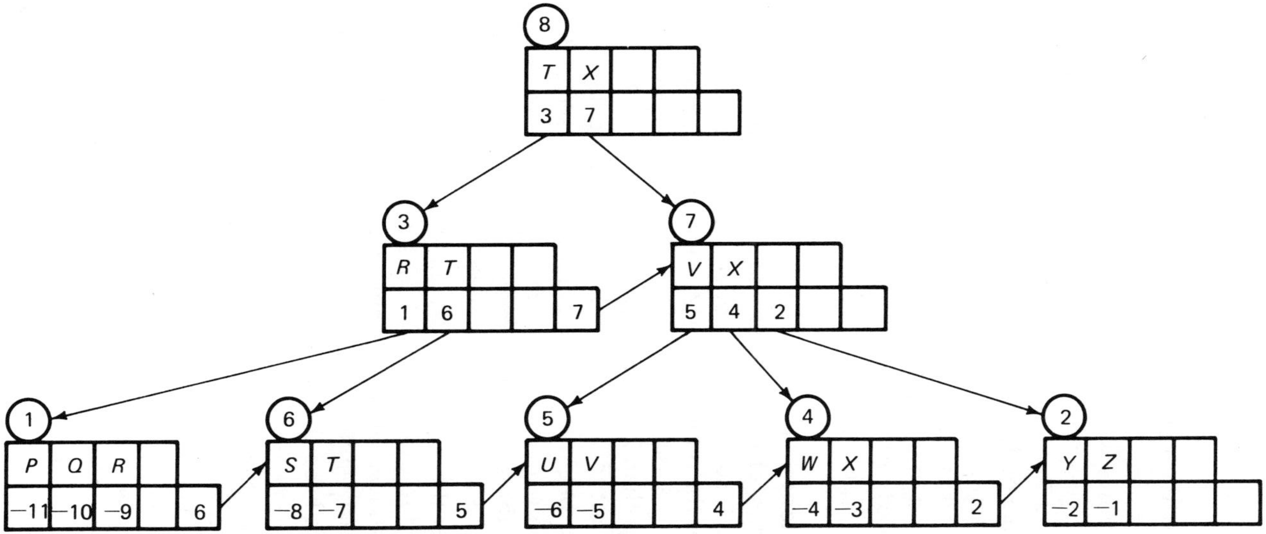

(e) Add S, R, Q, P and split interior node.

**Figure 7-4.** Growth of a B-tree.

(−1) record number is used to access record number (+1) in the master file.

Figure 7-4(b) shows the contents of the B-tree after Y and X have been added to the file. The master record containing Y is stored in record number (+2) and the master record containing X is stored in record number (+3).

Figure 7-4(c) shows what happens when the index file sector over-flows due to an excess number of entries. Each sector of the index file can hold 4 keys and 5 pointers to other sectors (records). Thus, when we put four keys into a node (node is the same as a sector) the node "over-flows." This is a signal to allocate more nodes to the index file (B-tree).

A B-tree node is split into two nodes (sectors) whenever it is full. Notice what happened to the split nodes in Figure 7-4(c). Half of the keys in node 1 are moved into a new node stored in sector 2. Notice that they are maintained in alphabetical order by using the fifth record number to point to node 2.

Now the two nodes are "managed" by a "parent" node which contains the largest key of each "child" node. In Figure 7-4(c), the largest key, X, is in node 1, so the parent node holds X and a pointer to node 1. The largest key in the other child is Z, so the parent node also points to node 2. It is not necessary to store Z in the parent node because there are no larger keys than Z in the entire B-tree.

Suppose we want to look up a record containing key "Y" in Figure 7-4(c). The search begins with the parent node in sector 3. The search key Y is compared with each key stored in the node in sector 3. Since Y is larger than X, the second pointer (+2) is used to retrieve the keys stored in sector 2 of the B-tree. In sector 2, we compare Y with the contents and discover that the first entry matches. The (−2) record pointer is used to retrieve record 2 from the master file.

Figure 7-4(d) shows what happens if we keep adding keys to the B-tree. A subsequent split of sector 1 produces another child node. The "horizontal" links keep the entries in the B-tree in alphabetical order.

Figure 7-4(e) shows even more splits as a result of continued growth of the B-tree. Notice that an interior sector (3) has been split into sectors 3 and 7. Also notice how the B-tree grows upward, adding a new parent node whenever it is needed.

Suppose we trace the search path through the B-tree to get the record number associated with the key value "X". The first node searched is at the top of the B-tree. Node 8 is searched until key X is found. This leads to the seventh sector of the B-tree. In sector 7 we search for X again. This time the search leads to sector 4 of the B-tree. Finally, the contents of sector 4 are searched until X is found. The master record is accessed as record number (+3)

The search for "X" took four accesses to find and retrieve the master file record containing X. This may seem excessive, but consider this:

1) the search examined less than half of the total records (11) stored in the system of files, and 2) the search is done in a way that guarantees an order on the keys. This last point is very important in database systems. Once the record containing X is found, all other records can be quickly retrieved in order from X to Z. This is done by reading the B-tree sectors "horizontally" following the fifth record number stored in each B-tree leaf. Therefore, keys Y and Z are retrieved in a single access through sector 2.

We used an example where each B-tree sector holds only four keys. The best size of a B-tree sector however depends on the length of each key. In most cases a 128-byte sector is able to hold eight or ten keys. This greatly improves the performance of a retrieval program because the number of disk accesses is roughly the following.

$$LOG_{N/2} \ (K/2)$$

where,

N     is the number of keys per sector
K     is the total number of unique keys stored in the entire B-tree.

Thus, in Figure 7-4, we used $N = 4$ and $K = 11$. The expected number of accesses is given by,

$$LOG_2 \ (5)$$

which is approximately 2.5.

## Features of B-tree Index Files

The B-tree structure has some advantages and disadvantages. We have emphasized its advantages, but to be fair we should acknowledge its weaknesses, too.

**Advantages.** A B-tree structure allows you to quickly retrieve a record by a kind of "divide-and-conquer" search method. Therefore, it is fast.

The B-tree structure also keeps the keys in alphabetical order. This makes it very easy to retrieve information as ordered lists.

The B-tree also makes it easy to add new keys with a minimum of reorganization. This makes insertion relatively fast.

**Disadvantages.** A B-tree uses redundancy to gain speed. Many keys are stored more than once. In fact, B-tree structures take up disk space in two ways: 1) the internal nodes of the B-tree hold redundant information, and 2) the leaf nodes of the B-tree are mostly empty.

Search and retrieval does indeed take more than a single disk access. Depending on the size of each node, it may take 5 or 6 accesses to disk just to fetch a single record.

You can examine the contents of an actual B-tree file by running the "Quick Dump" operation of the simple relational database system given in Figure 7-2. This program dumps the contents of all sectors in the B-tree. Each sector contains a FLAG field indicating whether the key is being used (FULL), not used (EMPTY), or deleted (DELETED). The ARC value holds a positive value if the record number points to another B-tree sector, and a negative record number if the ARC value points to a master file record. The LINK pointer points to the next leaf node in order.

## COMMON QUESTIONS

Q. What is a DBMS?

A. A Database Management System is a computer system with software for adding, deleting, and modifying large quantities of information. A typical DBMS consists of a physical file system, logical user's view of the data, a query language, and an I/O control subsystem for producing reports.

Q. What are the three kinds of logical user's views for a DBMS?

A. Network, hierarchical, and relational.

Q. What simplification does a relational DBMS provide to a user?

A. All data in a relational DBMS is stored in flat tables.

Q. What is a row and column in a relation?

A. A row is called a tuple, and a column is called a domain.

Q. How is a CRT screen form related to a relation?

A. The CRT screen form defines the domains of a relation. The screen form is subsequently used to enter a tuple at a time.

Q. What is a relational algebra?

A. It is a collection of operations on relations that produce a relation by operating on other relations.

Q. Isn't the word "relation" just a fancy word for table?

A. Informally, yes. Technically, the word relation should be used to describe tables that behave like relations whenever a relational algebra query is processed.

Q. Explain the difference between the physical and logical levels in the simple DBMS described in this chapter.

A. The physical level consists of a master file containing a relation, an index file containing a B-tree, and other files for holding the screen form, and miscellaneous parameters. The logical level is a single relation.

Q. The query language illustrated in the simple DBMS seems primitive. Is it really a relational query language?

A. No. It is an extremely simple question-and-answer query language fot illustrating the idea only.

Q. What are the two reasons to backup a database?

A. 1) Generate a backup copy in case the working copy fails, and 2) delete any unused records in order to save diskette space and processing time.

Q. How many B-tree index files can a single master file have associated with it?

A. Any number you want.

Q. Look at the B-tree of Figure 7-4(e). What percentage of the total disk space is actually being used to store information?

A. If we count all occupied and empty slots as taking the same space, then the utilization is 56 percent. If we count the keys in the leaf nodes as the only "useful" information then the space utilization drops to 15 percent.

# Chapter 8

# How Computers Work

"What do you have in the box?"
"A computer."
"What is a computer?" She was amused.
"See!" And he opened the box.
"But there is only another box inside," she complained.
"Open it then." he advised.
She continued to open one box within another, but every box contained a smaller box. Finally, a very small box was found and she opened it.
"What is it?" She was nearly exhausted.
"A *bit*," he grinned.

## BRAINS VS. COMPUTERS

It is no surprise that the human brain was used as a model of the first electronic computer constructed decades ago. In fact, today's small computers are made to operate much the same way as the first huge electronic machines—that is, like the brain. But if you were constructing an electromechanical equivalent of the human brain, where would you start? How does a brain work?

In this final chapter, we take a more detailed look at how computers work. It is not necessary to understand how computers work in order to use them, but the inquisitive reader might be curious to know more. Therefore, let's study the computer as a model of the human brain.

Actually, electronic computers are very crude approximations to a human brain. Much still needs to be known about humans before computers can simulate them, but at a simple level, the two "machines" are strikingly similar.

Brains and computers both accept **inputs**: sight, sound, touch, etc. for humans, and electronic signals representing data for computers. They both can retain information in the form of electronic charges in a **mem-**

ory (short term plus long term), and they both generate **outputs** in the form of speech, actions, etc.

Human brains are controlled by a consciousness (poorly understood) while computers are controlled by software (programs). The "programs", in either case, process information obtained from inputs and long-term memory and produce outputs. This simple input-process-output model is shown in Figure 8-1.

In Figure 8-1(a) a human is given visual input which is processed using long-term memory and the human consciousness (processor) to decide to run (fright). The output is a signal to the legs to run. Similarly the computer model in Figure 8-1(b) uses input data about an employee, a computer program (software), and long-term memory (files) to process a paycheck. The paycheck is output via a printer.

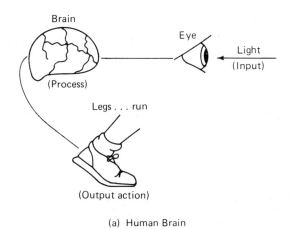

(a) Human Brain

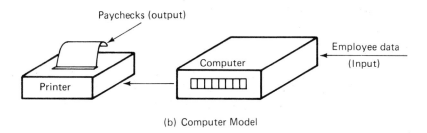

(b) Computer Model

**Figure 8-1.** Input-process-output model.

Clearly the model of a computer presented here requires three basic parts in order to become a reality:

1. Input devices like keyboard, disk drive, etc.
2. Processor like a microprocessor chip.
3. Output devices like screen, disk drive, and printer.

Let's examine each one of these parts in detail to see how they work.

## ELECTROMECHANICAL MEMORIES

Humans use short-term memory to momentarily remember a telephone number or keep track of current activity. Long-term memory is used to remember names of close friends, your home address, etc. The human brain actually manages a **hierarchy** of memories ranging from easily recalled "short-term" to hard-to-recall "long-term" facts. The idea of a hierarchy of memory is used in computing, also.

### Registers

The most easily recalled or **accessed** memory cell in an electronic computer is the memory **register.** A register is a collection of circuits that can store a **word** of information. A word is usually 8 or 16 **bits** of information in a small computer. Each **bit** corresponds to an "on" or "off" setting of the circuit. Thus, if the circuit is switched to its "on" state, electrical current can flow. The off position means no current can flow, just like the wall switch at home that governs the state of a reading lamp, on or off.

A word of 8 bits, for example, can be used to hold 256 possible combinations of on and off settings. Each pattern of settings corresponds to some meaning associated with the pattern. For example, the letters of the alphabet are made to correspond to 26 patterns. This is called **encoding** and is one of the secrets to the power of computers.

### Main Memory

The next level of memory in a computer is the "short-term" part. RAM (random access memory) is a collection of thousands of **bytes** (usually 8 bits in each byte). A memory of 64K bytes is one containing 64 times 1024 bytes because one K (pronounced kay) equals 1024 in computer jargon. An 8-bit computer is one in which each word is also a byte, e.g. 8 bits long. A 16-bit computer is one in which two bytes are needed to make a word.

The RAM main memory holds the program and data currently being used by the computer. If the program and data are too large to fit into this level of the memory hierarchy, then the next level must be used. The **disk file** is a form of "long-term" memory for computers.

## Disk Files

A magnetic disk device is a low-cost medium in which to store massive numbers of bytes of information. In fact, disk devices can hold millions rather than thousands of bytes. For this reason disk capacity is measured in megabytes. One megabyte, 1M, equals 1024 times 1024 or 1,048,576 bytes of information.

Unfortunately, disk devices are relatively difficult for computers to control and access. The information on a disk is stored as magnetic spots rather than on-off-switch circuits. The "spots" must be put into motion before they can be sensed by a read/write circuit. Thus, disk drives rotate the magnetic spots on the surface of the diskette under a read/write sensing magnet in order to access the information stored on the disk. This takes time to position the desired area of the diskette under the read/write magnet and so causes the computer to wait.

Secondly, the information stored on a diskette is usually not in a form that can be readily used by the computer. For example, hundreds of bytes may be grouped together into "bunches" called **records** in order to store the name, address, and telephone number of one person. A collection of records belonging together is grouped together into a **file,** and a collection of files is sometimes called a **database** or **library.**

Considerable effort and thought is put into file structuring in order to overcome the incompatibility between disk storage and RAM storage. One of the difficult tasks of a computer programmer, for example, is to select the best possible file structure for a given application. But due to the large storage capacity and low cost of diskette storage, the use of disks for "long-term" memory is guaranteed for a long time in the future.

## The Memory Hierarchy

Let's review the memory hierarchy momentarily and see how it is used to make computers work. First, the most immediate level is the register level. A typical computer has 2 to 10 registers which hold 8 or 16 bits of information while the computer is processing the information. Thus, it is the registers that hold sums, characters, etc. while the processor is performing an operation on the contents of the register.

There are too few registers in a computer to store a lot of data at one time, so some of the data is stored in RAM and the remaining data is stored in a disk file. Additionally, the computer must be told what to do next. Therefore, one of the registers must hold a word called an **instruction.** An instruction is a word that tells the processor what operation to perform (add, subtract, compare, move, copy), and what operands to perform it on (which register to modify).

Again, since there are not enough registers to hold all the instructions of a program, all but the **current instruction** are stored in RAM and in a disk file. A **program,** then, is a collection of words containing instruction information.

The RAM level of memory holds both data and instructions while waiting to be fetched and copied into a register. The instructions as well as data reside in RAM, so it is possible for an erroneous fetch to mistakenly fetch a word of data in place of an instruction or the opposite. Therefore, some memories are equipped with **tags** which indicate the **type** of information; whether it be data or instruction. But how does a computer know which is which?

## Encoding

The memory of a computer has very little "intelligence." In fact, as far as a computer memory is concerned, all information is stored as either an on or off setting. So, how can a computer tell the difference between the letter A, for example, and the number 5?

Computer systems use **encoding** schemes to *represent* information inside memories. This is one of the great secrets of how a computer works. The keyword is *represent,* because a **code** is simply a representation of information using on-off switches. Every number, letter, and special character in memory is stored as one or more bytes of on-off bits. However, numbers are encoded differently than letters, say, and the only difference between the two is the way in which they are encoded and then decoded by the computer hardware and software.

Most small computers use the following **types** of information. Each type corresponds to an encoding scheme which uses one or more on-off switches to represent information of the given type.

| Type of Information | Encoding |
|---|---|
| 1. bit | one on-off switch (one or zero) |
| 2. boolean | True (on), False (off) |
| 3. integer | two's-complement byte or word |
| 4. real | floating point format (word) |
| 5. character | ASCII code |
| 6. instruction | octal numeric |

Let's examine each of these types and their encoding schemes in more detail. A good understanding of these codes will give you a sound basis for understanding nearly all of the concepts of computing!

A **bit** is a **binary digit.** That is, it is a digit from the binary number system. Instead of taking on the values of 0,1,2,3,4,5,6,7,8,9, the binary digits take on only two values: 0 or 1. The on-off switch of an electronic memory is *represented* by a zero (off), or one (on). Thus a **bit** is the smallest piece of information that a computer can store.

Sometimes we encode information as a **boolean,** which means that a value of TRUE or FALSE is stored in memory. For example, we might store the boolean value TRUE if a certain employee has worked over-time last month, and FALSE if he or she has not worked overtime. As you can see, the encoding for TRUE is a one (on), and FALSE is a zero (off).

Integers are encoded using either bytes or words. Usually, 16-bit words are used to encode the values of $-32768$ to $+32767$ in memory. Several methods can be used, but in microcomputers the best method is **two's-complement.**

In two's-complement the integers from zero to $+32767$ are encoded as binary numbers, e.g.

| Decimal Number | Binary Number |
|:---:|:---:|
| 0 | 0000 |
| 1 | 0001 |
| 2 | 0010 |
| 3 | 0011 |
| 4 | 0100 |
| 5 | 0101 |
| 6 | 0110 |
| 7 | 0111 |
| 8 | 1000 |
| 9 | 1001 |
| 10 | 1010 |
| 11 | 1011 |
| 12 | 1100 |
| . | . |
| . | . |
| . | . |
| 32,767 | (15 ones) |

This table can be obtained by simply writing all the decimal numbers from zero to the largest number (15 ones) on a sheet of paper, then striking out all the numbers which *do not* contain 0 or 1, exclusively. For example, the first few are:

| Decimal Digits | Strike All But These |
|:---:|:---:|
| 0 | 0 |
| 1 | 1 |
| 2 | |
| 3 | |
| 4 | |
| 5 | |
| 6 | |
| 7 | |
| 8 | |
| 9 | |
| 10 | 10 |
| 11 | 11 |
| 12 | |
| 13 | |
| . | . |
| . | . |
| . | . |

The remaining binary numbers are renumbered as shown in the conversion table above. *Remember, computer memories can only store on-off (0,1) values.*

This takes care of the positive integer values, but what about negative integers? In the two's-complement code we store negative numbers by reversing all ones to a zero, and all zeros to a one as follows. Suppose we encode (−14) in two's-complement form using 8 bits. The steps are shown below.

**Step 1** Start with a positive number, +14

**Step 2** Encode +14 as a binary number (using 8 bits in this example). 14 is 00001110

**Step 3** Mark the right-most one bit and all the zero bits following it as the *unaltered* part of the number, 00001**110** (last two digits, 10, are unaltered).

**Step 4** Flip all ones to zeros and zeros to ones, except the unaltered part, 11110**010**

**Step 5** The result is the two's-complement equivalent, 11110010 is (−14)

To show that this is indeed the correct encoding for a two's complement integer we can add (+14) + (−14) to get zero:

$$
\begin{array}{rll}
& 00001110 & (+14) \\
\text{add} & 11110010 & (-14) \\
\hline
1 & 00000000 &
\end{array}
$$

Notice the carry-out of one. This is discarded to give a zero result. Remember that addition of $(1+1)=(10)$ because 0 and 1 are the only permitted digits.

The problem of encoding real numbers is more complex than the two's-complement encoding. We will not discuss it here except to note that it involves encoding two parts of a real number. The first part is the **exponent** (power of two), and the second part is the **fraction** or **mantissa**. For example, 14.5 is actually 0.145 times 10 raised to the second power. The fraction 0.145 is coded in one scheme, and the power of two is encoded in another scheme.

Character information is encoded in yet another scheme called ASCII (pronounced "ask-key"). The keyboard of a computer transmits an 8-bit byte of on-off bits in ASCII code each time you depress one of the keys. Let's study two keys and their ASCII code.

The letter A is encoded in ASCII (American Standard Code for Information Interchange) as follows:

A is 65 decimal or 0100 0001 binary
a is 97 decimal or 0101 0001 binary

The computer can mistakenly treat the letter A as an integer, real, or instruction since it is simply an 8-bit byte of on-off information. However, if the computer is programmed to *interpret* this as a code for the letter A, then it can be compared with other letters, output to a printer, etc.

Now, suppose we study the code sent to the computer when the keyboard key 5 is depressed. How does the computer interpret this character?

The numeral 5 is encoded in ASCII as follows:

5 is 53 decimal or 0011 0101 binary.

Surprisingly, the numeral 5 is not stored as an integer five when entered as a character. The computer must be programmed to convert 5 to either an integer five or a real 5.0.

## Structured Types

We have seen how simple bit, boolean, integer, real, and character information is stored in electromechanical memories. These differing types of information are all stored as groups of on-off switches, but their encodings are different. Indeed, it is one of the jobs or a programmer to translate from one type of information to another. One idea that makes a programmer's job easier is the idea of grouping information together into **structures**. A **data structure** is a collection of data that includes both information and structure. Let's look at two very important structures.

An **array** is a data structure which groups together one or more pieces of information all of the same type. For example, an array of integers is a sequence of words in memory containing two's-complement encoded values.

An array of characters is called a **string** because it consists of a sequence of letters and/or numbers. Each word of an array is placed in consecutive words of memory much like an array of post office boxes.

A second kind of data structure that plays an important role in computing is the **file**. A file is an array of records which typically is stored on a diskette. The records of a file can contain information of different types, for example, characters, integers, and boolean values. Thus a file may hold a mixture of different types of information.

The main purpose of file structure is to allow us to use a disk as a low-cost, high-capacity storage medium. However, since the method of disk storage is so much different than the method used in RAM (main memory), the information is stored in a file structure instead of an array structure. Again, it is the programmer who must translate from one method of storage to the other, and back.

## CHIP POWER

The power of a computer is in a miniature circuit packaged into a chip about the size of a fingernail. This is the **microprocessor** that can perform the operations dictated by an instruction.

In this section we discuss the fundamental concepts of processor operation. This will involve an understanding ot two things: (1) sequencing, and (2) computer arithmetic. These functions are the same in all computers; however, the details of how they are implemented vary from computer to computer.

### Sequencing

The idea of sequencing is very simple, yet very powerful in computing. Here is a recipe for how a microprocessor works:

*Repeat until the power is turned off:*

**Step 1** Fetch an instruction from RAM,

**Step 2** Fetch data from the registers that the instruction is going to use,

**Step 3** Do the indicated operation on the data as specified by the instruction

**Step 4** Compute the location in memory of the next instruction to be fetched in step 1.

The sequencer runs for as long as the microprocessor is turned on. The location of the first instruction in the program must be known. Also, the microprocessor must be given another program to work on as soon as the first program is **executed** to completion.

The first three steps of the sequencer recipe are straight-forward and easy to follow. The microprocessor simply fetches an instruction and the data to be processed (add, subtract, copy, move, compare), and then does the intended operation. For example, an instruction to add two integers together might be fetched and executed. The two numbers must be fetched, and then the addition (in two's-complement) is performed. The operation might produce a sum which is stored in a register. Another instruction might be used to copy the sum back to some word in RAM.

The fourth step is a little more complicated, but herein lies the power of the sequencing microprocessor. There are three fundamental ways to compute the location of the next instruction:

1. Use the next instruction in sequence,

2. Branch to some other location in the program by skipping part of the program,

3. Temporarily suspend the execution of the current program and execute another program. When the other program is completed, return to the current program and continue with the next instruction in sequence.

The first method A is called **sequential execution** because the microprocessor simply takes the next instruction in sequence as the next instruction to be performed.

The second method is called **branching** because the next instruction actually performed is dependent on a **boolean** value, TRUE or FALSE. There are two fundamental control schemes for branching,

1. if-then-else branching in order to make a decision,

2. looping in order to repeat a section of program over and over.

The if-then-else branching method is used to conditionally execute either one section of the program or else another section, depending on the outcome of a test. For example, *if* an employee worked more than 40 hours in one week, *then* compute overtime pay, *else* compute regular pay. Note that only one of the options is chosen, and not both.

Looping is used as a means of repeating a section of program. This is a valuable way to reduce the length of a program by using a section over and over again. For example, we might repeat the section of program which prints a single payroll check over and over for each of 100 employees. The loop terminates after a prescribed number of iterations, or when a certain condition is satisfied (for example, no more employees).

The third method is called **subroutining** and consists of two methods:

1. Program subroutine call,
2. Interrupt service routine call.

In the first method a programmer writes a program called a **procedure** (or subroutine) which is subordinate to the main program. This procedure is **called** by the main program using a special subroutine-call instruction. The idea is to "divide-and-conquer" by breaking the program into smaller (and simpler) procedures and then calling them one at a time as needed.

The second method is used by the computer system itself to take care of time-critical events like reading information from a disk, answering the telephone when it rings, etc. An **interrupt** is an unscheduled event which is usually signaled by an Input/Output device. Since we cannot always predict when an interrupt service routine will be executed, it is the microprocessor itself that calls this kind of routine. In short, an interrupt service routine is a procedure which is called by the hardware rather than a special instruction fetched from the program.

## Processors Galore

Most small computer systems consist of many microprocessors, rather than simply one. For example, a microprocessor may be used to control access to the disk drives, printer, and screen/keyboard. A computer system consists of a memory hierarchy which is accessed by several microprocessors.

In most situations, it is necessary for a microprocessor to be under control of a **permanent program.** That is, a printer may be controlled by a microprocessor which governs the print wheel (or whatever), forms control and so on. The printer microprocessor is in turn controlled by a permanent program supplied by the manufacturer. This program never changes and is the only program executed by the printer microprocessor. Therefore it is stored in a special kind of memory called a ROM (read-only-memory).

ROMs cannot be altered. That is, once a program is stored in a ROM it remains there forever. If the power is removed from a ROM, the program remains intact.

## Computer Arithmetic

A microprocessor sequences its way through a program by executing one instruction at a time, as discussed above. But exactly what does a microprocessor instruction do? In this section we survey some of the operations performed by a typical microprocessor.

Fundamentally, all microprocessors are the same. They all perform

- arithmetic,
- branching (boolean), and
- input/output operations.

We have already discussed the binary operations associated with integer encoding. The two's-complement code is used to represent positive and negative integers. Floating-point encoding is used to store real numbers.

Suppose we want to perform the following payroll calculation:

> Payroll Problem: Multiply the payrate times the number of hours worked. If the number of hours exceeds 40, add 50% of the payrate times the excess hours beyond 40.

This problem involves all three fundamental operations. First, we must input the payrate and the number of hours worked; next, we must perform the necessary arithmetic, and finally we must output the answer. These steps are:

**Step #1** Input PAYRATE and HOURS
**Step #2** Compute PAY = PAYRATE times HOURS
**Step #3** If HOURS exceeds 40
       then 3a). OVERTIME = HOURS − 40
              EXCESS = (PAYRATE/2) times OVERTIME
       else 3b). EXCESS = 0
**Step #4** Adjust PAY = PAY + EXCESS
**Step #5** Output PAY

The microprocessor instructions to do these program steps would look like the following (except we present them in English rather than on-off switch encodings).

### Step #1

   a. Wait for a keyboard key to be depressed,
   b. Input a character
   c. Convert the numerals to an integer or real

d. Do these steps for PAYRATE and HOURS

e. Store PAYRATE and HOURS in RAM

**Step #2**

a. Copy HOURS and PAYRATE into registers

b. Multiply PAYRATE times HOURS

c. Store the result in RAM at the location corresponding to PAY.

**Step #3**

a. Copy HOURS into a register

b. Compare HOURS against 40

c. Branch to 3a) if comparison is TRUE

d. Branch to 3b) if comparison is FALSE

**then 3a).**

a. Subtract 40 from HOURS and store the result in OVERTIME

b. Copy PAYRATE into a register and divide by two.

c. Multiply PAYRATE /2 times OVERTIME

d. Store the product in RAM at the location corresponding to EXCESS.

**else 3b).**

a. Store a zero in the RAM word corresponding to EXCESS

**Step #4**

a. Copy PAY into a register

b. Copy EXCESS into a register

c. Add the contents of the registers and store the result at PAY in RAM

**Step #5**

a. Copy the result from PAY in RAM and put it in a register.

b. Convert the real or integer value of PAY into a string of characters

c. Repeat until the string of characters have all been displayed on the screen:

   c.i. wait for the screen to catch up

   c.ii. output a character to the screen

These operations roughly correspond to the actual operations performed by a microprocessor. As you can see, the detail is painstakingly great, and yet this example is trivial. The chances of successfully managing such detail is slim unless we employ software tools that are more powerful than shown here. This is the reason for high level languages such as BASIC, Pascal, and COBOL. These tools give us a kind of "lever" for accelerating software production by hiding much of the detail.

Computer arithmetic is strangely different from the kind of arithmetic learned in grade school. Computer arithmetic is performed by moving information from one place in hierarchical memory to another, encoding and decoding on-off switches, and performing comparisons followed by branching. The actual operations of addition, etc., are only a minor part of computer arithmetic. In the payroll example, only about 16% of the operations actually involved arithmetic operations. In fact, the most common operation performed by a microprocessor is the copy operation. That is, about 40% of the work performed by a microprocessor is to move information from one place in memory to another.

## CHIP TECHNOLOGY

We have discussed how computers work, but how does an engineer construct a chip microprocessor to do the functions discussed above? To add another level of detail to this discussion, we must learn something about hardware.

The chip technology of microprocessor and RAM memory fabrication is an amazing combination of photography, chemistry, electronics, and mathematical logic. We will discuss this confluence of technologies in the most elementary terms.

Simply put, a chip is constructed by doing the following:

1. A circuit designer draws the circuits for a memory or processor using a graphics computer as an aid.

2. The circuit is tested using other computers to make sure they work.

3. The tested circuit is drawn on a photographical medium, and then reduced in size by a photo-reduction process. This reduction is a thousand-fold compression of the circuit so that a "large" circuit becomes a micro-circuit.

4. The micro circuit is "developed" onto a silicon substrate called a wafer. This is done by a multistep series of etchings using various photosensitive chemicals.

5. The etchings are washed and tested to find the ones that still work. The "yield" is then packaged into a dual-in-line chip. Such chips are ready to be used in a computer as processor, memory, etc.

The basic circuit that makes a chip work as either a microprocessor or RAM memory is a circuit that can "remember" an on-off state. A micro-circuit of transistors is used for this purpose. The idea is very simple. A transistor allows current to flow when it is "on" and prevents the flow of electrons when it is "off."

Figure 8-2 shows a simple diagram of a transistor. The base or substrate of the transistor is a silicon compound which has an excess of negative charge (too many electrons). This is shown as an N (negative) charge. The substrate has etched into it a channel, shown in the picture as an area with a P (positive charge or shortage of electrons). Also etched into the transistor is a metal gate shown above the area of P charge. This gate controls the flow of electrons across the channel by changing the potential ever so slightly.

As long as there is a shortage of electrons in the channel, the source of electrons will flow into the channel and if the destination potential is "lower" than the channel, they will continue to flow out to the destination (called a sink). If, however, a voltage is applied to the metal gate, the potential of the channel is changed so that the electrons are blocked by a "hill". This "hill" prevents the electrons from flowing, hence making the transistor turn "off."

For every bit in a computer memory we must construct one or more transistors which are turned on (1) or off (0). The revolution in technology called microelectronics makes it possible to imprint millions of these tiny transistors on a single fingernail-sized wafer. The next step is to connect these transistors together in ways that simulate computer arithmetic.

## The Boolean Connection

In order to make a computer add, for example, we must connect transistors together so that they obey the laws of logic. These laws were invented by George Boole, so we call them the laws of boolean algebra in his honor. To see how they relate to transistors, consider the following examples.

Boole formulated a set of laws which work especially well for on-off switches. These laws govern the algebra of AND, OR, and NOT circuits which are in turn implemented with transistors. For example, two transistors connected in series form an AND circuit, see Figure 8-3(a). Two transistors connected in parallel form an OR circuit, see Figure 8-3(b).

In Figure 8-3 we have connected the inputs x and y to the metal gate of each transistor so that when a voltage (as indicated by a one) is applied electrons cannot flow from source to sink. The absence of flow is a zero and the presence of a flow is a one. The inverter circuit reverses a one to a zero, and a zero to a one.

The tables show what is computed for every combination of input values. For example,

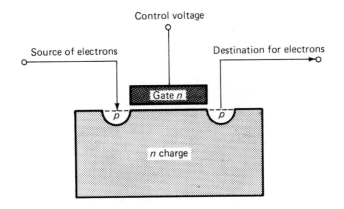

Figure 8-2. Simple model of a transistor.

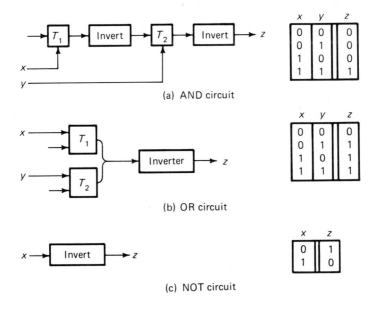

1   and   1 is 1
0   OR    1 is 1

because these inputs allow a flow (one) of electons.

The most profound feature of boolean circuitry is that it can simulate computer arithmetic. For example, the boolean circuit shown in Figure 8-4 can add two bits to get the sum and carry bits.

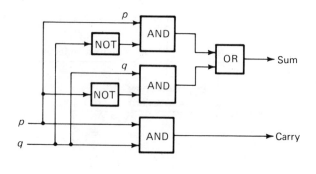

| p | q | Sum | Carry |
|---|---|-----|-------|
| 0 | 0 | 0 | 0 |
| 0 | 1 | 1 | 0 |
| 1 | 0 | 1 | 0 |
| 1 | 1 | 0 | 1 |

**Figure 8-4.** A simple (half) adder.

Eight simple adders as shown in Figure 8-4 are used by circuit designers to simulate addition of two 8-bit bytes. Each adder computes the sum of its input bits and produces a carry bit. The carry bit is added to one of the input bits and then the next pair of bits is added, etc.

This example demonstrates how boolean algebra is used to design circuits containing transistors etched on a chip wafer. The transistors are connected together to form a circuit which obeys a boolean expression. The boolean expression in turn, simulates the usual arithmetic we learned in school.

Of course the boolean circuits of chip computers are more complex than the ones shown here. The concepts are the same, however, and given enough time and effort anyone can design a circuit for computing whatever is desired. The boolean expression for the sum in Figure 8-4, for example, is

SUM = (p AND (NOT q)) OR ((NOT p) AND q)

and the carry is,

CARRY = p AND q

## Altogether, Now

Let's put it all together, now, and see how computers work. First, a collection of circuits is designed which uses the on-off switch transistor as the basic unit of storage. The connection network of these transistors form boolean circuits which obey the laws of AND, OR, and NOT logic. If properly connected, these boolean circuits can do almost anything including computer arithmetic.

An on-off switch transistor circuit holds a single bit of information. Collections of these bits are used to encode integers, reals, characters, etc. Some bits are also used to store instruction words. The microprocessor circuit uses a sequencer for executing the instruction words. The instruction words modify the data words stored in memory, and cause the computer to "compute."

Programmers design data structures and instruction sequences called programs which control every step of a microprocessor. These programs must translate from one encoding to another, control input and output, and control the branches taken within the programs. This is the job of software, in general, and leads to the need for tools to produce software.

Text editors, high-level language translators, and operating systems are all special-purpose programs used by programmers to aid in developing other programs. All of these software systems depend on the lowly bit for their operation, however. Thus, the bit and how it is used to encode information within a computer memory is the story of how computers work.

## COMMON QUESTIONS

Q. Why is it necessary to have registers separately from RAM memory?

A. It would be too expensive to connect every word of RAM to the microprocessor, so a small number of special words called registers are connected instead. Thus, every word in RAM that is processed must be copied into a register first, and then copied back to RAM after the operation is performed.

Q. Why are characters encoded in ASCII the way they are? For example, the character encoding of numeral "5" is equal to 53 instead of 5. Why?

A. The ASCII code was standardized for teletype equipment rather than computers. Thus, it was designed to simplify the construction of mechanical printers and mechanical devices which have long ago been forgotten.

Q. Computers are based on such simple mechanisms like transistors and on-off switching rules. So why do they appear to be so complex?

A. Two factors contribute to apparent complexity in computers: (1) abstraction and (2) size. The coding schemes of high-level languages, software, and the vocabulary of computer programmers lead to an enormous amount of abstraction. This form of abstraction is applied in layer upon layer so the beginner has difficulty separating the "real" machine from a coded abstraction. Secondly, computer systems are large collections of details, e.g., a lot of information can be packed into a 64K memory.

Q. What is the difference between a **byte** and a **word**?

A. A byte of information usually corresponds to 8 bits. A word usually corresponds to more than one byte, e.g. 2 or 4 bytes.

Q. What is the difference between RAM and ROM?

A. RAM is **alterable** memory, because it can be read or written into. ROM, on the other hand, is **unalterable,** because it can be read from but not written into.

Q. Why is it necessary for a computer system to incorporate a hierarchy of memory devices?

A. Cost. In general, the faster a memory device is, the more it costs to build. Therefore, a small, high speed device like a RAM chip is used for main memory, while a large, modest speed device like a disk is used for "bulk" storage. This makes sense because the cost-per-bit of disk storage is much less than the cost-per-bit of RAM.

Q. How does a computer separate instructions from data within its memory?

A. There is no difference between the way an instruction and a word of data is stored in memory. Hence, an artificial separation is enforced by the programmer. Alternately, a programmer could choose to execute data as if it were a program. However, this is a very risky way to control a computer.

Q. Why are so many coding schemes used in computers?

A. Partly for efficiency and partly because of historical precedence. In the case of integer versus real codes, for example, the hardware circuitry is more easily implemented if two's-complement is used for integers and floating point is used for real numbers.

Q. Why do computers use a binary number system instead of a decimal number system?

A. Efficiency. A few decimal computers were constructed in the past, but the most efficient coding schemes are based on binary representations. There are also secondary advantages which have to do with electronics. For example, it is much easier to construct an on-off switch than it is to construct a 10-way switch with a transistor.

Q. How is 57 written as a binary number?

A. Binary: 32 + 16 + 8 + 1 is 111001.

Q. What is the 8-bit two's-complement of binary 111010?

A. Flip all bits except the last (right-most) part beginning with the 1 bit. Hence, 111010 is 00111010 which is 11000110 in complement form.

Q. What is a **string?**

A. An array of characters.

Q. What is an **array?**

A. A sequence of values (all of the same type of information), usually stored together in memory.

Q. What is a program?

A. A sequence of instructions which controls the operation of a microprocessor.

Q. What is a subroutine?

A. Sometimes called a subprogram, procedure, or function. A subroutine is a program that is called into action by another program.

Q. How do transistors encode 1 bit of information?

A. By controlling the on-off flow of electrons; "on" is equivalent to a 1, and "off" is equivalent to a 0.

Q. How does a computer process alphabetic information like the letters of the alphabet?

A. By encoding the letters of the alphabet into numeric codes (ASCII), and then processing the numeric codes like any other numbers.

Q. What is a data structure?

A. A data structure is a collection of data along with information which tells a program how to access the values stored in the data structure. For example, an array is a collection of values; each succeeding value is accessed immediately following the current value in the array.

Q. How does a computer perform arithmetic, e.g. ADD?

A. Addition is simulated by a boolean circuit which uses AND, OR, and NOT operations. The adder circuit is designed to work with the encoding, whether it be an integer or real number encoding.

Q. How do computers work?

A. Very well, thank you.

# Index